50
GREAT READS

EDITED BY
MARK KEOHANE & GARY LEMKE

BUSINESS DAY SPORT MONTHLY 50 GREAT READS
First published 2010
© Business Day Sport Monthly, Highbury Safika Media (Pty) Ltd
2004 03/1056/03, Highbury Safika Media, 21st floor, Metlife Centre,
7 Coen Steytler Avenue, Foreshore, 8001, Cape Town, South Africa

Editors: Mark Keohane, Gary Lemke
Designer: Stuart Apsey
Senior Copy Editor: Philippa Byron
Copy Editor: Nick van Rensburg
Junior Copy Editor: Dan Gillespie
Proofreader: Simon Borchardt
Repro Manager: Karin Livni
Repro Artists: Donnevan van der Watt,
Adri van der Watt, Tammy-Anne Clarke
Printer: CTP Book Printers

CONTENTS

CONTENTS

CONTENTS

CONTENTS

CONTENTS

CONTENTS

CONTENTS

INTRODUCTION

I WAS LOOKING AT THE SHINING MEDIA ACCREDITATION BADGE confirming I was Beijing-bound for the 2008 Olympics when I got a call from Mark Keohane, then publishing director of Highbury Safika Media and a long-time friend. 'What will it take for you to join us?' he asked. As he's got it right so often over the years, Mark already had the answer: the creation of South Africa's first high-quality general sports magazine.

I was taking a quantum leap into the unknown. But, it was something I yearned to be associated with. Less than six weeks later I had said goodbye to the intoxicating smell of newsprint, following a career that had seen me hold sports editorships at the *Pretoria News*, *Daily News*, *Sunday Tribune*, *Cape Argus* and *Weekend Argus* as well as *The Independent* and *Independent on Sunday* in London. I also had to say goodbye to covering another Olympics, and for a Games junkie it wasn't without heartache.

The magazine world is radically different to the newspaper environment. But what South Africa needed was *Business Day Sport Monthly* magazine, launched in August 2008. Mark penned the magazine's first editorial, 'When Words Matter'. It's replicated in this first volume of '50 Great Reads' of *Business Day Sport Monthly*, and it remains the reason we produce the magazine.

People appreciate quality sports writing. There are 16 different writers in this first volume, yet anyone who has contributed to the 300-odd pieces that have so far appeared but didn't make the 'Best Of', is desperately unlucky.

The 'selectors' – Mark and myself – didn't have an easy job when faced with the work from some of the finest sports writers in South Africa and abroad. Our writers have been original, they've written with authority, humour and opinion. And they've never compromised themselves by dropping their own high standards. We've been controversial at times but make no apologies for telling the audience how it is.

INTRODUCTION

If you put writers of the calibre of James Lawton, Mark Kram Jnr, James Corrigan, Peter Roebuck, Tom Eaton, Mark Keohane, Clinton van der Berg and Mark Gleeson together in the same sports department anywhere you'd call it the best sports department in the world. Each and all of these writers compete for space in *Business Day Sport Monthly*, and as the editor and publisher of the magazine, the most difficult decision each issue is who to leave on the subs bench.

By the same token, though, through two years of the magazine we've challenged ourselves to nudge the bar of excellence ever higher. There is a highly competent editorial production staff at Highbury Safika Media who work with the words and they have to be thanked for their professionalism, while the design team have to take huge credit for making it a visual delight.

Readers have responded with great enthusiasm. Some have even flatteringly called the product the *Time* magazine of South African sport. Advertisers, including blue chip companies, have embraced the magazine through the recession which is another endorsement of the quality of the magazine.

Peter Bruce, the editor of *Business Day*, has always demanded the best from the product. He must also get immense credit and thanks for believing, along with Mark and the HSM chief executive officer Kevin Ferguson, that this had the potential to be something special.

Of course, we're not here to judge other publications. The vision has always been to focus on what we are doing and to do it to the best of our ability. In getting to the position where we can produce a book of '50 Great Reads' suggests that the hard work has paid off. The work doesn't stop here, though. The South African sports audience is an intelligent one, a demanding one and it is one that is appreciative when it has something to celebrate.

This book is about celebrating the journey we've been on in the first two-and-a-bit years. Long may the journey continue.

GARY LEMKE
Publishing Director

WHEN WORDS MATTER

DAN JENKINS IS AMERICA'S MOST CELEBRATED SPORTS COLUMNIST AND, as far as I am concerned, the wisest, because he knows and promotes the value of words. When one of his younger colleagues was being seduced by television's ability to turn a talking head into a celebrity, Jenkins told him never to give up his column.

'They respect you if you write,' said Jenkins. 'The dumber the world gets, the more the words matter.'

Sports writing has to matter in this country, but those wonderful storytellers we have are being relegated to an afterthought because of television's instant replays and quick-fix solutions. Why read about it when you've watched it?

I have an answer to that but American author, columnist and writer of several sports books, Michael Lewis, says it so much better than I do. 'What's reassuring about great sports writing is what's reassuring about great sports performances: facing opposition, and often against the odds, someone, at last, did something right.'

That is what I believe *Business Day* editor Peter Bruce did in pursuing a sports publication for his newspaper. He did something right for the industry and his readers and he found a willing partner in Highbury Safika Media's CEO Kevin Ferguson.

The industry needs quality sports journalism and it needs a readership that appreciates that words do matter and that words educate as much as they entertain. Sport is important and in our country it deserves closer inspection, celebration and cross-examination. Instant online journalism, rent-a-quote sound bites from robotically programmed athletes and coaches and two-paragraph back-page briefs have robbed us all of the storyteller in sport and by consequence, the story.

In this launch issue, we've found the storytellers again and they've told the stories that you won't read on the back pages of any newspaper. They're fearless, honest, informed and interesting. There is passion and perspective to their writing and already there is a commercial appreciation, from the advertisers to our brilliant sales team, that content remains king.

The imagery in this publication is powerful and sourced from the best in the industry and put together by a world-class design team, but it is the words that will entertain and challenge you.

I have never understood the simplistic view that sports reporting and sports writing are merely positive expressions or a platform for negativity, because the writer can only tell the story of what is being acted out. The characters are for real, as are the sports in which they play or govern. In the sports writing world, the positive is accentuated through the accuracy of the story and accuracy is coupled to credibility. The negativity is shaped by the misrepresentation of the story.

The athletes and players will always be the celebrities in sport, but any good story demands a narrator and subsequent discussion.

I've always loved playing sport and writing about it. As a teenager, I accepted my sporting skills would bring pleasure to a handful that included me, but I was not good enough to play for South Africa, which didn't mean I couldn't write about those who were faster, stronger and more talented. Imagine if there were no storytellers to record and articulate the story of every day sporting achievement and the despair of losing? I can't imagine a world without sport and one without storytellers.

Why do I love sports writing so much? Again I have an answer to that, but again Michael Lewis says it better: 'It enables the writer to cram on to the page an awful lot of life that otherwise might be left off. Sports is the literary category that tolerates the most outrageous liberties: the writer doesn't need to be relevant. He needs only to be interesting.'

The writers in this issue are interesting and they are relevant to the future of the sports they care and write about. They know that words – like sport itself – matter.

MARK KEOHANE
Publishing Director

BYE-BYE BENNI?
FAT CHANCE

By Mark Gleeson

BENEDICT SAUL McCARTHY IS ARGUABLY SOUTH AFRICA'S FINEST EVER footballer. He has won over 70 caps and scored more goals for Bafana Bafana than any other player. Before his 30th birthday, he had competed in some of the top European leagues and become the only South African to ever garner a Uefa Champions League winners' medal. His transfer moves and contract deals over the past decade have been worth well over R100 million.

Yet, in a country where adulation of footballers sometimes reaches fever pitch, he remains a divisive figure, derided for his perceived lack of patriotism yet revered for his obvious influence on the fortunes of the national team. In normal circumstances, his beaming face, complete with dark scar under the right eye and golden tooth, would be peering out from every conceivable advertising forum, yet there are few corporates willing to risk associating their product with as controversial a figure.

McCarthy has had more divorces from Bafana Bafana than Liz Taylor and Zsa Zsa Gabor combined. His future with the team, even with the World Cup less than two years away, remains far from certain. Perhaps most galling is that despite his recent lack of playing time, goals and his podgy frame, he remains the vital ingredient to any potential recipe for success. Plainly put, McCarthy has this country hostage, able to dictate his own terms and make everyone else dance to the vagaries of his personal agenda.

It is a situation that speaks volumes of the deep, dark depths to which the national side has plummeted in recent years. To be fair, there has been a dearth of talent over recent generations but it has not been helped by poor coaching at youth level, which constantly delivers players adept at crowd-pleasing antics but devoid of any ability to put the ball in the back of the net.

Ordinarily, McCarthy's impudence would never be tolerated. But with no other player able to score goals, he remains Bafana Bafana's most sought after commodity (next in the queue is 33-year-old Sibusiso Zuma, whose dodgy knee guarantees he is often sidelined). In June, McCarthy was selected to play a taxing schedule of four qualifying matches but evidently had no appetite for another month of football after the completion of his English season.

While the rest of his team-mates were cloistered up in hotels and on training pitches, as well as forced to travel twice to the humidity and discomfort of West Africa, McCarthy took up residence in the nightclubs of Cape Town, missing out on playing for his country because of unspecified 'personal circumstances'. But in August, he was back again, almost without missing a beat, for the London friendly against Australia, the loose fit of the garish yellow kit unable to hide the expansion of his girth. Yet despite the extra pounds, it was McCarthy who set up both South African goals with sublime back heels that would have graced the Brazilian side, almost nonchalantly reinforcing the value of his role to the team.

Controversy attached itself to Benni McCarthy almost from the first moment of his professional career when his amateur club wanted a bigger share of the spoils than the set of tracksuits and bag of balls they had initially accepted to allow him to join Cape Town club Seven Stars.

McCarthy was discovered by former Orlando Pirates great, Meshack 'Mr Executive' Mjanqeka at Crusaders of Hanover Park, the bleak flat land where McCarthy grew up among the drug lords, gangsters and nightly cacophony of stray bullets.

Mjanqeka was the coach at Seven Stars, a newly created second-division side owned by magazine publisher Rob Moore. McCarthy's pace and finishing ability has since proved the ticket for both himself and Moore to a previously undreamt of world at the cutting edge of the international game. From cold nights in Langa township, where Seven Stars played on a bumpy patch after the goats had finished trimming the grass before kick-off, to sparkling arenas across Europe, the fortunes of the two have been intertwined ever since, both having benefited lucratively from the relationship. The entrepreneurial spirit of Moore advanced McCarthy quickly across the South African league landscape to Ajax Amsterdam in the Netherlands. The Dutch club had been suitably impressed when he proved the star of the 1997 African Youth Championship in Morocco, seeing enough of his potential to sign him on the spot even though McCarthy managed to get himself sent off and miss the final, which South Africa then lost to the hosts.

In a way, McCarthy proved one of the central figures in the demise of Clive Barker as Bafana Bafana coach at the end of 1997. A series of poor results post-World Cup qualification suggested Barker was unable to take the team up the extra notch they needed to ensure a competitive showing in the world's biggest sporting arena. The coach was also accused of intransigence in picking new talent, McCarthy being central to the argument. Once Barker got the bullet, Benni rolled into the team, used almost as a publicity point by Jomo Sono to legitimise his appointment as caretaker coach.

It was at the 1998 Africa Cup of Nations finals in Burkina Faso, ironically the 'land of the upright man', that the 20-year-old turned himself into an overnight national hero. Four goals in a single game against Namibia and seven overall in the tournament saw McCarthy become the pivot as Sono's new-look national side surprised all and sundry to reach the final in Ouagadougou, where they lost 2-0 to Egypt. He came home to a hero's welcome, his name now known in all the country's households.

McCarthy was mighty fortunate to have lasted past the first game of the event. It took a supreme display of brinkmanship by the far from saintly Sono to save him from expulsion in the first game, a dour goalless draw with Angola in Bobo-Dioulasso. McCarthy was in serious hot water for a prominent part in a full-on fist fight in the first half for which he should have been promptly sent off.

But while the referee was still trying to sort out the melee, and issue two red cards elsewhere, Sono had McCarthy feign injury and then quickly stretchered off the pitch for supposed treatment. A swift substitution was made and in the resultant confusion, the referee never got around to issuing McCarthy a deserved dismissal, which would have ensured a mandatory two-match suspension.

Sono's swift thinking saved McCarthy for the rest of the tournament and the heroics to come. Months later he scored against his boyhood hero Peter Schmeichel in the World Cup finals in France and by October 2000, had quickly amassed 23 caps. It was then that he first flexed his new-found muscle, encouraged by his manager Moore and after a R50 million move to Celta Vigo in Spain, releasing a statement announcing his 'retirement' from the international game at the age of 21 years and 11 months.

'It worries me that my club career is suffering,' he said at the time, making it clear he was putting club above country. Had Moore not engineered the 'retirement', on the pretext of McCarthy having been forced to come back to South Africa to play a meaningless match against Saudi Arabia, McCarthy would have been forced to go to the Nations Cup tournament in Ghana and Nigeria at the start of 2000 and would have surely lost his lustre in Spain a lot sooner than he eventually did.

The conflict between club and country was born in the era before the co-ordinated international calendar, which now dictates which match days are specifically for club football and which for international duty. Less than a decade ago, each continent had its own calendar and often the African internationals clashed with league programmes in Europe. In that case, countries were allowed to call up players for a specified number of matches per year, a total that changed over the years but averaged at around seven.

For an African footballer seeking to establish himself at a European club, the irritation of having to miss key club games because of international duty was all too evident. Gone went the bonus money and more than likely a place in the first team line-up too. But any empathy with the young McCarthy's cause evaporated when he suddenly 'came out of retirement', conveniently close to the Olympic Games in 2000 and at a time when his career in Spain began to stall.

There is nothing quite like the international arena to polish up the glitter of your star. He played throughout the era of Carlos Queiroz and would not have dared to miss the 2002 Nations Cup finals in Mali, so soon before the World Cup finals in Japan and South Korea. It also helped that he was desperate to get away from Spain and by going to the Nations Cup tournament, he would be away from his club for an effective six-week period. Effectively he gave them a solid two-finger salute at a time when they were putting an unreasonable transfer fee on his head and dissuading potential suitors. When he came back from Mali, Moore had arranged a loan spell under Jose Mourinho at FC Porto and the change of scenery saw McCarthy score 12 goals in 10 starts.

In September 2002, Moore advised McCarthy against signing a contract the South African Football Association (Safa) demanded its national team players sign, one that allowed the association to exploit the player's commercial rights, as well as set down wages for national team appearances.

McCarthy said at the time: 'People can think what they want about me but it's the new generation of young players I am trying to protect from being exposed.'

Into exile he went again, but was brought back within six months, in mid-2003 for a prestige friendly against England in Durban. Of course, he scored in the match. McCarthy hung around long enough to collect a 50th cap, Safa missing the milestone but attempting in Pythonesque fashion to make up for the oversight by appointing him Bafana Bafana captain for his 51st game.

Then came 'retirement' again in order to miss the 2004 Nations Cup finals in Tunisia, a fallout with coach Ephraim Mashaba conveniently allowing him to concentrate on his career at FC Porto. Without the burden of national team duty, he was able to feature prominently in Porto's march to the Champions League title, including two brilliant goals against his favourite club Manchester United.

A third national comeback coincided with the tenure of Stuart Baxter as coach and helped McCarthy to get his competitive national team appearances up to the level of 75% required for a British work permit. His agent Moore was beavering away at a lucrative move to the English market. But when McCarthy was needed most by his country – for a decisive World Cup qualifier at home to Ghana in June 2005 – he was sitting on the rides in the sunshine at Disney World.

In the previous qualifier, in the Cape Verde Islands, he had contrived to pick up a caution in the final minute of the match, a second yellow card of the campaign that brought a convenient one-match suspension and an early holiday in the USA.

The South African side sans McCarthy lost 2-0 at home to a Michael Essien-inspired Ghana and tumbled out of contention for a place in the 2006 World Cup finals when they effectively needed just a draw to book their place.

In 2006, McCarthy went to the Nations Cup in Egypt with arguably the worst side ever assembled by South Africa and ran headlong into another dispute over contracts and payments again. It was the catalyst for another long period of exile, this time lasting 18 months and ending only when Carlos Alberto Parreira went to see him in Manchester. McCarthy was well ensconced at Blackburn Rovers by this time, having scored 18 goals in his first season in the English league. His return for Bafana Bafana came with a condition, however: to be left out of yet another Nations Cup trip, this time the 2008 finals in Egypt.

Now able to pick and choose his games, it came as no surprise when McCarthy's impudence hit an all-time low in June this year. Not even Moore was able to muster a customary soprano defence of his charge. Having lost his place in the Blackburn side, McCarthy could actually have done with the playing time. Without him, South Africa lost away in Nigeria and Sierra Leone and in a tired-looking display even failed to score at home against the feeble Leone Stars in Atteridgeville.

With the need to create a competitive side for the World Cup finals increasing, desperate officials have had to stomach the McCarthy agenda (he was even handed the captaincy for the match against Nigeria in Port Elizabeth). It is a situation that won't change until such time as any credible successor is found. For the sake of the sanctity of the game, the arrival of that blessed soul cannot come quick enough.

Benni McCarthy is the leading goal-scorer in South Africa's international football history – with 31. However, the last of those goals for Bafana Bafana came in October 2008. He has been the enfant terrible of the national team for years. He was consistently criticised by his English Premier League managers for being overweight and in September 2010 was fined for not losing enough weight. He was also selected for the initial 2010 World Cup squad, before being left out at the last moment. Despite his poor conditioning, McCarthy always seemed to get another chance at international level.

Mark Gleeson is a globally respected television commentator and editorial director of Mzanzi Football. He is an SAB award-winning broadcaster and commentates for SuperSport. He is an authority on African football and also works extensively for Reuters, among other organisations. He has an encyclopedic knowledge of the continent's football. He was once referred to by the former Observer columnist and renowned football author Simon Kuper, as 'the anorak's anorak'. Gleeson's garage at home in Cape Town holds his drum kit and plenty of footballing treasures.

PRECIOUS ONE
By Patrick Farrell

THE ACCENT IS HARD TO PLACE. PART PIETERMARITZBURG MAYBE, PART British Midlands. It's deep, mannered and refined. Not the thing to expect from a diminutive man who only stands 1.47m tall and weighed 56kg when he was a competitive weightlifter.

'Thank you for calling, young man,' says Precious McKenzie, the slight delay on the line to Auckland presenting the usual stop-start 'sorry, you go, no *you* go' international telephone conversation.

Small talk begins with the Olympics. He participated in three (1968, 1972 and 1976), representing Great Britain but alas was not among the winners.

'I didn't have much time to watch Beijing. I was in Australia on business [he is a consultant in the field of back injury prevention] but one of my New Zealand boys was there, Mark Spooner. I trained him. You know his parents said to me when I first started with him that they would fly me to the Olympics if he was chosen. They called me up and said it was all on to go to Beijing but I just couldn't make it. I had all these seminars booked. A pity really.'

He competed himself until two years ago.

'I broke five world records in 2006 in Las Vegas at the World Champs and then that was that. The hunger was gone. My body said to me "Hey boy, you've had enough".'

He had just turned 70 then.

Nine times British weightlifting champion, 10 times British powerlifting champion, five times world powerlifting champion and current World Masters powerlifting champ. He was inducted into the powerlifting Hall of Fame in Texas in 1981 and granted an MBE by the Queen in 1974.

Oh, and he also won gold in four successive Commonwealth Games – a record, the last one coming when he was 42.

Suddenly another phone rings in the background.

'It's the BBC,' comes a woman's voice – his wife Elisabeth.

'Sorry, would you mind calling back in an hour? I promised them I would do this. It's for Northampton.'

Born in Durban in 1936, he was baptized 'Precious One' because he survived a serious illness in the same year his father was killed by a crocodile in the Limpopo River. His mother turned to drink and he and his younger sister Gloria were given up to a series of foster families. Beaten and malnourished, he grew no taller than a child. Wiry and a natural athlete, he was encouraged to take up gymnastics at a Catholic mission school in Pofadder when he was 11. He returned to his mother in Pietermaritzburg at age 17 and worked in a local shoe factory, but Precious had another ambition: he wanted to join the circus. He laboured away at Steve's Gym, training at 5:30am every morning before work, but when the circus came to town he was told that his skin colour was wrong. He was classified coloured, you see.

So he turned to weightlifting instead. In 1957 he won the Natal bantamweight title and the next year the South African title. However, he was not selected for the Empire Games the same year because of his race, and again in 1960, when an all-white team was sent to the Rome Olympics, despite him smashing records at the non-racial Olympic trials. By then he was regarded as South Africa's best weightlifter, but he was not given full Springbok colours. In 1963, he became the first coloured Springbok when he was selected for the World Champs in Sweden, but he refused to participate when the colours came with conditions (he would have to travel separately from his team-mates, for example). So he left, turned his back on his country and went to another place that accepted him.

In 1964, he emigrated to the UK with Elisabeth and their two girls, Vanessa and Sandra. He left for Northampton ahead of them, only to be confronted with the news that he'd have to live and work in the country for five years before he could compete for England. Alone and disillusioned, he thought he had made the wrong choice but when his family joined him, Elisabeth encouraged him to stick it out. They lived in a tiny, one-roomed flat while he worked in a shoe factory but he continued training and competing.

As in South Africa, he dominated competitions and soon his achievements reached the ears of the British government. In 1966, the British minister of sport, Dennis Howell, fast-tracked his citizenship and Precious represented England in the Commonwealth Games in Jamaica, promptly winning a gold medal in the bantamweight division. That is still his proudest sporting memory, along with his induction into the world powerlifting Hall of Fame in Texas in 1981.

An hour later and that smooth voice is back again. 'Sorry about that. They wanted me to chat about the Olympics. It was on the radio and the chairman of the club where I used to train in Northampton was listening in.

'Oh yes, that medal in Jamaica. When I won gold there were tears in my eyes. I was happy but heartsore. Sad that I couldn't win it for my birth country because I was not white. But I went to a place that accepted me with open arms. My colour wasn't even a question. Emphasise that, young man, emphasise that.'

He has been outspoken for years on the questions of sport and race.

'It's something I've fought against. I've been firm about it. I believe strongly in ability, in merits, not colour. I left my country for this. If you say there must be more black people than white people ... there is no such thing. Quotas ... no, no, no.'

Forgiveness is a constant in his conversation.

'It's the Mandela attitude. We fought the same battles. You must forgive. Don't forget, but forgive.'

As he said of his mother: 'She was a woman who treated us so badly, she was the real devil but my sister and I have forgiven her. No matter who it is, you have to forgive eventually.'

Talk returns to the Olympics again and weightlifting.

'I detest drugs. Sportsmen who do that are not using their bodies. In those days we all knew fellows who were doing it. Russians and Bulgarians. That's why it was so hard to beat them. Their governments were providing the stuff for them.'

He keeps an interest in the world of weightlifting and does some training (his Kiwi, Spooner, finished 21st at the Games in the under-69kg division), but mostly these days he is tied up with his business.

He runs courses in New Zealand, Australia, Singapore, the United Kingdom, and the US, advising companies how best to avoid back injuries in the workplace. 'Most back injuries are not caused by lifting heavy loads,' is the catchphrase on his website. 'You can put your back out lifting up a set of keys.'

There are even a series of pictures on the site showing the dapper McKenzie in white dust coat demonstrating the right way to lift an object and mop the floor.

'Last year I travelled 5 000 miles throughout the UK by car. Rolls Royce, Airbus, they're all my clients.'

After the 1974 Commonwealth Games, which were held in Christchurch, he decided to emigrate again, to New Zealand, but this time for good. He won't be moving back to South Africa but he did pop over in December for his sister's 70th and will be back next year – 'I have to train the chap who is going to play me'.

Ah, the movie.

Wheels are in motion to shoot a film, simply titled *Precious*, about his life. New Zealand father and son Lance and James Morcan believe they have a powerful movie in the making that will have widespread appeal.

'It's a story that must be told,' says Lance.

'It's a reflection of his indomitable spirit, that no matter how bad things got – be it extreme poverty, violence, racial hatred – Precious remained unbreakable,' says James.

It was supposed to begin shooting in November but will now apparently start in January. Casting hasn't started yet but will present some problems seeing the usual Hollywood stars will be way too tall for the lead role.

Precious himself remains modest about his input, directing queries to the Morcans – 'They know a lot more about it than me'.

When it is released it will perhaps be the first time many South Africans will have heard anything about this tiny man, even though he was eventually inducted into the South African Sports Hall of Fame in 2006.

'Man, for my achievements to be recognised by my homeland was a dream come true,' he said at the time. 'Finally, I have got recognition from my own people.

'You're always remembered when you're dead. I'm just lucky people are remembering me now, while I'm alive.'

Finally when we say goodbye he muses about weightlifting, how it is still largely an amateur, minority sport despite the rigorous, dangerous and long training. 'Thank you for your interest, young man, thank you.'

South Africans are well aware of the damage apartheid did but every so often one needs reminding of what the country lost in the dark years. One sporting talent was the weightlifter Precious McKenzie. Born in Durban, he was forced out of the country of his birth but his desire and ability was such that he represented New Zealand and England internationally. This was an interview with a man just 1.45m in stature but a giant in life.

Patrick Farrell bowled like Michael Holding and batted like Viv Richards. At least in his dreams, although his parents did have a litany of broken windows to prove his prowess with the hook shot. Or more correctly the 'hoick'. Long since retired from Durban, the '70s, and backyard cricket, he works as a journalist in Cape Town where he is editorial director at Highbury Safika Media.

FOR KEV AND COUNTRY
By Peter Roebuck

KEVIN PIETERSEN'S APPOINTMENT AS ENGLAND CAPTAIN WAS THE culmination of a long, bold and hazardous journey undertaken by a player nicknamed 'The Ego' by former colleagues but feared by bowlers around the world. Far from shrinking under the weight of responsibility, the settler from Pietermaritzburg put into practice the attitude that carried him from the 2nd XI at Maritzburg College to the leading role in the country where bat and ball first fell into combat. Naturally he was delighted by his promotion. It had been a rough ride. In his early days in county cricket, he was regularly forced to stand in a corner and sing 'God Save the Queen'. Anything to put the loud intruder in his place. He did not baulk at it, understood he had to pay his dues. Later, his kit was thrown over the balcony by his captain and this time he retaliated. He has had his revenge on all who rejected him.

Recognition and a desire to be accepted have counted among Pietersen's driving forces. Throughout his time in England, he has done everything he can to demonstrate his commitment, scoring runs, tearing attacks apart, awakening the national team, helping them to win back the Ashes. He knew it was not enough and so went further, adding patriotic tattoos to his body, and displaying them to all who asked. It was an attempt to display permanence, to convince sceptics that he was not flying a flag of convenience, did not yearn for veld and beach or braaivleis and wors (though everyone knows he does). And he went even further, burning bridges with his former country, even picking a fight with Graeme Smith, denouncing transformation policies, portraying himself as a victim (not an easy task for a well-raised boy from a comfortable family who attended a prestigious school). In his mind, his country had let him down. Of course, it was an oversimplification but it has been a powerful motivating force.

His promotion to the captaincy was important because it indicated acceptance, almost dependence. He needed England and it needed him. Throughout he has been forced to fight for the recognition he thought he deserved. Repeatedly the world told him he was humdrum, and he always felt he was exceptional. England had the fortune to be his proving ground, the place where the upstart made his name. English cricket has been a beneficiary, not a prophet. And now it has had the sense to give him his head.

Throughout that first match in charge, Pietersen remained aggressive. He captained as he batted, choosing five bowlers and letting them loose on an opponent whose resolve had been weakened by its impregnable position in the series. Nothing was held back. But it was not all bugle and bluster. Pietersen is a street-smart cricketer. Most particularly, he understands the importance of seizing and retaining the initiative, and to that end is prepared to take risks. By and large, his gambles are shrewdly calculated. And inactivity is also fraught with danger. In the antipodean phrase, he is not the sort to die wondering.

Naturally he batted in the same forthright, apparently extravagant and yet calculated manner. There is nothing half-baked about him. Sometimes it gets him into trouble. His dismissals tend to attract excessive censure. Pietersen tries to dictate the course of events and that requires risk. Even his worst dismissals in the recent Test series can be defended. He was trying to impose himself. Another 10 minutes and it might have worked. Meanwhile, team-mates nibbled like aged hamsters. And anyhow, there is a fine line between a breathtaking counter-attack at the critical moment in an Ashes decider and an assault on a seamer that might have changed the game. Not everything can be judged by its outcome.

Typically, too, Pietersen ended up on the winning side. That has always been his aim and his expectation. Apparently he lost only two matches in an undistinguished school career. College, as his seat of learning is generally called, much as Gandhi is Gandhi and Dylan is Dylan, does not like to lose and makes no apologies for the fact. Hard work, high standards and a rugged culture are the cornerstones of the school ethic. Not long ago, the entire student body gathered on the main field to protest a demotion imposed on a head boy for caning recalcitrant Grade 8s. They were complaining about the oncoming softness. College is a tough place for tough people, and Pietersen thrived within its walls.

Although it is foolish to rush to judgement, the newcomer's performance in his first Test as captain boded well for his prospects. It was neither a safe nor a unanimous decision. Observers could remember Ian Botham's disastrous stint as captain and worried his equally brash successor might make the same mistakes. But Botham was young, reckless and self-indulgent. He convinced himself he could take everyone along with him on his adventure. It was a fantasy that became a nightmare. Pietersen is more ruthless, experienced and individualistic. He is prepared to make unpopular decisions. Indeed his career tells of little else. He was the right man for the job.

Yet his promotion was resented. Pietersen's relentless promotion of his own interests has not endeared him to everyone but he is hardly alone in that. Although cricketers nowadays join in huddles, it remains a starkly isolating game and players know they must perform or face the consequences. Sometimes the ambition is naked, sometimes it is guarded but it is seldom absent. In Pietersen's case everything is on the table. He sharpens the blades of his critics even as he loads the guns of his defenders.

Considering his extraordinary feats, it must seem as if Cricket SA blundered horribly when it allowed Pietersen to slip through its grasp. By no means is it as simple as that. Despite all the nonsense he has talked over the years, as a boy Pietersen was just another hot-headed hopeful. South African cricket had no particular reason to take him seriously. To his subsequent regret, his experienced school coach did not pick him to play for the 1st XI until his final term. Previously, Mike Bechet had preferred Matthew Cairns, a little leg-spinner who later emigrated to New Zealand. Eventually Pietersen was chosen as a hard-hitting lower-order batsman and useful off-spinner. He was big and upright and gave the ball a thump. That did not set him apart. So did almost all of his team-mates. It is the College way. His bowling was tidy but undemanding.

In short, Pietersen seemed no more likely to make his mark than 50 others taking part in school festivals. Most observers were surprised when he was chosen to represent his province in a youth tournament. But already he was a legend in his own mind. That took courage.

After school, Pietersen fought for his place in the KwaZulu-Natal side but again his performances were modest and his progress was slow. Overall he played nine matches for various provincial teams, collecting 222 runs in 13 innings at an average of 20 and taking 20 wickets at an average of 30. He only scored one fifty for his province, and that for the B side. It was hardly the stuff of legend. Yet belief did not wither. Next, he represented KZN on a pre-season tour to West Australia and took five wickets in a warm-up match. Aggrieved that his performance had been ignored in the newspapers, he confronted the reporter and was duly told he had bowled tripe and was lucky the batsmen were hitting out. Already he was impatient, confident and headstrong. In the words of Muhammad Ali, he was not 'conceited so much as convinced'. And yet there was one innings that might have rung bells. Playing against England in a 50-over match in 1999, Pietersen struck four sixes as he charged to 61 not out in 57 balls. Otherwise, he did not attract attention. Not that he was given much chance, never batting higher than No 8 in the strong A side.

And so Pietersen went off on in search of an opening. Already he had printed business cards introducing himself as 'Kevin Pietersen – Professional Cricketer'. In his mind, his destiny was not in doubt, merely his location. It was a bold outlook. Men like him must rise or face ridicule.

Now comes the part of his career that has been rewritten more times than Russian history. Following in the footsteps of hundreds of young South African and Australian cricketers, he went to England to spend a winter playing club cricket. Clive Rice had seen him play at a school's festival and, hearing he was around, invited him to sign for the county he was coaching, Nottinghamshire. Pietersen leapt at the chance to play competitive cricket for good money under a leader he respected. At this stage, he was not thinking about changing allegiance, did not understand a choice had to be made.

Soon Pietersen was forced to make a choice. He consulted past players, talked to KZN officials and flew to Joburg to meet Ali Bacher, always seeking reassurances. None were forthcoming. It could hardly have been otherwise. He wanted to know whether teams would be chosen strictly on merit. He had a career to construct and had played enough 2nd XI cricket. Although a junior contract was offered, no promises were provided. He was not in a position to demand anything. He heard that Gulam Bodi, a coloured spinner, had been lured to KZN and regarded that as a bad sign.

And so he packed his bag for England. At the time it seemed like arrogance. After all, he had hardly scored a run in serious company. Nor did he leave quietly, attacking South African cricket officials as he departed. His remarks did not go down well. Nor were they justified. He was not rejected. He walked out. Other promising white cricketers stayed and proved their worth. Even so, South Africa has been too harsh on him. He does not deserve to be singled out merely because he made it. Pietersen is not the only College boy, let alone KZN cricketer, to try his luck overseas. Ant Botha has been playing county cricket for years.

Pietersen joined Rice in Nottinghamshire, scored five centuries and two double centuries in his first season, and stayed for three years. It was his first move in pursuit of the greatness he felt within, an extraordinarily wilful and audacious step towards his destiny. Before anyone knew his name he was shouting it from the rooftops. In the UK, he delighted in driving around in a car with 'Kevin Pietersen – Nottingham Professional' blazed on its bonnet. At least he brightened up a city described by novelist Tom Sharpe, once an inhabitant, as 'half the size of a New York cemetery and twice as dead'.

Seeking greatness, Pietersen continued to surround himself with it, pursued it in every arena. He worked hard and took no prisoners. When Nottinghamshire did not meet his standards (after Rice departed), Pietersen walked out with a year left on his contract. Eager to rub shoulders with Shane Warne, he joined Hampshire. From a distance it might seem he was craving money and attention. Certainly he took every opportunity that arose. But it was not about glory or glitter. He wanted to be exceptional and could not abide anything less. It did not always make him easy company but it was uncompromising and courageous.

And now the boy from Pietermaritzburg has become captain of all England. Finally the radical has been warmly welcomed. England's new captain has dared to explore, even to expand, his horizons. It is one of the most hazardous undertakings known to man. He went in search of the supreme. It is exactly the journey England has been so reluctant to undertake. Captain and country may not like each other all that much, but they will rise together.

Kevin Pietersen had travelled an extraordinary route, turning his back on South Africa and starting a new life in England. He was never short of talent nor self-belief and after serving his qualification period in his adopted country, he was chosen to play for England. A sensational run of form and success saw him awarded with the captaincy. 'KP' had arrived.

Peter Roebuck played cricket for Somerset before settling in Australia. He has been writing on cricket for the Sydney Morning Herald and Melbourne Age for 25 years. He has written eight or so cricket books. It Never Rains was recently voted the third best book in the field. Nowadays he divides his time between Sydney and South Africa, where he helps 40 impoverished young Zimbabweans take their place in the world. However, parts of him remain in Bulawayo and India.

0.01 SEC
By Mark Keohane

MICHAEL PHELPS'S IMMEDIATE THOUGHT WAS THAT HE HAD BLOWN HIS chance at Olympic history in losing the 100m butterfly final. Milorad Cavic, a Californian who swims for Serbia because of dual citizenship, thought he had created his own bit of history in beating Phelps. The naked eye could not separate the two at the finish and technology declared Phelps the winner.

The conspiracy theorists made the point that Omega, for whom Phelps is an ambassador, made the equipment that determined Phelps' fingernail to be longer than Cavic's. The Phelps supporters ridiculed this theory, asking if Omega knew in advance that Phelps would be swimming in lane five of the final.

'Get serious and salute a true champion,' was the general sentiment of the pro-Phelps bloggers.

'Cavic touched first,' responded those favouring Cavic.

The debate was intense on the internet and Phelps supporters insisted there was no doubt and that their man would have crashed through a brick wall with the power he hit the touch pad, while Cavic, in their view, miscalculated the distance to the touch pad with his final stroke. Commentators were divided as to which swimmer got there first. Ironically, the swimmer who thought he had lost won and Americans had their Hollywood ending.

'When I took that last stroke, I thought I lost the race there, but it turns out that was the difference,' said Phelps. Cavic added: 'The hand is quicker than the eye. I am taking what I got and I'm happy. If we raced again I would win it.'

The Serbian swimming officials refused to be as accommodating of the Phelps phenomenon and appealed the decision. Cavic asked them to back off and accept the result.

Cavic, schooled at Berkeley, and resident in the United States, glided away from controversy with the same grace as he glided to the touch pad. Phelps' explosive final lunge in the 100m butterfly final was in keeping with his impact at the Beijing Games in becoming the first swimmer to win eight gold medals at one Olympics.

Sports writers declared Phelps the greatest swimmer of all time, but equally as many trumpeted Cavic as a champion who epitomises the values of sportsmanship and Olympic spirit.

Cavic may not have a gold medal but his type, they wrote, gave swimming and the Olympic Games integrity. Here was confirmation that it was not just about winning and that there was honour in competing.

Did Phelps touch first?

Video cameras record at either 25 or 30 frames a second and the margin determined by the touchpads in this race – the 100m butterfly final – was a hundredth of a second. There may be no definitive video evidence in existence to prove the touchpad technology got it right.

Some continued to question the validity of the Phelps win but Cavic pleaded with everyone to move on and hammered the media for not respecting the result.

Cavic, on his blog, wrote: 'I am completely happy, and still in complete disbelief that I was able to achieve this feat [winning the silver]. I'm not joking … It's a tough loss, but I'm on cloud nine. I congratulated Phelps and his coach Bob Bowman. I'm just glad the race was fun to watch for everyone. It was a pleasure for me, really.

'As for the filing of a protest: Yes, as you all saw, I almost won the gold, and if you ask me, the clock does not lie. I had nothing to do with this filing, and neither did my coach Mike Bottom. This is just another attack on my coach who has never wronged anyone in swimming, except coach foreign athletes [non-Americans] to Olympic medals. You all have to understand that any coach would have done this for their swimmer if there was any possibility of error, but I'm sorry to disappoint. It was my Olympic committee and swimming staff who did the filing.

'We're not "sour grapes" and we're not "pissed" … If you ask me, it should be accepted and we should move on. I've accepted defeat, and there's nothing wrong with losing to the greatest swimmer there has ever been.'

Phelps, in Beijing, went where no swimmer had gone before in bettering Mark Spitz's seven golds at the 1972 Munich Games, and his sponsor Speedo paid him $1 million for breaking the record, which consisted of five individual and three relay races.

Phelps has no equal in swimming, but even the great need help and if technology favoured Phelps against Cavic, the eight golds would not have happened without Jason Lezak's incredible swim in the 4x100m freestyle relay.

Lezak took more than one second off his fastest 100m split, to catch and beat France's Alain Bernard and win the USA gold to ensure Phelps would be a gold and a million dollars richer. Lezak, after the swim of his life, said he neither expects nor desires a cut of Phelps' cash.

Lezak at least got a gold medal, which is more than Cavic got, although you can't put a price on integrity and dignity. For that, Cavic will always be remembered as more than just another swimmer beaten by Michael Phelps in Beijing, if in fact he actually was.

The official photo finish in the Olympic men's 100m butterfly final confirmed Michael Phelps' standing as a swimming legend. The jury remained out long after the event though, with the naked eye unable to separate the American and his Serbian rival, Milorad Cavic. Conspiracy theorists had a field day. The timing of this article reflected the ongoing debate around the result.

Mark Keohane *is the founder of the multiple award-winning rugby blog* keo.co.za *and the author of books that include* Chester – the biography, Springbok Rugby Uncovered, Champions of the World *and* Monty. *He is a former winner of the SAB Sports Journalist of the Year award, among other accolades. He was a rugby journalist for 10 years before being appointed communications manager for the Springboks, a position he filled for three years. He lives in Cape Town and was integral to the creation and launch of Business Day Sport Monthly. He is currently chief operating officer at Highbury Safika Media.*

MONOPOLY MONEY
By Mark Gleeson

PATRICE MOTSEPE MIGHT BE A MAJOR CAPTAIN OF INDUSTRY, PEER OUT from the front cover of *Fortune* magazine and be accorded a seat among a distinguished few at the recent presidential inauguration, but it is highly likely none of these trappings of wealth and power come close to the aphrodisiac of owning his own football team.

It is no ordinary club, mind you. Mamelodi Sundowns is a side that has risen rapidly over just two decades, from almost provincial-like obscurity in a township on the fringes of Pretoria, into the closest South Africa has to a Hollywood-style collection of sports stars. Motsepe, too, has danced from the financial pages into the national consciousness, now easily counted among the most recognisable figures in the country, on the back of his involvement with Sundowns.

It is a public persona that has not come cheap.

He has become, at no small expense, the 'Roman Abramovich' of South African football, injecting a financial muscle into the game that astonishes, perplexes and irritates his counterparts, but has rapidly raised the profile and legitimacy of the domestic game, something even his arch-rivals begrudgingly admit.

Irvin Khoza calls him 'The Man'. The Premier Soccer League chairman, and Orlando Pirates owner, probably calls him a lot of other things, too, behind his back as Motsepe has brought turmoil to the transfer market and killed off the cozy dominance Khoza and his Kaizer Chiefs counterpart Kaizer Motaung so long enjoyed.

'He's killing us,' Khoza joked this winter as yet another proposed signing was lost to Motsepe's magnetic chequebook. Khoza said it with his toothy smile but you could feel the frustration.

Motsepe, who will be 47 in January, seems to take an almost perverse pleasure in 'gazumping' the pair, bringing to an abrupt end the stranglehold Chiefs and Pirates have held over decades of the domestic game. Sundowns shattered the record books with deal after deal in the off-season, eventually signing 11 new players in their bid to win back the Premiership crown.

Although there are no official statistics, it has been widely held that the record domestic transfer fee for a player moving from one South African club to another was R1.8 million.

Motsepe managed to splatter that record several times in the matter of weeks in a steady flurry of July activity, his biggest deal being a R5 million payout to SuperSport United for the Bafana Bafana pair of Siboniso Gaxa and Katlego Mphela.

His biggest coup, though, was the signing of Sibusiso Zuma, who was offered an extension of his contract at Arminia Bielefeld in the German Bundesliga but was offered the same money by Motsepe and made the rather easy decision to come home. Zuma's estimated annual earnings are R3 million, which would make him the biggest earner among those sportsmen who earn their professional income exclusively in South Africa.

Motsepe had a hand in all of the deals, some common sense and others eclectic. His hold on everyday affairs is all too passionate even if he sits poker-faced through most of his team's matches.

Despite this, there is little doubting the club has turned from a rich man's play thing into a time-consuming obsession. This on top of running African Rainbow Minerals and his sizeable interests in companies like Sanlam, which have earned him a personal fortune estimated at $2.4 billion.

Motsepe is increasingly almost always at Sundowns' home matches at the Super Stadium in Atteridgeville and frequently at away games too. At the MTN8 final at the Absa Stadium in Durban, he sat next to King Goodwill Zwelithini. Two days later, he was being ushered into a row alongside the country's political leaders for Kgalema Motlanthe's inauguration at Tuynhuys as South Africa's new president.

Just weeks ago, two Bloemfontein traffic cops sped Motsepe from the Free State Stadium back to the city's airport to catch his private jet back home to Johannesburg after a win for Sundowns over home side Celtic.

Sunday afternoon traffic in the Free State capital probably hasn't changed much since the Boer Republic and Motsepe is a private citizen, yet the city deemed it proper to accord the magnate a flashing escort along an empty highway to the small terminus. It had all to do with his pop-star appeal rather than any need to catch his flight on time.

At the Super Stadium, orange cones mark out the parking slot he commands at the front door of the home Sundowns share with SuperSport United.

Motsepe's arrival is met, these days, with regal protocol, a fawning swarm of attendants speeding him up to a high-backed chair in the VIP enclosure, where Motsepe will sit stoically through the game, almost like a schoolboy seeking to be brave on a visit to the dentist.

Afterwards, Motsepe comes down into the bowel of the concrete stadium and strides to the change room, often keeping his side stuck inside for an age.

From outside, there is the frequent sound of communal clapping, presumably accompanying the latest promise of a win bonus for which Motsepe has a reputation of exceeding generosity. He was also the first to pay a six-figure monthly pay package, in both cases pulling one over the ultra-cautious Kaizer Motaung.

First, he enticed away Chiefs' long-standing first-choice goalkeeper, Brian Baloyi, with the temptation of a R100 000 salary and then pipped Chiefs to the services of Peter Ndlovu in mid-2004.

Motsepe's considerable investment means he has no intention of being a hands-off benefactor, content to sit in the VIP box and occasionally glad hand the players and supporters.

In recent months, Motsepe has become more influential in team selection too, demanding, for example, coach Trott Moloto no longer pick the Uruguay import Bryan Aldave after Gordon Igesund had been fired in February.

Aldave might have not been the most gracious footballer but his ability to win aerial balls, draw defenders off team-mates and finish well made him a player Moloto had intended to use. But Motsepe did not think he was any good and Moloto was told to stop selecting him.

Sundowns players and officials, past and present, paint a picture of some eccentricity on the part of their boss, although none want to do so on the record.

Motsepe often summons his coaches and managers to his Bryanston home in the early hours of the morning to demand explanations and issue instructions. He once had a video of Brazil playing and wanted to know why his team didn't play the same way.

They look more and more like Brazil these days, if truth be told, if only because they both have the same kit sponsor.

Nike has replaced Diadora as kit suppliers in a switch that speaks to the brand-conscious nature of the owner and his courtiers. But Sundowns do not have a title sponsor, after their contract with MTN came to an end last season.

The cellular network had sought to renegotiate but Motsepe rejected the R20 million-a-year deal offer that would have left Sundowns well behind the commercial pull of Chiefs and Pirates. The Amakhosi and Buccaneers earn an estimated R45 million a year from their sponsorship deals with Vodacom, Nissan and Standard Bank. It speaks to Motsepe's all-consuming ambition to usurp the two Soweto giants that he would turn down a potential R100 million over five years and rather fund the club out of his own pocket, than suffer the slight of being sponsored to the tune of half the money his two major rivals are getting.

Particularly galling it must be too, if you are outmuscling them everywhere else; the transfer market, and on the pitch in the chase for trophies.

To have that big an ego demands a wallet of similar size but Motsepe's profile is exactly the tonic the domestic game needs. For decades the game has been a festering pit of shady operators, unscrupulous characters and men of violence and little moral fibre. The letter 'c' may appear twice in the word 'soccer' but there has never been any 'class' in South African football.

Motsepe, with his military bearing, benevolent smile and Tswana royal roots, has taken it up several notches at a time when the coverage of the Premiership had reached unprecedented levels. Just in the way Jose Mourinho and Abramovich have livened up the English game and turned it into even more of a world brand, so the arrival of Motsepe and his ilk in the South African game has propelled the Premiership to a new sphere of respectability.

Not that there are many Motsepe clones on the horizon. Another mining magnate, Mzi Khumalo, was flirting with Durban club Lamontville Golden Arrows but little has come of that connection, save for his name on the letterhead. Brian Joffe of Bidvest has taken over Wits University, and also invested considerably and played an active role, but is not a figure who commands publicity like the urbane Motsepe, who *Fortune* magazine dubbed the 'Prince of Mines'.

Rich Swedes have set up Thanda Royal Zulu, a reclusive German investor owns Moroka Swallows and sugar money propels AmaZulu. As the profile of the owners improves, so does the professionalism of the game and the quality of its personnel, on and off the pitch. But few can slap about the cash in the style Motsepe has, creating for the local game enthralling daily episodes that rival the twists and turns of the best written soap operas.

It has contributed to a growing rise in interest and the associated benefits of new sponsorship and TV rights money that all the clubs now enjoy.

The playing field is a lot more even although Motsepe will, in all likelihood, buy the league title for Sundowns this season, the depth of quality at the club arguably too strong for any of the other 15 Premiership clubs to challenge.

It is what Jack Walker did at Blackburn Rovers and Abramovich did for Chelsea; Massimo Moratti at Inter Milan and Jean-Michel Aulas at Lyon.

Sundowns have already carved apart Chiefs and Pirates' monopoly but their contribution in recent years is to add a sense of much-needed intrigue, style and glamour. The club was on the verge of relegation in the mid-80s when Zola Mahobe took over. He bought as liberally as Motsepe has, although it turned out later a girlfriend had been stealing millions from Standard Bank to fund the extravagance. Mahobe became soccer's equivalent of Robin Hood and continued being feted after serving a seven-year jail term.

The next owners, Abe and Solly Krok, who had made millions from harmful skin lightening creams, found that involvement with Sundowns shielded their profile from more serious scrutiny and gave them a legitimacy in the black market they did not deserve.

Motsepe, whose father named him after iconic Congolese leader Patrice Lumumba, comes with none of that baggage. Instead, there are respectable credentials given his family connections (brother-in-law Jeff Radebe is the minister of transport) and place among the first black lawyers to graduate from Wits University.

The danger of Motsepe is if his side ever achieves his ambition of all-conquering glory. There is no doubting that if they continue to buy as much quality as they have assembled of late they could enjoy a long period of success, giving a predictability to the local game that will kill its entertainment value.

But Motsepe's level of control means he will force judgement calls on his club that will stymie the search of total dominance. He already has too many advisers, consults too many other people and has picked his staff poorly. By meddling in team affairs he will force the experts he has employed to make decisions they would not ordinarily countenance.

Effectively, he will trip over his ego and ambition, thankfully ensuring a balance that is vital for the future of the prosperity of the game.

Forbes magazine had just published their annual list of 'Rich Clubs' which placed Manchester United in first spot, followed by Real Madrid. We decided to look at the South African landscape where Patrice Motsepe's millions had made Mamelodi Sundowns the envy of many. But would his money ultimately make a difference? The league title went to SuperSport United.

A STAIN THAT WON'T GO AWAY
By Stephen Brenkley

IN THE LATE AFTERNOON OF 7 APRIL 2000, HANSIE CRONJE WAS FIRST publicly accused of taking bribes. The reaction, when the information came across the news wires, was universal and it took about five seconds to express. How could the blundering plods in Delhi have got it so wrong? How dare they charge Hansie – upright, stoical Hansie – with such wrongdoing? When would they put their own house in order?

Perhaps the later indignation of those who had sprung to Cronje's defence was heightened by the guilt they felt at this response. Perhaps they felt doubly betrayed and are still feeling like this more than eight years later.

The original rush to discredit the so-called tapes of so-called phone conversations, and the readiness to agree with the hopelessly wrong assessment that none of the accents to be heard were of South African origin, reflected badly on all those rushing to judgement.

It was not good old Hansie who was bang to rights, it was the cops, went the thinking. Four days later, of course, Cronje coughed. He did not cough the lot, he never did, but in the small hours he sought out Rory Steyn, a security officer attached to South Africa's team and conceded that he had not been entirely honest. The ordure heaped on Cronje was therefore multiplied by the thought of the appalling earlier misjudgement.

Initially, this was the feeling of almost everybody – all those, that is, who had been prepared to believe the Indian police were dolts. But views changed, not gradually but quickly. In South Africa it seemed, it still seems, that many people were so astonished at the level of the betrayal that they were prepared to forgive too easily. Perverse but true.

It has seemed on visits to South Africa since that much of the population is either in denial or adopting the stance that it was all excusable because nobody died. So, pretty early in the piece, the fact that it was only money involved allowed plenty of tosh to be talked. A particularly slushy example was: 'When money talks, even the angels listen.'

To an observer from abroad, it remains pretty clear. And if the nature of the continuing antipathy felt towards Cronje is aggravated by the memory of that opening, angry response that he could not possibly have done it, then it is also compounded by the feeling that absolution was granted before justice was done.

There remains deep perplexity outside South Africa – certainly in England – that Cronje has been so easily forgiven in so many quarters. Everybody deserves a shot at redemption but it helps to do the time first.

His death a mere two years after the extent of his wrongdoing was brushed under the carpet served only to enhance his rehabilitation. There is a tendency to sentimentalise Cronje's life – there is nothing quite like a dose of the old schmaltz to conceal flaws – which merely complicates the difficulty in reaching an objective judgement on Cronje.

It may be an idea to view the new biopic, *Hansie*, which has been criticised for its candy floss approach, alongside a documentary film shown in Britain earlier this year called *Not Cricket: The Bookmaker and the Captain*, which had no film of Cronje swimming with dolphins. There needs to be a balance struck between condemnation and understanding.

Cronje, it can never be repeated often enough to those eager still to sanctify him, was guilty of the greatest betrayal. It is not simply that he had a fondness for money and was prepared to take oodles of it for distorting the progress of cricket matches. It is that he, a natural leader, entrusted with the direction of a team still coming to terms with its place in the world, was prepared to compromise his gifts.

Where the movie depicts his actions but seeks no explanation, the documentary makes a damning implication. It is uncomfortable, it may be easy to overlook because it is the conclusion of foreigners but it has continuing pertinence.

The business of quotas and the balance of black and white faces in South Africa's cricket team still haunts selection policy today. It affected Cronje too. He simply wanted to take on to the field the strongest team, regardless of colour or creed. But almost eight years after transformation, to general consternation in the rest of the cricket world, South Africa could still play a team consisting solely of white cricketers.

Persuaded but unconvinced that this could not be permitted, Cronje had to relent. But the documentary hints that Cronje, more or less forced to take part in a more sympathetic selection process, was adopting an attitude along the lines of: 'If you don't care if we win, then neither do I.'

The timing, which would give full credence to this assertion, is not quite right – since Cronje probably started taking money earlier – but it helps to build a picture of a man whose influence was beyond control.

There is another key element in Cronje's manipulative methods, one that also does not bear sympathetic scrutiny from those looking from afar. It is that he was prepared to use his power to persuade inexperienced players – Pieter Strydom, Herschelle Gibbs and Nicky Boje, all of them then wet behind the cricketing ears – or non-white players.

Indeed, Cronje's most strident critics believe there to be a definite pattern: the corruption increased, if it did not begin, after non-white players became a more regular part of the team.

To those who want to be led rather than to lead, which is most of us, Cronje seemed to have enviable gifts. He was strong, astute, aloof, talented, caring. He was from sound Christian stock who had been 'born again' and the wristband he wore bearing the initials WWJD – What Would Jesus Do – simply enhanced his credentials.

When South Africa matures as a nation, and it has some distance to go, it may begin to assimilate the lesson of Cronje. It may have been fortunate to have had the opportunity to learn the lesson so early. It is annoying, again to the outsider, that it has not yet done so. The captain of any cricket team must be given his head, but he must not be given free rein. Cronje, the spats over quotas apart, was allowed unfettered power. His relationship with Bob Woolmer, the coach, for most of his time in charge, probably allowed him to be overreaching.

Woolmer, a wonderfully trusting, open and frequently naive Englishman, knew South Africa well from his time as a player. He was to marry a South Africa girl. If he was the antithesis of Cronje – whom he described once as 'the epitome of the dour Afrikaner' – he was also in thrall to him.

In Cronje, Woolmer saw what everybody else saw, a natural leader who did not take easily to personal criticism, but because of his nature – Bob's glass was always half full – he was willing to overlook much. When the extent of Cronje's corruption began to unravel, Woolmer did not condemn, partly because he was bewildered at what had happened under his watch, but partly because Cronje was his friend.

A few weeks before Cronje died, Woolmer had dinner with him. Woolmer was touched by the fact that as he left, Cronje took him aside and told him: 'I never fixed one match in which I was captain of South Africa. Not one.' This may be true because under Cronje, it should always be remembered, South Africa won 27 out of 53 Tests and 99 out of 138 ODIs, a spectacular record. If he was fixing matches, he was better than even that record suggests.

This seemed to be enough for Bob. Well, if he had not fixed results then that was all right. Woolmer took this feeling to his own death. He, like so many other South Africans, was missing the point.

Cronje abused his power (in so doing he also abused Woolmer which seems to be overlooked). The English view of the crooked captain's misdeeds is obviously shaped by the events at Centurion Park in January 2000. It is not going too far to suggest that they felt duped.

To be at Centurion on that fifth day, when the match was drifting inexorably to a draw, was to be in the realms of the surreal. What we were to discover only a few weeks later put it entirely into context but at the time it seemed we were witnessing something brave, something indeed that might change the nature of Test cricket forever.

Few voices were raised in protest in the Centurion press box. The great Fleet Street veteran, Chris Lander, of the *Daily Mirror*, spent most of the final day telling anybody who would listen that it was a travesty. But dear old 'Crash' was not referring to any bribes being taken to ensure there was not a draw, he was simply suggesting that the rectitude of Test cricket was more important than giving the crowd their money's worth. How right he was.

In the years since, it emerged that Cronje set up the match in return for a few dollars and a leather jacket for his wife – it has become known as 'The Leather Jacket Test' – England have generally pretended to be unbothered. As far as they were concerned, they were playing to a one-innings Test and did so.

South Africa set England 249 and they got them when a seriously hungover Darren Gough, who had been strutting his stuff until the small hours in the bar of the Sandton Sun Hotel, drilled a boundary to long on. Nobody on the England side, and for that matter, nobody on South Africa's side except for their captain, knew why this had happened. But that night, amid some memorable English celebrations, the general mood was that Cronje had done something remarkable for the game of cricket. Good old Hansie. No typical dour Afrikaner him.

After years of reflection, it is that match above all for which Cronje could never atone. In coming to a shabby agreement with a bookmaker that he would indeed endeavour to ensure there was not a draw – remember, it mattered not who won, just that one of the teams did – he sold the purest form of the game down the river.

His greatest tragedy and the biggest flaw in the readiness to redeem in the Cronje apologists is that he could not recognise the magnitude of what he had done.

Maybe this is just a conned Englishman reaching an embittered conclusion but it still rankles down the years. Any win would have done at the time – England were in a real mess having lost at home to New Zealand in the previous summer – but the manner of the duplicity remains breathtaking.

At the very least South African cricket, which is in a state of constant turmoil, should learn from history (of course, it is a human foible that we never learn from history). Cronje was simply permitted to be too unaccountable. The job of captain, an honour, appeared to have grown to be his by divine right.

Graeme Smith, the present captain, is an admirable man. Given the job too early (as possibly was Cronje – you never understand that you knew nothing when you were 25 until you are 40), he has grown into it. On SA's tour of England this summer, Smith was outstanding as a leader and a player. He does not have Cronje's aloofness or his moody monotone. But he does have power and he is sure of his place. Smith will not do what Cronje did – he is too robust a character – but South Africa would do well to be wary of allowing him too much rope because it always ends in tears.

It seems the rest of the world can give up on Cronje's own nation coming to terms with his misdeeds. The commission chaired by Edwin King, set up in the wake of those first damning charges, never finished its business, in essence because there was not the stomach for it. The film *Hansie* cannot (as it has done) deliberately gloss over the bad parts, or by any standards be an objective assessment. South African cricket is strong again partly, maybe largely because of Smith, but it is still suffering because of Cronje.

The new biopic, Hansie, had taken to the screens which prompted this commissioning of a veteran respected English writer. Hansie Cronje, the disgraced former South African captain, still invokes the strongest feeling among global cricket lovers, many who feel cheated that closure wasn't attained before his untimely death.

Stephen Brenkley was appointed cricket correspondent of The Independent in succession to Angus Fraser after serving on The Independent on Sunday for a number of years. He is a veteran travelled journalist with strong views. In June 2008 he and ECB chairman Giles Clarke had to be separated at a dinner during a Test match in Nottingham. Conversation had turned to discussing Zimbabwe. Things grew increasingly heated until Clarke grabbed Brenkley by the collar.

THE PROS (AND THE CONS)
By Iain Fletcher

THERE IS A DESPERATE GAME OF BRIDGE, AN INFAMOUS LORD AND THE omnipotent presence of that most revered of commodities, gold. And yet the truth is that spread betting is a simple financial tool hijacked from the stock markets and adapted to bets across finance, sport and politics. It was Stuart Wheeler, bridge companion of Lord Lucan, who founded IG Index in 1973 to allow traders to circumnavigate the draconian tax and financial laws to bet against the price of gold. No one actually bought the gold, they just bet on the price of it and in the company's infancy they were so successful that Wheeler won at the bridge table and swiftly paid out his winnings to some traders. If he had not, the credibility would have gone and spread betting would not be so prevalent today.

Cricket is near to the perfect sport for spread betting because it offers numerous markets with their own scores, plenty of opportunity for wild price action during a game and importantly, plenty of games.

Britain is the core market and the biggest sports spread betting company is Sporting Index. Their head cricket trader, Justin Swift, believes their annual cricket turnover to be in excess of £50 million and despite 14 or 15 markets being offered on every match, the majority of money is wagered on the runs markets of teams, individual batsmen and the exciting first 15 overs of an ODI.

These markets also serve to exemplify how similar spread betting is to share price movement.

During the South Africa-England Test series this year, each innings of each match would have offered three major markets as the players walked on to the field. The team innings score (320-340 runs), Graeme Smith's innings score of around 48-52 runs and Neil McKenzie's innings score of 45-49.

Those who wanted to support or 'buy' any of these markets could have done so at the higher price, so for Smith at 52, and they would nominate a stake level per run, say R100. If he was dismissed for a duck, they would lose 52 multiplied by 100 which is R5 200.

But this is where spread betting is like the stock market and with every run, Smith's price would have changed. When he reached 10, his new price would have increased. It would now be 58-62 (from the original 48-52) and a buyer could sell and guarantee a profit.

He bought at 52 for R100 a run, he sold at 58 for the same stake, so he made six runs multiplied by R100.

Old Mutual does the same every day on the markets and of course, just like the stock market, there would have been sellers or people who believed Smith would fail. They would sell his runs at the lower price and the spread between is the bookmakers' profit.

That is spread betting. There are two prices, a sell and a buy price and punters decide their own stake level and with the huge increase in ODIs and live cricket on television, the industry has grown rapidly.

'For an ODI, I offer about 30 markets pre-match,' explains Swift, 'but the truth is most people bet on runs or the number of sixes. Also, the runs in the first 15 overs are popular because the market only lasts about an hour and there are punters who are used to horse racing and quick results. For Test matches it is a slower process and the potential price swings can be huge. Sellers of Brian Lara [ie, those who believed he would "fail"] when he scored 400 would have suffered and this shows why choosing a sensible stake level is so important for punters.

'In cricket, runs markets can end up 100 or 200 runs higher or lower than the bet and that can prove expensive or profitable but that is why so many people like spread betting as opposed to fixed odds ... you get rewarded more for being right.'

But as the warnings go, losses are not capped and because the industry is regulated by the same authority as the stock market, the FSA, there is no escape.

At £50 million, though, the legal and trustworthy market is dwarfed by the illegal betting on the subcontinent.

Lord Condon, head of the ICC Anti-Corruption Office, has publicly stated that $1 billion can be traded illegally on an important ODI at any given Cricket World Cup.

'Who knows for sure because it is run by organised crime,' explained Swift, 'but I do know within the gambling industry people genuinely believe the illegal cricket market in Asia turns over about $9 trillion a year.' And it is in this dark world that Hansie Cronje was snared.

'Most of it isn't spread betting, though,' Swift continues. 'It is line betting, so a batsman's market may be whether he scores more than 20 or not and the win and loss level are fixed. The problem is the potential for fixing, which is where the massive corruption in cricket came from. The hope is now with the money on offer in the IPL [official Indian Premier League] and ICL [rebel Indian Cricket League] and Stanford Twenty20 that players won't need to be bribed to make good money.'

At the 1999 World Cup in England, one international bowler told me under strict anonymity that he had been offered $50 000 to bowl a wide on his first delivery. It was more than he was getting to play in the whole tournament and he could earn it in one delivery. (And no, he didn't agree and he didn't bowl a wide.)

'Spot markets like that are the easiest for crime,' explains Swift. 'Spread betting firms don't offer markets like that for that very reason.'

Spread markets can be decided in a single ball, that is the nature of cricket, but they are not offered like that. It needs integrity to continue to thrive and that means the players doing their best at all times.

With the prize money on offer now they have no reason not to, apart from greed and that is something the financial markets know plenty about.

As an extension of the Hansie Cronje piece and the obvious connections with the betting underworld in cricket, the writer – an author of books on betting exchanges and spread betting – took the reader into the world of someone who wants to bet on cricket's developments.

Iain Fletcher *is a former professional cricketer with Somerset CCC (14 first-class matches in the English County Championship), city broker and a regular rugby and cricket correspondent for* Scotland on Sunday, *is the author of many books on sports betting and poker. One of them is* A Spread Better's Diary. *It tells the story of how he was given £7 000 by Sporting Index and 11 months to see if he could make a profit. If he did, he could keep it.*

THE RISE OF A STALLION
By Gary Lemke

I MET VAR WHEN HE WAS BETWEEN JOBS FOR THE DAY. IT WAS APPROACHING 1pm and he was standing quietly in his stable, with a mouthful of hay. He was four hours away from his next assignment. One down, and one to go on this warm Cape spring Monday. All things being well, he had already netted his owners R35 000 and by the end of the day another R35 000 would drop into the account. Sometimes the daily figure reaches as much as R105 000.

You see, Var services mares, and in the first three years of his new life, he's a natural. He's successfully covered (ie, impregnated) over 300 mares and his 'success rate' of impregnation is in the upper 90s. Var is still just nine years old and can expect to remain an active stallion until he's in his 20s. It's nice work if you can get it.

Then again, Var is not your ordinary stallion. He's no five-minute 'wham, bam, thank you ma'am' individual, like most of his peers. He's a sensitive soul who knows how to make a mare feel special. And afterwards – and there have been cases when it's been before and during – he gets a couple of polo mints for his efforts. The mints calm him down, and it's always been this way, a tip passed on by his former trainer, Clive Brittain, who discovered the trick during the colt's distinguished racing career.

Var stands, for that's the correct parlance, at Avontuur Estate outside Somerset West. It's been his home since he arrived in South Africa in 2005 from France, where he was celebrated as Europe's finest sprinter, the quickest racehorse to have set foot on the famous Longchamp racetrack outside Paris. And he once carried the world's most famous current jockey, Frankie Dettori, to victory on Prix de l'Arc de Triomphe day.

'This is a very, very fast horse. He was three lengths up after the first furlong [200m] and when I asked him for his effort in the final furlong he gave me two lengths on the rest,' the Italian said after Var's defining moment on the track, a course record over 1 000m.

THE RISE OF A STALLION

Quite shortly we will know whether or not Var's career speed has carried through to his progeny, the first of which should hit the ground running later this year. It's his first batch of colts and fillies, and the racing world is watching whether or not the offspring have his genes. For if they do, the stallion's stocks will rise. Right now he 'charges' R35 000 for about 10-15 minutes 'work', but the potential to cash in is there. His father was Forest Wildcat, and his grandfather was Storm Cat, the world's most successful sire, who commanded a fee of $500 000 every time he was asked to cover a mare.

Var's story itself is one to tug at the heartstrings. Pippa Mickleburgh, the Avontuur Estate stud manager and the person who controls Var's sex life, as she puts it, is never far from the animal who means so much to the estate.

'Mr [Tony] Taberer lost his life to cancer last year, but Var gave him an extra couple of years. Mr Taberer [who bought the estate some 18 years ago] was extremely ill but was determined to fulfil his 20-year vision. He invested in high-quality mares for our stallion, Dominion Royale, and then, four years ago, said he was going to buy the best horse out there to continue the progression. So he bought the best champion sprinter in Europe, fending off strong opposition from the Middle East and the USA.

'When Var got here he caused a real scene. More than 250 guests arrived for his "unveiling" only three days after he had landed in his new country. But it was as if he was born into the role and he has touched the soul of everyone he's come into contact with. He was five years old when he pitched here and was a rarity, an unknown horse [in South Africa] and an unproven stallion. He had never had a "child" and yet his fee for covering a mare was R35 000. Normally it's nothing like that high for an unproven sire.

'In his first "season" here he covered nearly 100 mares. In his second it was 120 and in his third it has been 140. At this year's National Yearling Sales he averaged R300 000 per foal sold. There are 44 shareholders who have invested in Var [at R120 000 a share] and the return on that has been phenomenal,' Mickleburgh says.

Indeed, at the 2008 Yearling Sales, one of his offspring, Valetta, was bought by trainer Michael Azzie for R850 000. 'In total, 13 of Var's progeny were sold for R4.37 million, which puts him top of the list for first-season stallions and we are very happy with the support we received from buyers for his exciting debut,' says Mickleburgh.

'It is sad that Mr Taberer will never get to see the offspring of Var on the racetrack, because to him Var was like a baby he mollycoddled. But I'd say we are close to fulfilling his 20-year project,' she adds.

Now, it's a case of run, babies, run. 'By February or March next year we will know for sure the true value of Var. As a stallion, his direct opposition is [former champion middle-distance horse] Victory Moon, but in his first-season stats and returns I can say, touch wood, Var was the top performer.'

Avontuur Estate is a family farm nestled in the hills on the wine route just outside Somerset West, and Var's presence has raised the attention of those tourists who drive through the gates. He was named after a region in Provence, in the south of France, and the fact that he was so well-performed as a sprinter adds to his appeal. 'People come from all over and they want to pet him. He's such a gentleman,' Mickleburgh says. 'I always keep a roll of polo mints at hand, just in case he needs calming when the visitors get close to him,' she adds, 'but generally he is well mannered. He's not like most stallions, who can be rather aggressive in nature.'

His calmness is a trait which immediately comes to the fore. I wasn't expecting to get within five feet of him, but here I was, able to walk into his stable and pet him on his big white blaze running down his face. He was more interested in the roll of mints Pippa had in her hand than in me.

'Come boy, you need to get some rest. You've got a big mare coming round to see you tonight and you have to have your strength,' she tells him. 'Now that he's into his third season of making babies, is it like a job for him?' I ask Pippa.

'No, he really, really enjoys what he does,' she says. That might seem rather obvious to most red-blooded males, but most often a stallion doesn't care much for the opposite sex. He wants to get on with it, and then off with it.

Where many stallions have 'teasers', those horses who get the sacrificial mare 'in the mood', Var prefers to get the ball rolling himself. 'He is quite sensitive,' says Mickleburgh. 'He prefers to do the teasing, and where others will take five minutes from start to finish for the act itself, he is in the region of 10-15 minutes. The other day he was at 45° to quite a feisty mare he was covering and was becoming distracted and disinterested. So I popped him a polo mint and he completed things in style. He just needed a bit of calming down, for he does feel the stress.'

Clearly, Var is revelling in his status as a stallion on the rise, so to speak. 'Often when he is outside and sees a horse float pull up near the stables, he starts to get excited. He thinks it's another mare being sent for him,' Mickleburgh laughs.

When one looks at the young colts and fillies spending their hours in the paddocks at the estate, you can virtually identify which are his. Many have inherited the white blaze and dark coats, while some have the white socks (he has three). There are times when Var is called upon to perform three times a day.

THE RISE OF A STALLION

'Most of the time when his diary is booked it's twice a day, around 7am and 5pm,' says Mickleburgh. 'But it can also be more. I just have to get the timing right that six hours elapse between coverings.' That, and ensure there's a fresh roll of polo mints to keep him happy.

The imported former European sprinter Var had arrived as a new stallion in South Africa. Standing at Avontuur Stud in Somerset West, we visited him and reported on the experience. Var went on to become a champion sire in his first season. This work formed part of a winning 2009 SAB Sports Journalist of the Year and Feature Writer of the Year submission by the author.

Gary Lemke started journalism in 1981 out of desperation for a job. He joined the Daily Dispatch in East London, on R300 a month. He has won the prestigious SAB Sports Journalist of the Year award, and has worked in other sports departments on newspapers in Pretoria, Durban, Cape Town and London. He wrote an autobiography with swimming legend Penny Heyns, and is currently publishing director at Highbury Safika Media. He has covered events as diverse as Wimbledon, the British Open, Daytona 500, the Olympic Games, Commonwealth Games, world swimming and athletics championships and world championship boxing.

AN INCREDIBLE JOURNEY

By James Corrigan

REGARDLESS OF WHAT ANY OLD-FASHIONED GREGORIAN CALENDAR MAY suggest, the marketing men have decreed that the last golfing year is over and the new golfing year has already started. Yet, even that belligerent breed would surely allow Trevor Immelman to draw his own line in the sand when he at last returns to South Africa this month. Sun City, December 2007. One life ends. Another begins.

Ostensibly, the Trevor Immelman who stood on the 18th green of the Gary Player Country Club celebrating his first victory in the Nedbank Golf Challenge, was the same Trevor Immelman who, the very next week, was in a doctor's surgery waiting to find out why he had just doubled up and been unable to breathe at the SAA Open at Pearl Valley. Except it wasn't. It couldn't be. When a 27-year-old is informed he has a tumour the size of a golf ball lurking deep within, something profound changes. Existence had been a given, a lifetime had been forever. Then Immelman discovered differently. It's all about the moments. White jackets, green jackets ... the images of one staggering sporting year.

'Even now as I talk to you I have to pinch myself when I think back to what's happened over the past 12 months,' Immelman told me recently. 'It was the craziest year ever. Winning that tournament [the Nedbank] put me on cloud nine, and then – bang! I hit earth so hard when I'm diagnosed with this tumour. Then the next week, having it cut out and the elation of hearing it was benign after two days of being in that hospital bed just waiting, then starting the rehab and then coming back and getting off to a real slow start and then going ahead and winning The Masters. Well, it was a series of unbelievable highs and unbelievable lows. I said at the time it had been a rollercoaster, but I'm not sure that did it justice. However you want to describe it, it's been one incredible journey.'

Of course, it is a journey that has yet to finish, a statement that sounds simple enough, what with Immelman not even being 30 yet and in terms of a professional golfer barely out of his nappies. But if the threat of cancer had given him all the focus that perspective invariably brings, then the fulfilment of a boyhood dream was inevitably going to skew the objectives for a while.

'It took me a long time afterwards, two or three months, to really come to grips with the fact I'd won The Masters,' admits Immelman. 'Everything was such a blur and it really was difficult to concentrate on my game, because of all the extra stuff coming at me. Yeah, that's the same for everyone who has just won a Major but because of what happened in the run-up it probably did seem more surreal to me. There I was, answering the questions of what it means and everything when I didn't really know. It's funny. All I ever wanted to do was win Majors and to do that at the age of 28 ... well I really had to stand back and go "wow". You know, I'd achieved a lifelong dream and it takes a while to sink in and then think "right, what next, where can this take me?"'

Wisely, it was not the $64 million question (plus sponsors' bonuses) that Immelman sought to address all on his ownsome. While 'Mr Player', as Immelman continues to refer to him, was the credited driving force behind his three-stroke victory over Tiger Woods at Augusta (nice ring to it, that) and will always be there for his young countryman, Immelman went to a more contemporary champion for advice.

If anyone has proved that the first Major does not necessarily have to mean the only Major, it has been Padraig Harrington these past 16 months. 'Padraig has definitely been an inspiration and a big help to me since The Masters,' acknowledges Immelman. 'First of all he's very approachable, we have spent lots of time together with me asking him this, that and everything. But it's the example he sets that has been the thing to me. You know how hard he's worked and now it's only too clear to see it's paid off. That makes you feel good because it makes you think, "well, if I put all the time in, it will happen to me too". That sounds easy, but it isn't. You must realise that just because you've won once, does not mean you are entitled to win another. Padraig says, if anything, you must work harder.'

But surely the experience stands a Major winner in good stead? 'That's the other side of the coin – the confidence you can take out of it,' explains Immelman. 'I know that when I play my best golf I can beat the best players in the world. Now, a lot of players "think" they can do it, "believe" they can do it, but until they do it they don't actually "know" they can do it. But they "know" I can. They will see your name on the leaderboard and think, "Hey, Immelman's done this before, he's experienced this heat and survived it. I've yet to do that". That is a massive difference right there and that has to work to my advantage whenever I can get into the hunt. So for me the goal now is to be able to bring that form to the big tournaments more regularly, just the way Harrington did in the last two Majors. I know that it will happen again and that I will put it all together and have a strong chance. The question is how many times can I do this?'

If one of Immelman's longest-held convictions is correct, the answer to that will be many, many times. When he was five, he informed his startled parents that he was going to become a touring professional and ever since then he has had a timetable to work to. He was right on schedule when he won his U10s tournament in America aged six, when he had his first hole-in-one at eight, when he represented his first senior South Africa side at 14 and then all the way up through the ranks until he became a fully-fledged member of the European Tour as a 20-year-old. Yet, even this precocious child did not foresee the events of April.

'I've always believed that my best would come in my thirties, purely because there are so many nuances to the game, and purely because experience counts for so much,' he says.

'The more you play, the more you learn and those things serve you so well in the intensity of battle. Perhaps that is why it happened at Augusta for me because, although I wanted it so much, I hadn't yet demanded it of myself. I always told myself to remain patient because I believed that as a golfer in your twenties you're trying to figure your game out, your swing out, the courses out, your life out even. That's why now, when I take stock of everything, it's so important that I've done it early and sort of nicked one before I'm due. I've got many years ahead of me. Harrington's 37.'

And Ernie Els is 39 and Retief Goosen soon turns 40. Emerging from any shadow results in a warm glow, but what about from the gigantic one cast by the Els-Goosen cartel that spreads across every South African fairway? Well, let's just say that Immelman has basked in the brilliance of this new light. 'It was nice for me, no not "nice", brilliant for me,' he says. 'Obviously, in the past 15 years it has been Ernie and Retief who have really been the guys who have been flying the flag for us and have been put up there on a pedestal. So it meant so much for me to step up and give South Africa another Major champion. That was really a fantastic feeling.'

For a man who was accused of arrogance as a boy ('How many kids do you know who don't believe in themselves?' he says in relation to that charge, 'When you're that age you feel you're bulletproof.') Immelman understandably stops short of comparing himself directly to Els and Goosen. Yet he would have every right to.

He was the first South African to win The Masters since Player in 1978 and just the second of all time. It was a big deal globally as he became the first player currently under 30 to hold a Major, so imagine what it added up to for his own country. As the son of Johan, the former commissioner of the Sunshine Tour and the brother of Mark, a much-respected college coach in America, Trevor is steeped in his nation's golfing history and quickly realised the significance of his success.

'I thought about it as I was walking up the 18th,' he says. 'Not just what it could mean for South African golf but also how it would be viewed at large. Any time our sportsmen get a result it gives the country such a jolt. Obviously, we've been through tough times in the past 10 or 15 years, trying to get everything in place and running. I was down there when the Rugby World Cup was on last year and I watched the final against England with a few mates, saw them lift the cup and it was just great, incredible. I knew what it did for me. It keeps you going, makes you excited to go to work in the morning, whatever you do. Such an awesome energy erupts.'

At least Immelman will feel the back-end of its fallout when he returns. A schedule that has gone from packed to overloaded, from The David Letterman Show in America, to tournaments and yes, publicity shoots in Hawaii and China, has meant the postponement of many visits home with his wife Carmenita and their two-year-old Jacob. And not only is Mark a short hop from Orlando up there in Ohio, but Immelman's parents have recently settled in Charlotte, North Carolina, where Johan helps run the Sbonelo Foundation, which provides scholarships for South African students. It is fair to say the homecoming parade is overdue.

'No I haven't been back down there since I won, but I've done a lot of interviews with South African journalists and broadcasters and have received a lot of messages,' he said. 'According to family and friends it was fantastically well received and I'm looking forward to getting back and seeing everyone and kind of reliving the story again.'

He will no doubt begin his tale at Sun City and the final-hole victory over Justin Rose that was worth so much more than the fat cheque. 'For a South African to go and win that tournament, well it's quite a big deal for us,' he said. 'It's an event that the young guys have grown up watching and wanting to play in, so to win that event really is something special for a South African player. It was obviously special for the crowd, too, as the atmosphere when I was battling it out with Justin down the stretch was amazing. You know, somebody told me that only Bernhard Langer and Seve Ballesteros have held the Nedbank and Masters titles at the same time and they're Hall of Fame players. Like I said, I have to pinch myself. I look at other sportsmen in others sports who have achieved their ultimate goal and have to stop and say "hey, I'm on that level". It's surreal.'

But it's also deadly serious. Immelman accepts that life is unrecognisable this time around. There will be more autographs to sign, more pictures to pose for and more hero worship to justify. It comes with the glory of Georgia, if not with the agony of the Western Cape four months before.

'I'm conscious of the fact that I'm coming back as a Major champion and as the defending champion and that brings responsibilities,' he said. 'Yet I want to keep things in perspective. I look back and think I've been extremely fortunate, with the tumour being benign and everything. If I had got the wrong results then I wouldn't have been playing golf this year at all. There would have been no Augusta, no green jacket, none of this. I would have been getting all sorts of treatment, radiation therapy and stuff. So I kind of say to myself "man, that was a pretty big bullet you dodged there". That keeps things nice and real.'

The past year had been one of white jackets and green jackets for South Africa's only current Major champion. He won the Nedbank Challenge at Sun City and the US Masters at Augusta – and dodged a health bullet along the way. This was an emotional time for Trevor Immelman whose life in one year had taken more twists and turns than many people experience in a lifetime.

James Corrigan has been with The Independent newspaper in London since 1996. He has been voted Welsh Sports Journalist of the Year and shortlisted as Features Writer of the Year in the British Sports Journalist awards. He covers a wide range of sports, including rugby union, golf, horse racing and football. A passionate supporter of Cardiff City and the Welsh rugby team, one of his other great loves is golf and these days he travels the world writing on the subject.

WILTING MATILDAS
By Tom Eaton

ITS ATTACKS REPULSED BY THE AUSTRALIAN EMPIRE, THE REBEL ALLIANCE has retreated to the small desert planets of Bloemfontein and Centurion where it has kept its eye in by shooting Bangladeshis in barrels. However, its leader, young Biff Widechaser, and his mentor, the mystical Mickey Wan Kenobi, know that another fateful confrontation is coming ...

I know, I know. If it's going to be blockbuster allusions it's got to be James Bond, and a litany of clangers about how South African cricket is looking for a quantum of solace after years of living to die another day in Australia, with an aside focusing on Brett Lee's thunderballs and how glad we are not to be facing Shane 'Octopussy' Warne.

But somehow, after four trips to Australia and eight series against cricket's evil empire since readmission, those macho Bond titles don't seem quite up to the task. Where South Africa-Australia Test series are concerned, tomorrow always dies, the best view to a kill is from Bay 13, and the only goldfinger on display belongs to an umpire who has just been asked by an Australian whether the ball was hitting middle halfway up.

In fact, to look back at that grim list of chances fumbled and half-chances throttled is to start feeling that the past 14 years have just been eight instalments of *The Empire Strikes Back.*

But the rebels won in the end, didn't they? Didn't the little guys blow up the Death Star? Is it just possible, as the Proteas travel to a universe far far away, that Biff Widechaser and his motley crew might score a direct hit this time? It's possible. In fact, it's more than possible. And this time it's not science fiction.

According to current wisdom, any discussion of the prospects of a series against Australia must begin with a dutiful analysis of their ragged form in India. I agree that this does make some sense, and we will need to know whether we are facing a champion team experiencing a hyperspeed wobble, or a cluster of fading stars rushing towards a black hole. But that's not where this discussion starts. This one starts in Graeme Smith's head.

In 2005, at the zenith of Brave Cricket, or what many of us called Stupid Cricket, Smith had the following to say to *The Independent* in London: 'Australia's top three batsmen are their strength, so being able to knock them over is important. That exposes their middle-order, which has experienced pressure in domestic cricket but maybe not in Tests (as much). If we get things right, we will be putting Adam Gilchrist under pressure at No 7 too.'

Try to stop laughing for just a moment and allow me to paraphrase in *Star Wars* dialogue:

'OK, Blue Section, the Empire's top three fighter pilots are their strength. That's Lord Vader and his two wingmen, and they've killed every Rebel pilot they've ever come up against. But if we can overcome Vader's psychic stranglehold and shoot down all three while avoiding the flak turrets on the Death Star, well, then we'll be through to the main swarms of TIE fighters, who haven't killed quite so many Rebels because Vader has done most of the killing.

'But if we manage to get through them, by shooting down 400 each, then we'll be putting quite a lot of pressure on the impenetrable wall of flak from the Death Star itself. OK, so that's the plan. Got it, Blue Two? Hello, Blue Two? Blue Three? Anyone out there?'

Meanwhile, Mickey Wan Kenobi kept murmuring in the skipper's ear, 'Biiiifff, use the force ...' and Chewbacca Symcox bellowed inarticulately from the sidelines, telling journalists that the South Africans were going to 'target' Warne and that it was 'payback time' for the leg-spinner.

In short, it was all looking a little bit like a B-grade Saturday afternoon space adventure, aimed at teenagers and people who think sport is war. But somewhere something changed, and the silliness fell away. South African cricket emerged from the matinee performance into a pleasant afternoon in the real world.

The 'story so far' of the first paragraph is wildly unfair, because Biff Widechaser disappeared and in his place appeared Graeme Smith – solid bloke, good captain, excellent batter. Mickey Wan Kenobi had Brave Cricket stuffed down his throat by Darth Ponting, but from the little heap of brown robes stepped Mickey Arthur – decent coach, good man-manager.

Perhaps they both lost enough matches to have their bluster and childish, insecure South African nonsense burned away. Perhaps they simply feel more secure in their respective jobs. But whatever the reasons, Smith and Arthur, and by osmosis the team, are no longer the yapping 'Japies' that the Australians love to patronise.

The clearest sign of this new mindset is that I can't remember the last time either man said something stupid. Instead, what I do recall – apart from a sequence of superb innings – is a reassuringly sensible comment by Smith.

At the start of the season some scribe asked him what he thought of the Proteas' chances in Australia. He could have galloped away into fantasy, speculating on the decline and fall of the Australian empire and promising a 2-0 series win.

Instead, he simply said that there was a 'realistic opportunity' of a South African series victory. If ever one needed evidence that Stupid Cricket is gone, this was it. What seems to have replaced it is Pragmatic Cricket. And that, more than Australia's current flaccidness or South Africa's rising confidence, is why the Proteas have a real shot at victory in the next few months. But beyond experience and a settled team structure, there is another possible reason for Smith's remarkably measured attitude, and that is the critical distance.

Since readmission in 1993, the prospect of a series victory against Australia has only floated before South African teams like the Holy Grail. The analogy is not used loosely. Meetings with Australia quickly took on religious subtexts as a team led by charismatic Christians did battle against notoriously earthly atheists and agnostics.

Indeed the crusading nature of our cricketing relationship with Australia was revealed in Old Testament starkness in 1994 when Warne poured bile over Andrew Hudson at the Wanderers. It couldn't have been clearer: the baddest of the godless Australians, apparently possessed by demons, persecuting the holiest and meekest of the South Africans.

Even for those of a more atheist bent, the Australians seemed to possess an otherworldly aura, and the harder we fought them the more effortlessly they pounded us. Steve Waugh is the icon of the era, a slit-eyed barnacle oozing disdain for the histrionics of the Japies around him, but for me the epitome of that terrible, frustrating, inspiring time was his brother Mark, perfect as a statue, ethereally contemptuous, like one of those dispassionate and omnipotent seraphim one finds in Medieval altar-pieces.

When Warne and Glenn McGrath retired, the last of that great generation were gone and South Africans were left unavenged. We will beat Australians in the future, perhaps even in the near future, but the Waughs' Australia, around which we built so many hopes, will forever be out of reach.

But the odd thing about Grails is that they're only tempting when they're just out of reach. Put them out of sight, and they quickly slip out of mind. Suddenly a series win in Australia is only that. It's not a triumph of righteousness or any of the other stuff we loaded it with. And for the first time since 1993, we seem to have a captain who understands that. There's no doubt that Smith would give a great deal to beat Australia, but he'd stop well short of giving his soul. For this captain, this time around, it's not about casting Beelzebub into the pit. It's about playing 15 days of good cricket.

Certainly there are fresh terrors waiting that will worm their way into Smith's mind and tempt him to lose perspective all over again. There's the insatiable hunger of Mike Hussey, for one thing, and of course the monstrous hand-eye co-ordination of Andrew Symonds. But if he stays as calm as he seems at the moment, he and his team will meet these threats as cricketers playing to a plan, and not as knights-errant (or worse, Jedi knights-errant) trying to slay a dragon. If all else fails, Smith can stand at mid-off knowing that he has played more Tests than both Hussey and Symonds combined.

The Proteas know how to win, and it would be extreme arrogance on my part to offer technical or psychological advice to further their cause. But if there is one piece of commonsense I can offer, from a professional writer to professional sportsmen, it is this: don't believe anything the media says over the next three months.

There are probably three journalists in this country who have the faintest idea of what's going on – technically and politically – with the Proteas and world cricket. I am not one of them. The rest of us indulge in sophistry bordering on fraud, making predictions as open-ended as that great con artist Nostradamus on his most evasive day ('The game might go five days, but ultimately the side that takes 20 wickets is going to win').

Indeed, I still stand by my much-derided prediction, made in last month's edition, that spin is on the way out, but thanks to India's performance I now have only belief rather than evidence.

The role that the profoundly fickle media can play was never clearer than in England earlier this year. For some reason Fleet Street decided that the Saffas were bringing the Four Horsemen of the Apocalypse with them in the pace department. All we and the English read was about how Dale Steyn and Morne Morkel were going to crack skulls. It was a completely arbitrary decision to punt South Africa's bowling attack: it had done very little in the preceding months to warrant such adulation.

But clearly our bowlers bought into it in varying degrees, and when the ball didn't rip off English grilles and seer off bat-handles into third slip's chest, but instead came onto the bat encouragingly and dribbled away into gaps in the field, there wasn't a backup plan.

There is currently another media version of reality doing the rounds, and that is that Australia are on the way out as a cricketing superpower.

It is a view being perpetuated largely, I suspect, by disgruntled Australian writers, spoiled by a decade of Warne and McGrath and not used to watching their fielders fetch leather. But it's a version that might appeal to South Africans, prone as we are to veering between extremes.

Having thought of the Australians as unbeatable warrior gods for so long, we are in danger of lurching in the opposite direction and willing them to be a ragtag collection of ageing show ponies and young undisciplined hotheads.

The reality is that they are neither. We don't really know what they are. But the good news from a South African perspective is that they don't know either. Mickey Arthur put it nicely when he described them as 'a bit bruised, physically and emotionally'. To our advantage, the Australians don't seem to know how and why they were bruised.

Which is why South Africa's first series win in Australia since forever might also be one of its most ill-tempered and attritional series in recent memory. Australia without direction and easy answers might suddenly resort to conservative field settings, defensive bowling, cautious batting. In short, it might play a brand of Test cricket it has derided as typically South African for the last decade.

South Africa are confident, but South African confidence tends to go slightly rigid when it walks into the shadow of the Melbourne Cricket Ground.

We will revert to old methods. But at least they're our old methods which means they're tried and tested. This will be a series hinging not on success but on mistakes: when teams are evenly matched it's the errors that weigh most heavily, and South Africa are more familiar – and therefore comfortable – with making mistakes.

We've been here before, and we've stumbled. But somehow this feels different. Something is with us that wasn't there before. Biff Widechaser might have called it The Force, or Brave Cricket. But now it feels more like maturity, and destiny.

With perfect timing, the author made a courageous statement that while beating Australia's cricketers on their home turf is easier said than done, there was strong evidence that suggested that Graeme Smith's players had matured to the point where victory Down Under was their destiny. What followed was a riveting series – won by South Africa.

Tom Eaton was educated at Westerford High School and the University of Cape Town. As an undergraduate he majored in English and Afrikaans/Netherlandic studies, before completing an honours degree in English literature. By 2001 he was the South African editor of the Cricket365.com website. In 2005 his cricket writing expertise led to an approach from publishers putting together a groundbreaking coaching manual, written by the late Bob Woolmer, professor Tim Noakes and Helen Moffett. Eaton has also established himself in South Africa as a published author of fiction.

THE PEOPLE'S CHAMPION
By James Lawton

IT SHOULDN'T REALLY BE A CONTEST, AT LEAST NOT ONE FOR THE RIGHT to be proclaimed the best footballer on earth, because the young man in the red corner is big, 6ft 1in, as beautiful as Adonis and almost ridiculously gifted in all aspects of the game. Cristiano Ronaldo can do anything with power and the easiest accomplishment. In flashpoints of the most acute action, opponents simply shrivel before your eyes. He doesn't so much beat as engulf them.

The one in the blue corner is 5ft 6in and still as scrawny as a street urchin after years of treatment for a growth hormone deficiency. Unlike Ronaldo, he doesn't run the gamut of football skills. His inability to make any impact in the air was, unfortunately and irrevocably, settled in the womb.

However, the little guy, Lionel Messi of Barcelona and Argentina, has drawn such a brilliant bead on Ronaldo of Manchester United and Portugal that the latter's triumph in the voting for World Footballer of the Year, to go along with the European crown he collected in Paris in December is, in the view of some hard judges, and not least Diego Maradona, quite possibly his last ultimate stride in an extraordinary rush of glory.

Ronaldo, aged 23, has two problems. One is Messi, who is two years his junior and currently playing the football of the gods. The other is himself. If Ronaldo was beset by any more hubris he might well, in the interests of consistency, seek out the nearest cliff edge. As it is, his behaviour on the approach to his season of awards lurched from one example of self-indulgence to another.

One stunning instance came at Old Trafford on 13 December, on the eve of Ronaldo's trip to Paris to collect his European trophy. United were labouring to inflict themselves on a Sunderland team made desperate by the defection of their manager Roy Keane, who apparently could not bear to visit the stadium, which he had ruled for so long as arguably the most influential player in the history of the Premier League, and display the net result of his £70 million worth of player recruitment.

Ronaldo sustained a hip injury in a collision with Sunderland midfielder Andy Reid. He played on, irresolutely, for nearly 10 minutes, before side-footing the ball into touch with an expression of absolute disdain for all that was going on around him. He then walked directly off the field and to the dressing room. There was no consultation with the United dugout, which was caught completely unawares. The result was that United were required to play several minutes while a man down. Later, United manager Sir Alex Ferguson argued that his superstar had done the right thing in pursuing treatment at the first opportunity. The statement was as predictable as it was risible from a man who has been desperate to humour a player who has made clear his desire to move on to Real Madrid in a barrage of innuendo and petulant body language.

We saw more of that last commodity the following Saturday at White Hart Lane, where United – who had been obliged to wait until the last minute to secure the win against Sunderland – again struggled, this time to a scoreless draw, against Spurs. Ronaldo's most eye-catching contribution: an artful little tripping of Michael Dawson after the Spurs player had beaten him in a tackle.

Twenty-four hours later, in the Nou Camp in Barcelona, we saw a rather different contribution from the other half of the mano-a-mano contest which is now expected to dominate the football winter of Ronaldo and Messi, just as the duel of the great matadors, Luis Dominguin and Antonio Ordonez, enlivened a dangerous Spanish summer half a century ago.

Messi was inevitably the point of most intense focus in El Classico – the match pitting runaway leaders Barca against visitors Real Madrid. The Madrilenos were plainly terrified of the destructive force of Messi's dribbling. It blazed through the first phase of the game before dimming under the sustained weight of some brutal tackling. However, Messi kept himself under the firmest control as his impossibly frail body was repeatedly draped across the Nou Camp turf. There was no diving, no gesticulation, and not even a martyr's sigh. Messi simply stayed with his task, rounding off victory with the second of Barca's unanswered goals in added time.

For many this was a key round in the fight for the hearts and also the minds of the world's football public.

Yet if Ronaldo continues to paint himself in the most garish of colours, if he appears set on alienating all those who had so warmed to his astonishing season of 2007-08, when he swept his team to the league title with a record 42 goals and scored with a superb header in the Champions League final against Chelsea in Moscow – a feat beyond, surely, the much more intricate skills of his younger rival – there is no question about his enduring threat to all opponents.

It is now, more than at any time since he arrived at Old Trafford as the £12 million teenage signing from Sporting Lisbon programmed to largely obliterate the memory of David Beckham, a question of how much restraint can be placed on a nature in which a capacity for self-analysis, if it ever existed, has simply been burned away in the glow of his fame.

A kind of breaking point, it was hard not to believe, came in Moscow in the spring when United prevailed over Chelsea in that Champions League final that stretched, with outrageous tension, into a shoot-out – one in which Ronaldo had apparently blown his team's chances by so untypically firing a shot wide. The player's face flooded with disbelief at the possibility that for once he might be cast not as a hero but a hapless agent of defeat.

Such a development would have been a disastrous companion to his barely concealed flirtation with Real Madrid.

After the salvation of Chelsea captain John Terry's missed kick, Ronaldo reacted angrily when was asked to describe his emotions when he failed to score from the spot.

For English spectators the shock of the miss was compounded by the memory of his nonchalant dismissal of their team in another shoot-out in the quarter-final of the World Cup in Gelsenkirchen two years earlier. On that occasion he had revelled in his position on centre stage, having earlier winked at the Portuguese bench after his United club-mate Wayne Rooney had been sent off for stamping on centre back Ricardo Carvalho. Ronaldo plainly believed he was about to inherit the football world, an impression that only gained ground in the next game, the semi-final against France.

It was as though Ronaldo, the tricky dribbler of United with a fierce finish on the ground and in the air, had graduated to an entirely new level of accomplishment. He looked immense as he bore down on the French cover, but then he also spent a lot of his time diving for advantages which might have come more easily if he had stayed on his feet and exploited both his strength and his touch.

In Moscow, however, it seemed that Ronaldo had indeed moved on to a separate planet. He still dismayed purists with his diving antics and his loose sense of team. Yet there was the supreme redemption that at the most vital times the boy from Funchal, Madeira, could announce unplayable talent. He did this with the goal that sent United surging into the lead and when he was reproached about the missed penalty his eyes were filled with indignation. 'Why do you talk about the penalty and not that great headed goal?' he demanded to know. His anger blazed again when he was asked if he was ready to commit his future to United. 'I don't make any promises to anyone,' he said. 'Not even my mum.' Then he strode into the Moscow night. This, surely, was the time of Ronaldo.

But now, in ultimate terms, is the time of Ronaldo passing, partly because of the intensity of Messi's purpose in the brilliant Barca team and partly because of a failure to grasp that the truly great players are great not because of some brief flood of virtuosity but because they understand that the best reputations – the ones that span the football ages – are built from game to game, year to year.

Ferguson seems to be willing to grant him near instant membership of the pantheon of the great players, but sometimes when he makes such a declaration – recently he said that Ronaldo had already joined the company of Pele and Johan Cruyff – he seems to be indulging in nothing so much as wish fulfilment. Perhaps he thinks, you have to muse, that if he says it often enough it will happen, Ronaldo will indeed have elected himself to the tradition of the fabulous United triumvirate of Bobby Charlton, Denis Law and George Best.

Meanwhile, though, Messi chips away, often exquisitely, at the idea that Ronaldo is a player occupying his own unique terrain. He did this superbly at Old Trafford last season in the Champions League, when United managed to progress for the basic reason that Messi's extraordinary performance lacked only reasonably efficient support from his Barca colleagues.

While United vainly sought inspiration from Ronaldo – their triumph came from one moment of opportunism from the veteran Paul Scholes – Messi relentlessly applied his skills. For much of the time it seemed that the ball was attached to the little Argentine's toes.

Beside the slight but mesmerising figure of Messi, Ronaldo dwindled that night.

However, he had recovered his momentum soon enough, leading United to victory in Europe and at home and cheerfully declaring that he saw his election as the world's best player as automatic last year as it would be in the future. It was a commitment to himself that Ferguson, who recently suggested he was ready to set aside £40 million to the retaining of Ronaldo's services, can still only yearn will one day be extended to the club that invested so much confidence in his footballing future.

Messi, though, is scarcely without his champions. Most notable is the recently appointed manager of Argentina, Maradona. Many Argentines believe that his most natural successor is not Messi, but Sergio Arguero, the brilliant young player of Atletico Madrid, not the least of whose achievement is fathering Maradona's first grandchild. However, the great man is emphatic. Messi is the one.

Maradona, who was appalled that Messi was left on the bench when Argentina's challenge for the 2006 World Cup lapsed into indecision after a luminous start, believes that the little man from Rosario, who was whisked to Europe on the promise that Barca would pay for his expensive growth treatment, has already shown evidence of genius. 'Messi is not so big,' says Maradona, 'but his talent is huge. In his skill and his ability to judge speed and space, he is unmatchable. He also has a great temperament. Messi is the future of football.'

Confirmation could come quickly enough if, as so many hope so fervently, United and Barca are drawn together once again at some point in the current Champions League.

The most recent evidence suggests strongly that Messi might well be in position to deliver a knockout blow. Under the guidance of coach Pep Guardiola, Barca are not only dominating the Spanish league, they are illuminating the entire game. With Thierry Henry finding some of the best of the form that entranced the Premier League for so long, Barcelona's football is beginning to achieve levels of expression that some say was last seen when their bitter rivals Real built their empire back in the '50s.

If it is true, and the football heavens know it is a lot to say, there is no doubt about who is exerting the most thrilling influence. It is the little guy in the blue corner. The one ready to take over the football world that Cristiano Ronaldo presumed, maybe a little prematurely, belonged only to him.

The extravagant Portugal winger Cristiano Ronaldo had walked away with the 2008 Fifa Player of the Year award. The author made a compelling case as to why the judges had got it wrong – and that the real winner should have been the diminutive Argentinean who plays his club football for Barcelona.

James Lawton is the chief sports writer of The Independent. He joined the newspaper 10 years ago after performing the same role for the Daily Express for 14 years. Before that he worked for the Daily Telegraph, the Express and the Vancouver Sun. He was twice voted Britain's Sports Writer of the Year and was also

named *Sports Columnist* and *Sports Feature Writer of the Year*. In 2008 the first volume of Lawton's collaboration with Bobby Charlton won the *Sports Biography of the Year* award. He has written 11 other books, including biographies of Lester Piggott and Lennox Lewis, and worked with England World Cup-winning stars Nobby Stiles and George Cohen on their autobiographies.

THE BEAUTIFUL GAIN
By James Lawton

THE ROLL OF THUNDER CAME DOWN FROM THE VAST TERRACING OF THE San Siro each time Kaka touched the ball and when he did it most beautifully, on one occasion striding easily beyond two Fiorentina defenders, the noise became a keening.

It was as though the red and black garbed tribe of AC Milan were attending a hero's funeral, a passing no less poignant because the one who was being mourned, the lithe, God-fearing and perfectly balanced Brazilian, christened Ricardo Izecson dos Santos Leite in São Paulo in 1982, was about to become rich beyond the dreams of any of the great players who had come before him.

There had been so many ... Franco Baresi, Ruud Gullit, Frank Rijkaard, Marco van Basten, and, still alongside him, the peerless defender of the ages, Paolo Maldini.

Now the Brazilian was being plucked away, this artist of football who had been identified as an easily accessible commodity if you wanted to shatter every record in the imprecise science of estimating the value of a professional footballer.

It seemed that you could have him for no better reason than being given more money than had ever before been devoted to the making of a football team.

You didn't have to have a tradition stretching back through the decades and founded on lustrous skill and the highest competitive standards. You couldn't walk into the Louvre, make your bid and then leave with the Mona Lisa wrapped under your arm. But you could come to the San Siro and take away Kaka.

This, apparently, was the *fait accompli* as his Milan team-mates embraced him at the end of the 1-0 victory – and headlines in England and Italy announced that Kaka's move from one of Europe's top teams to Manchester City would provide the ultimate evidence that now every club, every player had been seen to have a price.

It was a price – £100 million for Milan, £24 million a year for Kaka – that seemed in San Siro about so much more than City's new status as the richest football club on earth under the patronage of Sheikh Al Mansour of Abu Dhabi. For who could not argue that it also spoke of a future when classic principles of team building, of the best players naturally gravitating to clubs most equipped to house and complement their genius, would now run second to another imperative: the one which simply demanded, 'show me the colour of your money?'

Such, anyway, was the reigning certainty for another 48 hours. Then, around 10pm, an astounding development: Kaka, and more closely, his agent father, had seen the colour of City's money and whether it was because it had not been piled up in sufficient quantities, or indeed the player had looked into the future and seen things he didn't like, the deal was off.

Kaka would continue to wear the Rossoneri shirt, and return to his first instinct that he wanted to grow old in these colours, and City would think again about their belief that if you put enough money on the table, or talked beguilingly enough of the potential of image rights, you didn't have to prove to a great player that you had the means to preserve his place at the top of the game in the only place that truly mattered, the field of play.

In the cafes of La Galleria and the squares around the huge bulk of Il Duomo, the reaction was straight forward enough. It was one of rejoicing. For football, though, there were wider questions – and a debate which, weeks after the sheepish return of the City officials without their prey, shows no sign of slackening.

The issue goes to the heart of football and, when it seemed that indeed Kaka, who wears a T-shirt which proclaims, 'I belong to Jesus' was about to become football's No 1 disciple of Mammon, even its very meaning.

Some argued that what City had attempted to do was not only a perfectly reasonable statement of suddenly empowered ambition but also a thrilling expression of a potentially fast-changing order. Why should the Milans, and the Manchester Uniteds and Real Madrids and Barcelonas, be allowed to luxuriate in the strength of accumulated success?

The opposing view is that before the wielding of huge amounts of money, before the right to cherry pick the likes of Kaka simply because you have received, out of a clear blue desert sky, an astonishing windfall, there must be team building, an understanding that you cannot suddenly implant a super-talent and expect it to radiate into a corner of a team still palpably under-equipped to compete at the highest level.

The case advanced by those who scorned the City initiative, and in turn were dismissed as dreamy traditionalists detached from a new reality, was best served in the denouement of the proposed deal – and the reaction of the man who had talked it up so vigorously, the club's chief executive Garry Cook.

Cook was reported to have been rebuked by his boss, the shadowy sheikh, for his accusation that Milan and their president, the Italian prime minister Silvio Berlusconi, had at the crucial moments of negotiation 'bottled it' or, if you want a precise translation from this rough Cockney rhyming slang, lost control of their bowels as the protests grew. Cook's statement was coloured by disappointment and perhaps even a sense of personal humiliation, but it immediately provoked speculation that Sheikh Al Mansour might already be reviewing his suitability as the guardian of football's greatest concentration of hard cash.

It was a theory that the merest glance at Cook's statement did little to weaken. He reported, 'We had gone through a three-or-four-stage process in which Milan made it quite clear that Kaka was for sale and we made it clear we intended to bring him to Manchester City. As we got to the next stage there were questions they could not answer and I think public and political pressures made them change their conditions. We never ever met the player. We met his representative, his father, but we had discussed commercial terms only. The agenda we thought we were on was about Kaka coming on a journey with this club, but in the end the only journey they were on was a fiscal one.'

Then, extraordinarily, Cook added, 'Kaka's father was very interested in the project and we talked about humanitarian factors, but then those issues took a back seat and financial issues came to the fore.'

Humanitarian factors? Apparently before becoming bemused by the image right projections of Cook, who made his reputation with Nike on the mega account of basketball's Michael Jordan, Kaka Snr was told that City would set up a foundation with which the already charitably inclined player could develop his interest in good causes. Cook, it seemed, was bruised by the Brazilian's failure to understand the scale and the sophistication of his plans for a player who in 2007 was voted the best in Europe and the world. Inevitably, though, such fineness of feeling was consumed mostly by a wave of derision.

There was Kaka, and his employer Berlusconi, running with the idea that they were being seduced by nothing more complex than a scarcely believable mountain of cash and here was a complete stranger attempting to dazzle them with the sheer breadth of his business intellect.

Berlusconi, as the average cunning politician would do quite automatically, simply exerted damage control when it emerged that Kaka was underwhelmed.

The golden player would stay in Milan, and he would be re-embraced by his public. Fiesta would replace the funeral rites.

Elsewhere in football the impact of the Kaka affair, and the implications of a global economic meltdown, continued to invite questions about the future and the purpose of the game.

It was not as though the Kaka business lacked a hundred precursors, albeit at less outrageous costing, most notably at Manchester United where ever since Cristiano Ronaldo followed his starring role in the 2008 Champions League final by fluttering his eyelids at Real Madrid, Old Trafford manager Sir Alex Ferguson has been fighting to placate Kaka's successor as the most celebrated player in the world.

For some, City's lunge for Kaka was a natural development. What were they supposed to do with their Arabian gift? Why shouldn't they do what the strongest clubs have always done? And who really worried that Kaka would be paid at the rate of, say, Sir Paul McCartney, if that is how his value had been assessed?

According to this argument, City were merely reacting to their new situation and, commendably, attempting to provide their long-suffering fans with a supreme reward for their loyalty. If you said all of that quickly it might have a certain power of persuasion but then you thought of Kaka operating in an unformed team which had been recently ransacked 3-0 in an FA Cup tie in front of their own fans by lower league Nottingham Forest, and the picture was not of virtuous improvement but football illiteracy. One image was of Queen Anne chairs being dumped in the foundations of a house still to be built.

It did not help that Mark Hughes, a manager with a creditable record with Wales and Blackburn Rovers, was widely seen as a casualty waiting to happen amid talk of a coach whose glamour might match that of some of the intended superstars – someone like Internazionale's Jose Mourinho. The problem with the Kaka move was not that it was at odds with the reality that the great players will always find their way to the richest clubs but that never would there have been starker evidence that money had become the sole arbiter of their destiny.

City, or so Kaka believed, had come to Milan with no greater claim on his services than the ability to pay him wages that he could not have have dreamed of when he first arrived in Europe. City had not worked for a place at the top of football, they couldn't offer him, for several years of the prime of his career, the reward of Champions League football – the natural habitat of the world's best players. Their plan was to sign Kaka, make him a Pied Piper for a Mancunian version Los Galacticos of Madrid, and from there success would flow quite naturally.

It was a project quite without the underpinning of precedent. No one ever made a great team by solely shopping for footballers as you might fancy items along Rodeo Drive, and all else in the debate tended to shrivel beside this essential point.

Manchester United, on whose achievements City have for so long been impaled, currently boast the reigning World Player of the Year, Ronaldo, alongside three players who cost around £30 million: Rio Ferdinand, Wayne Rooney and Dimitar Berbatov. Carlos Tevez's services are priced at £11 million over two seasons, with a further £20 million if his signing becomes permanent. Anderson and Nani, who so often ride the bench, cost around £17 million each. But none of them arrived as the foundation stone of a team, the starting point of a climb to a significantly competitive point. They came to augment a team of settled strength. They were not required to step down from the level they had claimed as their own.

In the shadow of the Kaka misadventure, the former great player Gianfranco Zola, now manager of West Ham United, offered a telling reaction to City's £14 million swoop for his own key player, Craig Bellamy.

Zola, who once turned down a huge offer to return to a Chelsea newly enriched by Roman Abramovich because he had made a verbal agreement with his hometown club Cagliari, shrugged his shoulders and said, 'I hate transfer windows because they are only in place for the benefit of rich clubs. I just wish we could keep them for a season without interference. Then we could see who really knows how to make a team. Of course, when I say this I know no one will listen because football is now all about money. Whenever we look up we see this.'

It was a conclusion that was maybe only briefly contradicted when, 24 hours later, Kaka said that he would stay in Milan. Still, that was not likely to quell the thunder in San Siro. A funeral had been transformed by a miracle. A great footballer had, after all, said that for him money could never be the only thing.

At the time Manchester City arrived on the scene as the new free spenders of world football, their owners flashed the chequebook in the faces of many of the sport's big names. Their prime target was the Brazilian superstar Kaka. They offered AC Milan a world record £100 million and the player himself £24 million a year. He turned down the offer, preferring to play for a lesser wage at AC Milan.

HYPE HYPE HOORAY
By Tom Eaton

AND LO, A CHILD WAS BORN IN A STABLE, AND LAID IN A MANGER, AND THREE wise men visited him bringing gifts of gold, frankincense and a cricket bat. And yea, he did cast the Australians from the temple that was the MCG, and truly, he did turn Powerade into sweat, and it was good. And so it will be, forever and ever, amen.

To read the cricketing press you'd be forgiven for thinking a Messiah had arrived. A new gospel is being spread everywhere you look: the Gospel of Duminy. From Melville to Melbourne the new devotees are choking up describing the wunderkind from Cape Town, surrendering en masse to his spell, and going on bended knee to worship before his stroke play.

Cricinfo, probably the most authoritative cricket website, declared that Duminy was a 'once in a generation player marked for greatness'. Fans, thrilled and awed by his response to pressure, are clogging online forums with mentions of Brian Lara and Steve Waugh. Another particularly weird form of worship has also emerged on the same forums: calls for JP to be referred to by his full name, Jean-Paul. As in Belmondo or Sartre. Clearly there is some form of romantic fervour behind this Francophile demand, or at least a yearning to idealise the lad into something more sophisticated than a skilful athlete whose job it is to thump a ball with a block of wood.

It's the sort of stuff that makes us Doubting Thomases start reaching for our bullshit detectors. There are three rules to live life by, all unrelated and all learnt by bitter experience. First, don't invest your own money in show business. Second, never go upstairs to look at the etchings. And third, when the mainstream media and its cohort of bloggers start telling you that the Messiah is come, it's time to be a heretic. Where they see signs and wonders, you need to look for smoke and mirrors.

But the search for empirical evidence has been startlingly short. The disciples of Duminy had barely howled at a full cycle of the moon before a far worldlier admirer of the young star pitched in with almost irrefutable evidence. The accountants and talent-spotters of the Indian Premier League (IPL) don't go in much for sentiment, so their endorsement of Duminy in early February couldn't be attributed to hype. Instead of superlatives the IPL produced a single number that spoke volumes: $950 000. Duminy's price at the IPL auction made him, at least in raw dollar terms, the third most valuable player in the 20-over game after Kevin Pietersen and Andrew Flintoff. The two hard-hitting Limeys went for $1.55 million each, but $950 000 ain't exactly chopped liver.

And yet there is something not right about accepting the IPL's word when it comes to Duminy. Those who set his price know how much money he will make them, but you can't help feeling that's all they know. The big wheels of the IPL are cricket's horse traders, tugging at teeth and poking ribs to see if the filly will make them a fast buck. They operate at the sharpest edge of the game, which means they probably don't spend much time exploring cricket's less clear-cut regions. They know money, and they know winners. But one can't help feeling that the IPL and everything it stands for doesn't have the faintest idea about class. And class is what we're dealing with when we consider JP Duminy.

To understand what class is, you have to understand what it isn't. Advertising executives would have us believe that malt whiskey, German cars, Swiss watches and Manhattan penthouses are the embodiment of class. Of course, advertising executives also once told us that cigarettes were good for you, and they continue to tell us that we can trust bankers. So much for advertising executives. But the reality is that if it's for sale and is on television it's just a thing: attainable by anyone with money, and made by professional middle-class people who are not necessarily good at anything other than making machines run properly.

True class comes from having a talent that fewer than one in a million possess; being able to turn that talent into performance; not allowing it to run away with your head; and making it look easy. But it's also about discipline. Test cricket is an infinitely more worthwhile sport than the 20-over stuff because it creates pleasure out of anticipation. It is the realm of the sophisticated hedonist, who delays pleasure so that when it finally comes it is so much sweeter. And Duminy, it seems, is the sophisticated hedonist's reward. His class has been worth the wait.

This, then, is why people who should know better have thrown themselves with religious zeal at the feet of Duminy, and fill newspaper columns with Messianic drivel about the new Lara. It's understandable, really: in a game increasingly clogged with banal and pointless players and games, the arrival of a genuine thoroughbred seems like a sea change of the 'Yes we can!' variety.

Of course, when that sea change is trumpeted by the likes of Richie Benaud – who compared Duminy to southpaw legend Neil Harvey – 'Yes we can!' becomes the Second Coming. (I would add that anchorman Mark Nicholas said Duminy reminded him of a young Brian Lara, but Nicholas has shown that if you catch him in the right mood, when he's high on life, a cow pat can remind him of a young Don Bradman, so don't read too much into it.)

All of which asks the question: hype aside, and looking past the natural infatuation with a new bright young thing in our midst, could Duminy be our Lara? Has our prince come?

It's hard to resist these seductive what ifs. Duminy's start in Australia was sublime. He is left-handed and fluent on the off-side, two facts that automatically add five runs to any good Test batter's average. That first innings aside, where he was bounced out, he is a superb judge of line and length. But if we are to see the future, we probably need to understand Duminy's past; because that's where some fascinating insights lie.

There's an anecdote doing the rounds at the moment that speaks volumes. It seems that Duminy was on shaky psychological ground in his first couple of seasons in the big time. Not yet 20, he was playing alongside his idol Herschelle Gibbs at Western Province, and, according to some, was learning more than just how to hit sixes over extra cover. Gibbs is an extremely likeable person, which perhaps made his vices seem less pernicious, and it would have been very difficult for a teenaged Duminy to resist being drawn towards a rock star view of the world.

When he made his ODI debut in Sri Lanka in 2004, some Gibbsian notions about his place in the world may have been clouding his judgement. Coach Eric Simons reportedly had a less than stellar impression of Duminy's commitment to fitness and training – both telltale signs of a 20-year-old diva who has sensed his talents but hasn't the faintest idea what to do with them.

Not surprisingly he was soon shown the door of the Proteas set-up, and returned to Western Province a more or less shattered player. And it was there that he was reportedly cornered by national treasure and general good bloke Gary Kirsten. According to the official version, Kirsten took the kid aside and read him the riot act, telling Duminy, 'You have more talent in your little finger than I have in my entire body, so use it.'

The paternal echoes here are too loud to ignore. Gibbs and Kirsten, so often together at the top of the order both for Western Province and South Africa, would have been Duminy's role models – cricketing parents, in a way. Duminy might have wanted to be Gibbs, but he would have found it impossible to ignore Kirsten; and so the final piece of the mentoring puzzle was inserted, and the 'son' could begin his journey to replace and exceed both 'parents'.

Frankly, he couldn't have asked for better: if early indications are anything to go by, Duminy has Gibbs' hands and eyes, his desire to show off his talent and to be audacious, but Kirsten's determination not to give an inch, to wring every run from every bowler, and to leave the field spent. (Again, the seductive what ifs: I might just have described Lara back there.)

And so why maintain the façade of suspicion? Why remain a Doubting Thomas? Why not just throw myself into a maelstrom of praise, and start planning what I'll write when Jean-Paul (*mais oui, mon amis!*) scores his 10 000th Test run and takes his 200th Test wicket?

Because Duminy's greatness is not a done deal. Not by a long shot. And the thing that could yet derail him is precisely the praise that is pouring in right now.

Clearly Duminy has developed an iron will since he lost his national spot half a decade ago. People don't suddenly become humble and hardworking at 24 if they were profligate at 20. Instead what happens is that they learn to sit on their urges and gag the noises in their head. In a way it's more admirable that Duminy has hauled himself back onto the straight and narrow than if he never left the path to start with. But accolades, and the expectations that they imply, can rust iron wills.

This is not to say that Duminy is going to turn into something out of the English Premier League, a spoiled overpaid brat. On the contrary, I think the Duminy we've seen so far – mild and modest off the field, blow-torch-determined on it – is what we're going to get for a good many years. But where the rust can take hold is where his talent is rooted: in his confidence.

I suspect that the parts of Gibbs that make Duminy so good also make him more vulnerable than if he'd just been a talented white boy from the 'burbs. What makes Gibbs exceptional is that streak of raw bravado that makes him as aggressive as any quick bowler. Often it fails, but when it succeeds, it's worth the price of admission alone.

I don't know enough about Cape Town's cricket culture and history to write definitively, but there seems to exist a unique, intensely competitive and entertaining world of 'coloured' cricket. Sit on the grass at Newlands and you'll get a glimpse of it. It's part real, part myth, a culture defined by extreme aggression, dazzling flair, a swagger and a wink. Vincent Barnes was its epitome in the '80s, and Gibbs took over the mantle in the '90s. Duminy is now its torchbearer, although the reckless fire has been tempered with contact with a more conservative mainstream approach. But even though Duminy has heeded Kirsten's advice, there remain forces at work under the steel, like fire and steam raging around in a boiler. And the fire is fuelled by confidence. Extinguish that and the whole thing goes to pieces. When Jacques Kallis' confidence is low, he falls back on technique. When Gibbs' is low, he falls back on the floor.

In short, Duminy must be allowed to fail, and he must learn that he's allowed to disappoint us. He must know that we don't expect him to average 60 in Tests, or score a hundred every fourth time he bats. When he falls, it must be back into a safety net of understanding and compassion. When Lara couldn't scratch a run in 1996 or 2000, the consensus in the West Indies and the rest of the cricketing world was that the temple curtain had torn asunder and that the end of the world was nigh. It must have taken indescribably depths of resolve, fire and fight for Lara to come back from both slumps and to reassert himself as the greatest batsman of his age.

Duminy's fightback in Melbourne was the sort of thing people do after they've just been exhorted to head once more to the breach by Henry V, and seemed to suggest that whatever fires burn inside him might match Lara's in heat and intensity. But we cannot assume that he can come back from failure just because he's fighting hard while his confidence is up. When Duminy slumps – and he will – he will have far enough to fall without us having added an extra few fathoms to plunge by building him a pedestal.

But that is for another day in the future, perhaps far off; because Duminy is here to stay. Can he be great? Yes he can. Will he? Only he knows that. For now we can rest assured that he is not the Messiah, but a champion in his own right. He's not the second Sobers. He's the first Duminy.

JP Duminy had signalled his arrival on the international cricket stage with a phenomenal series in Australia, playing a huge role in helping the Proteas win a series Down Under for the first time. He had even been compared with Sachin Tendulkar. This piece accepted that the country's latest sporting Messiah had the talent to become a modern great – but argued that he would have to keep his feet on the ground and pick himself up from the lows that would come his way. Which they did over the next season as he struggled to maintain the hype.

FLIGHTS OF FANCY
By Roy Collins

HAVING WON A DARTBOARD ENCASED IN GOLD FOR THE FIRST-EVER televised nine-dart finish at the Stan James World Matchplay tournament in Blackpool in 2002 (not to mention the £100 000 prize), the first thing Phil Taylor asked the following year was what goodie was on offer for a repeat. 'You'll see,' said James, leading him to the stage where an £80 000 top-of-the-range Mercedes was parked right next to the oche, not so much in the players' line of vision as tattooed onto their corneas when they threw.

Taylor made the mistake of boasting that he would be driving it home at the end of the week, so each night he failed, James would shake the keys in his face and tease: 'I've still got them'. The key jangling stopped on the final night when Taylor began with seven treble 20s. But before he could repeat the previous year's feat of switching downstairs for a treble 19 and up again for a double 12 out, he hesitated and the chance was lost. The only occasion, he says, when he has been distracted on a big finish.

But who needs a car when Taylor, who swims to keep fit, can also jog on water, according to his legion of fans, comprising all ages and sexes, after winning a record 14th world title in January at the age of 48? Even boxers do not see that as retiring age these days, but contrary to public opinion, fitness and youth now count as much in darts as other sports.

Despite the mental mathematical agility that all darts players possess, Taylor, the greatest player in history, now needs an abacus to chart all his triumphs. As well as the world titles, he has won nine World Matchplays, eight World Grands Prix, four Las Vegas Desert Classics, two UK Opens, four Premier Leagues (he was unbeaten in 44 matches during the first three), one World Series of Darts and two Grand Slams. And if you asked him to take out a partridge in a pear tree, he could oblige with a single arrow.

Ask any multi-winning champion such as Roger Federer, Tiger Woods or Lennox Lewis to name their sweetest triumph, however, and they will inevitably name their last. As does Taylor, who had failed to win the world title for three years and before January's triumph, had opponents openly mocking him. Squeezing past a table of players on his way to the oche, he overheard one say: 'I hope I get that Taylor next. He's crap.' Even the bookies deserted him, though it was a cautious retreat, odds of 11-2 hardly putting him among the also-rans.

Many others were claiming that the man they call The Power was running low on competitive juices, so he upped his practice hours, swam half a mile a day (walking the other half mile) and cut down all exhibition work, costing him thousands of pounds. That was not easy for a man who has never forgotten working in a factory as a ceramics engineer for £74 a week. He says: 'I used to run round the country four or five nights a week until the early hours. I had to to survive. When you suddenly go from £74 a week to £300 a night, how many nights will you do? Eleven. And I would have done lunch-time sessions if I could have.'

Taylor was inspired by former world champion Eric Bristow, who slipped out of the game after suffering from dartitis, an inability to let go of the dart, who also sponsored him during his formative years. One version of the story, perhaps instigated by Bristow, is that he peeled off £10 000 in notes to his protégé. But you do not earn the moniker The Crafty Cockney by handing out such largesse to a newcomer. Instead, air tickets to tournaments would drop through Taylor's letter box and he would arrive at hotels to find the bills settled in advance.

Bristow, restoring his Crafty credentials, wanted every penny repaid, which suited them both. Taylor says: 'I loved that because it made me into a winner. If I played a weekend tournament, Eric would ask me to phone and tell him how I got on. One Sunday, I phoned to say I'd been beaten in the final and he slammed the phone down. After that, he told me only to ring if I'd won. I was getting £50 or even £100 for winning tournaments, which was massive for me. Everything in my house was second hand, it was all givers, so I would come home and ask my wife Yvonne what we needed. We'd get a new carpet on the winnings, a new set of saucepans, some new towels. Eventually, we did up the whole house. It was really exciting.'

With his career earnings now around £5 million, Taylor could upgrade his modest house in his hometown Stoke and fill it with antiques. But having been brought up in a council house with an outside toilet, he has vowed that his family will live in comfort. He has already bought homes for his mum, his in-laws and two of his four children, with a third in line to receive a set of house keys.

Before the big cheques arrived, Taylor used to get home from his factory job at four in the afternoon to find queues of people wanting him to do welding jobs on their cars so that they could pass the roadworthy test. He also worked in a bar for four nights for the grand sum of £22. He is still welded to those working-class values, which explains why such a consistent winner has not seen the fans' love turn to hatred. He says: 'Sometimes, even I think it would be nice to see someone else win for a change. But I'm hooked on the competition and winning titles, and with annual prize money getting close to £10 million, I'm not quitting yet. I'll quit when I start getting beaten in the first round of tournaments. That would break my heart.'

Taylor is now as famous around the world as football players and rock stars. Fans from China send letters addressed to 'Phil Taylor, world's greatest darts player' and they drop through his door. Not averse to a bit of name-dropping, he tells how he was recently walking around Los Angeles with Robbie Williams, when they were besieged by American autograph hunters. But they only wanted Phil's, not even recognising Williams. He was also asked to go on the reality show *Strictly Come Dancing* but had to turn it down because three months of it would have impinged on the day job.

Warming up to the name-dropping, he recalls playing a match at the Palace of Westminster against firebrand Labour MP Dennis Skinner, known affectionately as the Beast of Bolsover. Taylor says: 'I asked that old chestnut about whether he considered darts a sport and he hedged for a while. Then he twigged. He said, "I can see where you are going with this one. If you're not a sport, you're a pastime or a hobby and you don't pay tax on those." Exactly.'

Rivals will do anything to turn The Power off: sledging, talking, slowing down, speeding up, clicking the darts behind his back. He says: 'George Best [another one slips to the floor] once said to me that if a player tried to kick him, he knew he'd got him. So when players try to cheat against me, I think the same. Try and nail him with a big score.' After his infamous row with Northampton's Kevin Painter a few years ago, Taylor humiliated him by scorning a bull finish to the match, instead using an extra dart to set up a double.

Taylor's only career regret is that he has allowed his weight to yo-yo over the years, instead of presenting a sylph-like athletic image. It offends his own professional checklist. He says: 'It was hard to eat healthy food in the early days because when you finished at midnight, fish and chips and Chinese takeaways were all you could get. I lived on those. Now you can get healthy stuff almost everywhere. I can shed the pounds easily enough but I get bored after six months and put it all back on again. For my own image and that of the game, I wish I could have looked good all the time. As world champion, I ought to go on stage looking a million dollars, like David Beckham.'

The other subject to avoid is prize cars. At a tournament in Holland, Taylor's driver failed to turn up at the airport after writing off his car in a crash and seriously injuring himself. Says Taylor: 'I felt sorry for him and as there was an Opel sports car on offer for a nine darter, I said that if I won it, I would give it to him. I was playing crap at the time and thought there was no chance. But I did it and as they were handing over the keys, I saw my driver, who could hardly walk beforehand, almost sprinting to the bottom of the steps to take them off me.'

The best darts player the world has ever seen was on the wrong side of 48 but his appetite for success had not been dulled by the advancing years. Phil 'The Power' Taylor is a 15-time world champion and followed his 2009 success – after a three-year hiatus – by winning again in 2010.

Roy Collins was chief football writer of the Sunday Telegraph from 2003-2008 and was shortlisted for the Sports Journalist Association's 2005 Sports Diarist of the Year award. Before that, he worked for the Guardian and between 1986 and 1995, was chief sports writer at Today. He currently writes for the Sunday Times but has worked for every national newspaper in England, covering four football World Cups, three Rugby World Cups, three Olympic Games, plus numerous athletic World and European Championships, Formula One grands prix, Wimbledon and world heavyweight fights, including Mike Tyson's defeat by Buster Douglas in Tokyo in 1990, regarded by many as the biggest upset in boxing history. He also wrote George Best's bestselling autobiography Blessed.

IT SHOULD BE ABOUT NADAL
By Mark Keohane

THE INDULGENCE OF ROGER FEDERER HAS TO STOP. THE TEARS HE SHED after another Grand Slam defeat against Rafael Nadal should not be glorified as those of a hurting champion. It was an act of selfishness made even worse by Nadal's concession that it was hard to feel elation when confronted by Federer's tears.

Nadal, in what should have been his finest moment, apologised to Federer. He then reassured Federer he was the greatest champion and that he would go past Pete Sampras' 14 Grand Slam wins. As he spoke, the cameras cut to an emotional Federer, who played the audience.

Federer, the tears flowing, nodded his appreciation. That is what spoilt boys do when things don't go their way. They manipulate a situation and Federer in his last three Grand Slam final defeats against Nadal has never allowed the moment to be Nadal's.

When Nadal beat Federer in the French Open, all the attention was on Federer having never won the French Open and how victory at Roland Garros would confirm his status as the best ever. Federer predictably lost, predictably cried and predictably was pitied for not being able to win on clay when it mattered most.

A few weeks later and Federer, aiming for a record sixth successive Wimbledon title, lost in five sets to Nadal, who had never won at Wimbledon. Nadal, as he would do in Melbourne a year later and as he felt compelled to do in Paris, reassured Federer he was still the master and that he would win many more Wimbledon titles, and there was an apology for ending Federer's chance of a record.

Federer's response was to tell the world how much it hurt to lose and how it hurt to be called the world's No 2. It was ironic that the guy with a 68% career advantage against Federer was the one always doing the apologising for winning.

Federer's bullying in the past decade of a top 10 whose players – with the exception of Nadal – would have struggled to make a top 30 in previous eras, created a sense of Grand Slam entitlement. Winning, before Nadal's arrival, was so easy for Federer that every time Nadal beats him in a Grand Slam final, the question invariably seems to be what was wrong with Roger and not what was right with the guy who beat him.

Nadal, at this juncture in their careers, is the better player. Federer has lost five of the last six Grand Slam finals he has played against Nadal and 11 in 15 career finals against the world No 1. He has also lost 13 of their 19 match-ups. Nadal is five years younger than Federer and has won five more Grand Slams than Federer had at 22.

Yet when greatness in tennis is mentioned, Federer is accorded God-like status and his fallibility against Nadal, and in the past year against Andy Murray who has beaten him five times in eight, is glossed over; hence the tears in Paris, London and Melbourne, and the continued pity and apologies.

The situation needs perspective, as does the claim that Federer is the greatest to have ever played the game because, if the latter is true, then on which planet does that put Nadal?

Federer simply doesn't know how to beat Nadal at the moment and in losing five successive times to him has taken the same game plan into battle and been undone every time. Surprisingly, very little is made of Federer going it alone without a coach since 2007, and whenever it does get mentioned, Federer rejects the need to have one, saying he knows his own game better than anyone else and that he knows tennis.

Everyone needs a guide, a mentor, a coach … a someone who provides another perspective, and the evidence is overwhelming that Federer is not an exception to the rule. In the two years that Tony Roche coached Federer, the player lost nine matches from 182. In the two years since they split, Federer has lost 24 from 158.

Federer is good enough to surpass Sampras' Grand Slam record, but he knows there will always be hollowness to any record that does not include the French Open, and there will always be questions about any claim to greatness when there is another guy out there he can't beat.

Expect more tears from Federer, especially in Paris, but don't indulge them because if the Federer-Nadal rivalry is to prosper in a way when you don't know who will win then Federer needs to stop crying and start fighting for the right to be called the greatest ever.

It is not Sampras' record that will define Federer. It is Rafael Nadal, the world's best player.

IT SHOULD BE ABOUT NADAL

After Rafael Nadal beat Roger Federer to win the Australian Open, the Swiss broke down in tears on court as the trophy went to his opponent. In the moment, the crowd's sympathy lay with Federer and this column argued that Nadal should have been allowed to bask in the immediate glory of victory.

DIRTY MONEY
By Peter Roebuck

ALLEN STANFORD HAS BEEN EXPOSED AS A FRAUD AND THE SPORTS PEOPLE around him have been exposed as fools. No other conclusion is possible after authorities in various countries closed Stanford banks as depositors desperately tried to retrieve money entrusted to the fake mogul and posturing philanthropist. Meanwhile, the Securities and Exchange Commission in the US served documents alleging that the noisy Texan had been involved in a multi-billion dollar scam. As it turned out, they had been investigating him for years. Governments in South America opened investigations of their own in an attempt to trace money and punish corruption.

None of it was new. Although the public was in the dark, various agencies had been trying to pin Stanford down for a decade. The willingness of his Antiguan bank to accept money laundered by Mexican drug lords had drawn him to their attention. As usual, Stanford blustered and bluffed his way out of it. In the end he was caught with his snout in the trough, just another wide boy taking the mugs for a ride. And he might have lasted even longer but for the global financial meltdown. It is harder to keep shuffling money when it is worth less with every passing day. And the swindler knew that a big lie is easier to seal than a small one.

And he did put on quite a show, with his private estate and marina in the northern reaches of Antigua, his airstrip and jets, his castle in Miami, his mansion, his girls, his profligacy – unsatisfied with the quality of the dry cleaning on his home island he flew it overseas – and his exuberance. As it turned out it was all a colossal bluff. He was running a Ponzi scheme and meanwhile living on the hog.

In hindsight, his locations rang a warning bell. He started his vast operations in Montserrat, an island renowned for its lack of financial oversight. When even Montserrat began asking questions he shifted to Antigua, a supposedly genial cricketing island famous for its beaches. Antigua's reputation has fallen almost as far as its tycoon's. But, then, its image was false. It is an angry, seedy beach resort run for decades for its own purposes by the Lester Bird family, currently and unusually in opposition. Stanford greased pals, giving ministers $100 000 each, not as a bribe you understand, but to help them uplift the people. When the FBI insisted on a probe into the dubious practices of the local banks, Stanford was invited to lead it. A member of his own board was aged and incoherent, another was a former car dealer. A fox might as well have been put in charge of a chicken run.

Now Stanford sits alongside Bernard Madoff and numerous other charlatans as a man driven by greed and guided by cunning, a man without principles of any sort, an impostor eager to cut a fine figure even as he massaged the actual figures. Of course he is not the only casualty of the period. Indian, Australian and other companies, American insurance companies and Swiss banks have likewise been revealed as all surface and no substance. By and large, though, they were not swindlers, merely reckless and overpaid gamblers. Recessions may not have much to commend them but they do demolish houses of cards. Stanford, Madoff and company, though, were not inefficient. Quite to the contrary. They were brilliant conmen. Every hour of every day they played to the gallery, kept up their act. And they were helped by henchmen, often family members and lovers. Charm was their main weapon. A lot of people have suffered terribly because they put their trust and their life savings in the hands of plausible rogues. Lock them up and throw away the key.

But Stanford's conduct and correction are not our immediate concern. Sport, and especially cricket, hardly covered itself in glory in this distasteful and damaging episode. One minute cricket officials were laying down their coats so that Stanford need not dampen his shoes in a puddle and the next they are admitting that he took them for suckers. One minute they allow him to land his helicopter at Lord's and haul a trunk of money across the famous turf, the next they belatedly discover his true nature and promptly refuse to resign. Indeed Giles Clarke, the endlessly coiffured and buffoonish chairman of the England and Wales Cricket Board (ECB), said that he 'wasn't going anywhere'.

Governance has always been the biggest issue in cricket, a game best played by a wide range of nations, including two involved in the Iraq war, one dying under a sickening dictatorship, another suffering civil war in its northern regions, another emerging from apartheid, one enduring abject poverty and two others involved in skirmishes in Kashmir and elsewhere. All the more reason to expect that England officials might take responsibility for their mistakes, especially the howlers. But what has changed? No leader resigned when the weapons of mass destruction were not found, while soldiers and civilians die. Still, no one is going to listen to these England officials lecturing about right and wrong.

Retired champions were not much better. One minute they were slapping Stanford's back and hastily cashing his dubious cheques, the next they were condemning their boards as grasping and naive. Some supposed giants did everything except jump into bed with him. So long as he paid their bills and fed their egos they did not care. Ian Botham and Viv Richards were prominent in backing the bankrupt billionaire. He chose them well. At one stage this pair pandered to the Sultan of Brunei, with his mansions and largesse. They pretend to care about the common man and mix with the wealthy. Richards has spent most of his retirement strutting about. Whatever remained of Botham's dignity was lost when he was pictured guffawing with the American only to demand the sacking of the ECB for trusting the same man. But, then, he has much in common with Stanford, including an inability to tell fact from fiction. Astonishingly, the management group asked to recommend the next England coach says it will consult this myth.

A phalanx of other past players took the money, hundreds of thousand of dollars apiece, and paraded around with the swindler. Stanford used them to boost his ego and reinforce his bluff. He cast himself as a larger-than-life character surrounded by other larger-than-life characters, and they were delighted to play their parts. Doubtless they will return these ill-gotten gains so that ordinary citizens can get something back from the debacle.

If anything, the conduct of the England players at Stanford's preposterous match for a million dollars each was even worse. Whereas the West Indies, repackaged as Stanford's Superstars, chased the money, they tried to look sheepish, embarrassed by the stakes. Chris Gayle and company went into a six-week camp by way of preparation, England arrived with the sort of glum expressions more often found in dentist's waiting rooms.

Not for the first time Shane Warne was right – he told the visiting English to lighten up. After all, they were playing an evening match for a million dollars a man. Inevitably England lost. A lot of fuss was made about Stanford cuddling up to the players' wives and disporting himself but that was hardly the issue. The entire project stank to high heaven.

Could the debacle have been avoided? Obviously. Due diligence was required. Boards are supposed to attend to that. There is nothing wrong with accepting money from outside forces. Cricket has always welcomed benefactors. Over the years, tournaments and teams have been sponsored by cigarette companies, beer manufacturers and even banks. Aristocrats fond of the game have organised tours and arranged festival weeks. A hundred years ago Lord Sheffield gave the Australian Cricket Board the Shield awarded to the top state at the end of every domestic season. It's been around a long time and has done more good than harm.

But a game ought to look gift horses in the mouth. The ECB and WICB did not bother with that. England was anxious to placate players frustrated to be denied the IPL loot owing to domestic commitments and to that end decided to bring the lolly onshore. Stanford was supposed to set up a tournament in the old country. The Texan must have laughed to see all the traditionalists licking his boots. England's other motivation was equally small minded, a desire to put one across an Indian board prepared to flaunt its power and wealth after decades of knowing its place. And so, to cite another cliché, the ECB did not look before it leapt. So at the very least, it ought to cost its chairman and inept CEO their jobs.

Of course cricket is not alone in accepting money from all comers. Premier League soccer clubs have been bought and sold by Russian billionaires of vast riches and dubious reputation. Now they dominate other clubs reliant on takings at the gate and TV contracts. No one worries that the money might be laundered. Best not to ask any questions. So long as their team wins, supporters could not care less. Admittedly sport has never been the ideal world occupied by saints portrayed by romantics. But the days of the brown bag in football boots have long gone. Now it is all about secret accounts and tax havens, and the numbers are huge. As the songster put it, 'money does not talk, it swears, obscenity who really cares?'

Stanford also sponsored golf tournaments and players, including Vijay Singh. He reached far and wide in his search for cover. Needless to say, players were let down by this unscrupulous man. Many from various sports invested in his unit trusts and so forth. Indeed Shivnarine Chanderpaul and Ramnaresh Sarwan, at least, accepted their million-dollar reward for winning the match in Antigua in the form of holdings in his financial operations; they will not see any of their money.

For that matter the Texan bought paintings and assisted charities. It was all a front. As it turned out, he was just another greedy man taking everyone for a ride, just another high flyer with clay feet.

Maybe the credit crunch will curtail this custom of using sport to gain legitimacy. Certainly shysters are being called to account. Respectable businessmen are also under the yoke. Several rebel ICL franchises are in trouble and the IPL owners are looking for partners and reducing their spending. But surreptitious money with its excesses, fixed matches and gambling has taken a hold on sport. More likely the loudmouths will be outed and the cunning will continue. Money is a necessity that becomes a way of life.

Allen Stanford was lauded as cricket's ultimate sugar daddy but the manner in which he flaunted his money, particularly in the Caribbean, always seemed suspicious. He even used his money to buy favour with players, and the sight of him bouncing the pregnant wife of England's Matt Prior on his knee in the players' balcony was gut-churning. Then the Texan's world came crashing down, but not before he'd taken many innocent parties down with him.

BARRY BARRY BAD

By Mark Kram Jnr

UNTIL NEW YORK YANKEES SUPERSTAR ALEX RODRIGUEZ BECAME THE junkie *du jour* with his unexpected admission in February that he used performance-enhancing drugs, Barry Bonds owned the headlines in the American sports pages with his anticipated perjury trial that stemmed from his denial of having ever knowingly dabbled in the stuff. The key word here is 'knowingly', which is to say that Bonds asserts that he had no inkling whatsoever that the potions provided for him by his weight trainer were illegal. But how could that be, you are surely wondering, given that athletes of his calibre are cared for as if they were show poodles?

Good question.

Some men and women in San Francisco with expensive briefcases are just as curious.

While I do not know Bonds personally, which is one of those unaccountable small blessings that the heavens occasionally bestow, I did happen to be at Citizens Bank Park in Philadelphia the evening in May 2006 when Bonds slammed his 713th career home run, which left him one shy of the legendary Babe Ruth and within 42 of the all-time home-run champion Henry Aaron. Given that questions concerning his alleged drug use were decreed off-limits by his public relations staff, Bonds appeared in the press room later with an uncommon air of congeniality, unmoored from the eye-rolling churlishness that has always stamped his persona. It was not until a voice shouted out in the back that the 'inner Barry' oozed out, and we were reminded again what a small man occupies that large body. The voice belonged to the fellow who caught the ball – one Carlos Oliveras, who had been ushered into the press room by security.

'Can I get you to sign the ball?' asked Oliveras, a young airman who just happened to be scheduled to ship out the following week to Iraq.

Bonds squinted at him and snapped, 'No, man. I never do that.'

Even before a jury renders its verdict on Bonds, the court of public opinion has weighed in. With the possible exception of his solitary fan in Philadelphia, who still proclaimed his devotion to Bonds in the face of that unseemly brush off, the apparent evidence arrayed against him is so compelling that no one for a second believes that his 762 home runs were not aided by pharmaceuticals. While his case has been delayed due to an appeal by the prosecutors of some pre-trial rulings, there is general agreement until proven otherwise that his accomplishments on the baseball diamond have been an utter sham.

But what has everyone in a state of uncertainty is what to do with him. Even if Bonds escapes a prison term, any formal admission or discovery of guilt will render him a pariah in a sport that is brimming over with them. Bonds is just the apex of a scandal that has ensnarled the stars of what is now called 'the steroid generation'. One by one they have been 'outed' or accused: Mark McGwire and Sammy Sosa, who in 1998 engaged in a stirring showdown for the single-season home run record; Roger Clemens, who won 354 games and seven Cy Young Awards during his career; and Alex Rodriquez, who once appeared to be the very player who by virtue of his unsullied status could redeem the sport. But with his disclosures that he splashed in the same cesspool with Bonds and the others, A-Rod – or as he is now called, A-Roid – will be just another thinning echo in an era of empty apology.

Cheating has always been looked upon by baseball fans with a wink and nod. Generally speaking, it has been considered a kind of gamesmanship, of taking the edge on your opponent wherever you could get it. With the exception of gambling on the game by the participants, which led to full-blown scandals such as the 1919 Black Sox and years later the exile of all-hit leader Pete Rose, the ruling powers viewed throwing spitballs or corking bats as transgressions along the same lines as exceeding the speed limit on the highway. Usually, violators were levied a small fine or suspension and were back in the line-up accordingly. The prevailing view is that boys will be boys.

But the scandal that now looms over baseball is quite another story. While attendance continues to increase across the American and National Leagues, which indicates to some that no one ultimately cares what the players injected into themselves, Bonds and his cohorts have shamed the sport in the same way Bush II shamed the American presidency. Urged on by ego and the quest for one dollar more, the players were ushered to the edge of the cliff by the very agencies that should have prevented it. With their sport in decline in the wake of the 1994 labour dispute that led to the cancellation that year of the World Series, both the baseball commissioner and the union that represented the players were only too obliging to look the other way when interest was ignited again by the eternal spark of the long ball.

Until McGwire and Sosa began slamming baseballs into the ionosphere in 1998, home-run records used to stand forever. When Roger Maris set the single-season home run record with 61 in 1961, he eclipsed by one a standard that had been held by Ruth for 34 years. Maris had held the record for 37 years when McGwire and Sosa not just bettered it but obliterated it. With two weeks remaining in the season, both of them had passed Maris, whose widow and adult children cheered them on as Americans became enlivened again by baseball. Well, yes, it was strange that not one but two players broke such a long standing record in one season – McGwire had 70 home runs, Sosa 66. And yes, some attempted to explain it by saying the pitching was not what it used to be or that the baseballs were 'juiced up' and not the players. Only a few conjectured that drugs played a part in it, but no one seemed unduly worked up over it, especially when the popularity of the sport soared even higher with the challenge by Bonds just three years later.

No one had a better baseball pedigree than Bonds. His father was Bobby Bonds, a talented but eternally unhappy player who bequeathed his son an abundance of both playing skill and surliness. And Barry had an even more impressive godfather, none other than the irrepressible Willie Mays – 'The Say Hey Kid' – whose stagey cheerfulness always belied a tendency toward pettiness. But Willie was a star of uncommon luminosity, and he ascended to that station with the aid of nothing stronger than a cup of black coffee. It is a matter of sad irony that Barry would one day eclipse his career home-run total of 660 under a suspicion of steroid use, fuelled in part by his astonishing transformation from a slender young player to an apparent laboratory specimen with an outsized head. The Say Hey Kid would never utter a peep in condemnation of Bonds then or ever, but that would not be true of Aaron when Bonds topped his all-time record in 2007. Hammerin' Hank could scarcely contain his bitterness when he observed of the upstart Bonds, 'Let me say this: Any way you look at it, it is wrong.'

But before Bonds challenged the legacy of Aaron and Mays, he took aim at McGwire, who had been found in 1998 with a jar of the steroid precursor androstenedione in his locker by an Associated Press reporter. In the book *Game of Shadows: Barry Bonds, Balco and the Steroids Scandal that Rocked Professional Sports*, reporters Mark Fainaru-Wada and Lance Williams of the *San Francisco*

Chronicle asserted that Bonds began using steroids under the supervision of his weight trainer, Greg Anderson, because of his intense jealousy of McGwire. While Bonds conceded that he used 'the clear' and 'the cream' provided by the Bay Area Laboratory Co-Operative, he said with a straight face that he had no idea that either were steroids. But in *Game of Shadows*, the authors claim that Bonds recognised McGwire as 'a juicer' and decided that 'he, too, would begin using what he called "the shit".'

Eye-popping projectiles soared out of what was then called Pacific Bell Park in the summer of 2001. Some of them carried so high and far that they landed with a splash in San Francisco Bay, where fans patrolled the choppy surf in canoes in expectation of snaring an exceedingly valuable souvenir. The 70th home run by McGwire had sold at auction in 1999 in New York for better than $3 million, so it was no surprise that the hysteria in stadiums became pitched as Bonds approached and surpassed the records. Indicative of just how frightening it had become were the circumstances surrounding the final home run Bonds slammed – No 73. While the ball fell cleanly into the outstretched glove of one Alex Popov, he immediately found himself drawn under by a wave of charging flesh. The ball popped loose and ended up in the possession of another fan, Patrick Hayashi. A judge ordered that the two evenly split the $450 000 that the ball eventually commanded at auction.

'I realised 20 or 30 seconds into it that things were getting ugly,' Popov told me. 'All these people were on top of me and suddenly it dawned on me that they were attacking me for the ball.'

Pretty soon, it would be the players who found themselves in a scrum not of bodies but of accusations. Even as baseball commissioner Bud Selig proclaimed the era 'the golden age of baseball', and even as his union head Donald Fehr obfuscated in the face of increasing evidence that membership was juicing up, the deception that players had weaved began to unravel with the ongoing Balco investigation and the publication of the 2005 book by former player Jose Canseco – *Juiced: Wild Times, Rampant 'Roids, Smash Hits, and How Baseball Got Big*. While quite a few observers looked upon his confessional as a sleazy grab by Canseco for a paycheck now that his career had ended, the essence of what he had to say was later substantiated: That some of the top players of the 1990s had joined him in his search of a better body by drugs. When Congress hauled McGwire, Sosa and others before a House Government Reform Committee later that year, McGwire declined to comment upon the advice of his attorney, and the bilingual Sosa suddenly forgot how to speak English, allowing his lawyer to read a statement that denied that he had ever used illegal drugs. Clemens was one of approximately 85 players identified in an investigation by former Senator George Mitchell on behalf of baseball in 2007.

One player who was conspicuously absent from that unsparing account was Alex Rodriguez, who fans looked upon as someone who would one day rescue the all-time home run record from Bonds. He was young enough. But whatever hope he seemed to embody was shattered in February, when *Sports Illustrated* published a report that he had come up positive for two anabolic steroids in a survey test conducted by baseball in 2003. A-Rod did not deny it. In an apology that seemed somewhat lacking in contrition – in that he accused the reporter of stalking him and said that he did not even know if what he was using was illegal – A-Rod said he only used the stuff between 2001 and 2003 and only because his $252 million contract had placed him under intense pressure.

The equivocating A-Rod shrugged and said, 'I was young and dumb.'

Ordinarily, Americans are suckers for an apology – even a half-cocked one. Give them a forlorn face, a few lines of remorse and usually the slate is wiped clean, especially if not forgiving would interfere with the simple-minded understanding that fans have with their superstars. By hook or crook, the bottom line is winning. In the case of A-Rod – who it should be pointed out was not 'young' in 2001 and has never been accused of being 'dumb' – the prevailing view of some percentage of the public was enunciated by a fan who greeted him as he walked out for the opening day of spring training. The *New York Times* reported that the fan said: 'Get us a championship, and everything will be OK.'

Well … perhaps not. The drug culture that has stained baseball is a troubling affair that speaks to far more than just a lapse in judgement. In fact, it was a concerted effort on the part of the finest players to get an unfair advantage – and that is precisely what happened. Players who did not use illegal drugs were under an unspoken pressure to use them if they wanted to try to keep up. Given how harmful this stuff is physically – and steroids will surely lead to the early deaths of some of the players who have used them – observers have expressed concern that Bonds and the others have sent a disturbing message to children. But no less alarming is the message that has been sent to the adults who care for them: Winning big requires risk, of doing whatever it takes. The American financial world is full of such cautionary tales.

The tragic piece enfolded in this moral collapse is that it was just so unnecessary. Given what they had achieved even before they started using illegal drugs, Bonds,

Clemens and some of the others would have been elected to the Hall of Fame. But that has become uncertain as the sportswriters who vote for it wrestle with issues far larger than home runs. Myself, well … I do not have a vote. But I wonder sometimes what that young airman who caught No 713 did with the ball, if he placed it in his duffle bag as he headed off to Iraq. Whatever he did with it, I do know where it belonged: the garbage.

Baseball's most prolific home-run hitter was facing complete ignominy, although the writer reasons that we may never really discover the full truth behind what is now the tragically tainted career of Barry Bonds.

Mark Kram Jnr's work has appeared in The Best American Sports Writing *(Houghton Mifflin) five times: 2008, 2005, 2003, 2002 and 1994. The Associated Press Sports Editors have awarded him with first place honours the past two years – in 2009 for Explanatory Writing, and in 2008 for Feature Writing. A sports writer with* The Philadelphia Daily News, *he has worked previously at the Detroit Free Press and the Baltimore News American. He is at work on a book for St. Martin's Press, provisionally entitled* In the Grasp, *the story of a quadriplegic former high school quarterback who persuades his younger brother to assist in his suicide at the hands of Dr Jack Kevorkian. The book is scheduled to be published in 2011.*

FIGHTING DEMONS
By Roy Collins

RONNIE O'SULLIVAN SNR, FATHER OF THE WORLD SNOOKER CHAMPION, IS expected to end his long stretch as a tenant of Her Majesty The Queen later this year when he completes a minimum 18-year prison sentence for murder. But in a classic case of the sins of the father being visited on the son, the latter has been serving time as painfully as the man chalking off the days on his cell wall and unlike his dad, freedom is not guaranteed to solve all his problems.

In some ways, O'Sullivan Jnr's form of incarceration has been harsher. While his father has been forced to adapt to the locked door, the deprivations and the sheer grinding monotony of prison life, young Ronnie has become imprisoned by his own thoughts, emotions, anger and obsessions, which have led him to darker corners than most murderers visit.

Depression took such an unyielding grip on him, exacerbated by his fondness for drugs, that at one time he was seeing three different psychiatrists at once, and given the prices they charge, it is doubtful you can ask for clearer proof of madness than that. He took Prozac for years until he decided the doctors were trying to prolong his illness so as to keep collecting their fat fees (no paranoia there, then), turning instead to Buddhism and Islam, which only added to the Tower of Babel in his head.

O'Sullivan, 33, says: 'Some days I think one thing, the next day I think something else. It's like there is this damn committee going on in my head. Shall I? Shan't I? Am I up or am I down? Am I doing the right thing? Should I carry on? Should I go home? Have I done enough? Have I had enough? Do people really care? Do I hate snooker? Do I love snooker? Have I had a good time? Is it time to move on? Have I got another five years in me? Should I give up now? Arrrrgh! I've got all this shit in my head to deal with.'

Snooker is both his salvation and his ball and chain. That much he understands. He knows that his success in the sport has sustained he and his father during the long years of imprisonment, but he also believes that if his dad had not gone inside, his career would have proceeded on a serene path to world title after world title, much in the manner of Steve Davis and his hated rival, Stephen Hendry.

The problem is, he cannot prove that, so he continually directs his rage at his sport, threatening to walk away from it on an almost monthly basis. His latest manifestation of self-harming is cutting off cue tips after tournaments, which is at least preferable to his actions at the 2002 UK Championships, when he chewed off the tip, though escaping a charge of ungentlemanly conduct.

In 1996, he was fined £20 000 for assaulting an official at the World Championships and then insulted Canadian Alan Robideux by playing left-handed. Robideux refused to shake hands after the virtually ambidextrous O'Sullivan won 10-3. The following year, he was stripped of his Irish Masters title after a drugs test revealed marijuana traces, but his most unforgivable snooker crime was committed in the 2006 UK Championships against Hendry, the man he has accused of having 'a sad little life'. Trailing 4-1 in frames in the 17-frame match, O'Sullivan messed up a shot, shook a bemused Hendry's hand and walked out, an incident now commemorated on YouTube.

O'Sullivan's outrageous natural talent first emerged as an eight-year-old when he began beating his dad and uncles and by 10, he had knocked in his first century break – the youngest ever to do so – while standing on a milk crate. O'Sullivan Snr then decided to give his son a formal snooker education by taking him to Brooksby's Snooker Club in Hackney, East London and allowing world amateur champion Marcus Owen to coach him in the arts of spin and ball control.

Owen, who many believe was the finest ever to chalk a cue tip, is a story in himself, a fabulous player who liked a drink but in the closed shop mentality of the times, was never allowed to turn pro because he might have beaten all the established stars. Instead, for the price of all the Guinness he could drink, he taught young Ronnie from 10 in the morning to six at night, when the latter would find victims on whom to practise his new found skills. Often, when his dad returned from his Soho sex shop in the early hours of the morning, he would find his son asleep under the table.

Some days, Ronnie would help his dad stack the porn magazines in his shop, which no one in the family seemed to find remotely unusual. 'Ron's me name and porn's me game' was O'Sullivan Snr's boast and it seemed as natural for him to enrol his young son in the family business as it would have been to a banker or a lawyer.

On the road, cleaning up at local tournaments, O'Sullivan says he and his father were more like brothers. 'We were just so close,' he says. 'We were like partners really. He was my backbone. He used to make me laugh, crack me up like no one else could.' Then, just after he turned professional in 1992, aged 16, his world fell apart when his father was sentenced for stabbing to death Bruce Bryan, the driver of Charlie Kray, elder brother of the notorious East End gangsters, The Kray Twins. Because Bryan was black, the judge deemed it a racially motivated crime and set a minimum tariff of 18 years, twice that served by the average murderer. The racial contention was overturned in 2003 but not a day was removed from the sentence.

Four years later, Ronnie's Sicilian mother Maria was sentenced to a year inside for tax evasion and snooker suddenly slid down his list of priorities. He says: 'I really went off the rails for a while. I started drinking a lot, doing drugs and hanging out with people I thought were friends but were only ever hangers-on. My weight ballooned from 12 stones to 15 [76kg to 95kg]. I was supposed to look after my 12-year-old sister Danielle but I had to get a friend's mum and dad to take care of her.'

The man on the inside now had to save the man on the outside. Casually, O'Sullivan Snr asked his son to get four tickets for the UK Championships in Preston for a Liverpudlian friend called Willie. The pair, presumably as O'Sullivan Snr had expected, got on like a house on fire, so much so that Ronnie moved in with Willie, his wife and three daughters. He says: 'I stayed for 18 months. He got me off the drink and the cannabis and I rediscovered family life. I ate meals with them, and his wife even ironed my suit before I went out to a tournament. And I developed the same father-son relationship with Willie that I'd had with my dad.'

Heaven knows what the psychiatrists made of that. But the real father-son relationship should resume later this year when O'Sullivan, 54, is released. In March, he was allowed out on home leave to prepare him for his formal release, spending his time in his £1.5 million Chigwell mansion, doors away from his son's own home. Ronnie Jnr says: 'All these years, I have visualised my dad and I having barbecues until two in the morning and having a laugh and a joke with his friends. Now they seem more real.'

He has also attempted to clean his own life up, joining his local athletics club in Woodford Green and taking part in 5km and 10km races at weekends. He says: 'Running has led me away from temptations and things I was doing before. Like going down the pub in the afternoon, watching the football, having a fag, carrying on until the night time, thinking there was no point going home. That lifestyle was getting on my nerves.'

O'Sullivan knows that three world titles, the first in 2001, represents a modest return for a man who is as natural a potter as anyone can remember, another source of his angst but one he tries to excuse by saying: 'I have definitely underachieved. But I haven't got the drive to win seven or eight world titles. I haven't got the passion it takes to be a Hendry, a Michael Schumacher or a Phil Taylor. And I'm not going to be a slave to snooker. I can't see me playing in five years' time.'

He also has important family reasons for winding down his snooker career, and not just because his dad is about to become a central plank in his life again. He has two children with Jo Langley, whom he met in a drug rehabilitation clinic eight years ago, and although the couple split up last year, they are continuing to live together for the sake of their daughter Lilly and their son. O'Sullivan also has a daughter, Taylor-Anne, from a previous relationship. Inevitably, he named his son Ronnie, and as he only turns two in June, the Ronnie O'Sullivan story could have several more decades to run or even, depending on the toddler's lifestyle, become a perpetual fable.

Ronnie O'Sullivan is in his early thirties but he walks a tightrope in life. This was a time to look back at a snooker champion and reflect on the things that troubled him. Here was the sport's most celebrated player but one who also had the most mental baggage.

THE LAST GREAT ADVENTURE
By Chris Hewett

JOHN BENTLEY STILL TALKS ABOUT IT TO THIS DAY. NOT ALL THE TIME, BUT whenever he is asked, which is approximately eight times an hour. He can remember receiving the ball somewhere in the back end of downtown Johannesburg, setting sail towards the bright lights marking the corner flag at Ellis Park, beating at least 14 of the 15 Gauteng players on the field (some of them twice) and veering towards the posts to complete the greatest try since great tries were invented, probably by one of South Africa's mighty Morkel brothers in nineteen-hundred-and-frozen-to-death.

It was the score that saved the Lions, the touchdown that made victory over the Springboks – the reigning world champions, the team of Os du Randt and Andre Joubert – a possibility. It was, in truth, one of the miracles of this sporting life.

And what glittering prize did Bentley receive for his efforts? A seat on the replacements' bench for the first Test in Cape Town. Thanks a million. He must have felt like pushing off home on the next plane – home to the godforsaken Yorkshire muckopolis of Cleckheaton, where, as the man himself confessed just recently, 'pigeons fly upside down, because there's nothing worth shitting on down there'. (Bentley did not push off home, of course. He stayed put in South Africa, larger than life and much funnier, to await his rightful reward, which duly arrived in the shape of a starting place in the second Test in Durban, where the Lions wrapped up a series no one thought they were capable of winning.)

Why wouldn't he keep the flame alive with his conversation? People have dined out on a lot less. Yet when Bentley discusses that trek through Springbok country a dozen years ago, he does it in the round. Yes, his try in that midweek game – a game that propelled a batch of outside-bets into Test contention – was as special as special gets, but it was just one of the many good things that were happening all round. Up here in the cold and wet of the British Isles, the '97 trip is remembered by all who experienced it, from management and players to medical staff and media (not to mention the zillions of paying followers who, in the face of all previous scientific evidence, proved it possible to get drunk on South African beer), as the last of the feel-good tours. And the longer ago it was, the better it feels.

Bentley's famous try marked the point, half-a-dozen matches into a programme that had already asked severe questions of the tourists, at which the mood changed. Suddenly, the tone and tempo of the trip seemed right: the Lions had the measure of themselves, and would now set about getting the measure of the Boks. Before Bentley, the visitors had struggled. There had been a laborious victory over an unrated Border side on an East London bog; a win over Western Province that had identified more problems than solutions, particularly in the scrum; a thoroughly nasty game with Mpumalanga, whose players kicked anyone who moved and kept kicking even after they had stopped; and a defeat in Pretoria, at the hands of Northern Transvaal. (Weirdly, the Blue Bulls do not have a fixture against this year's Lions. No one in these islands is complaining, but that doesn't mean they understand the South African thinking.)

After Bentley, there were spellbinding outbreaks of brilliant attacking rugby. The Lions put more than 40 points on the Natal Sharks, more than 50 past the Emerging Springboks (coached by Nick Mallett, no less) and rattled up another half-century against Free State in Bloemfontein. This last performance was jaw-droppingly good – so good, indeed, that those who saw it still wonder whether centre Allan Bateman and second-row forward Simon Shaw ever played better. Will Greenwood was pretty good too, until he crashed head-first into a rockhard pitch and damned nearly killed himself. It was a sure sign of the Lions' growing self-assurance that they dealt with the trauma of the Greenwood incident so calmly.

Lest we forget, they also won the Test series during that golden run. The images are still fresh in the mind: the bare-faced cheek of Matt Dawson's try in Cape Town, the riveting build-up to Jeremy Guscott's decisive drop goal in Durban, the tumult of Scott Gibbs' defence in both cities. By the time they returned to the highveld for the last week of the tour, the thing was done. They knew the last match of the rubber was a contest too far – so many of them were in pieces, they could barely raise a quorum – but as it was party time, who the hell cared? Joburg had never been more fun for a touring rugby team.

One of the fascinations of this year's return visit is the fun element. Does it still live and breathe as it did in '97? Is it possible for a professional rugby player to enjoy himself even a quarter as much as his amateur predecessors? South Africa is the place to find out. Far more so than Australia, where interest in the union code is so limited and the standard of competition so uncertain. More so even than in New Zealand, where fun and South Island weather are not natural bedfellows. In the land of the Springbok, the whole of life and the best of rugby come together in bold, brash coalescence. South Africa is the supreme touring venue for those who love the union game.

It has been considered thus for well over half a century. Before his death 13 years ago – eight months or so before a trip he would have relished as much as anyone – Clem Thomas painted a memorable word picture of his own experience as a Lions tourist, under the Irish forward Robin Thompson in 1955. 'The South Africans were kindness personified to us,' he wrote in his warmly received *History of the British Lions*. 'No people are prouder of their country, which is not surprising given its beauty and enormous variety of climates and contrasting regions ... The hospitality was overwhelming. One farmer actually kept a leopard, which had been decimating his cattle, alive for a couple of weeks so I could shoot it! Jack Siggins, the manager, heard about it and decided to ban my involvement, but the farmer shot it anyway and gave me the cured skin. It was not so politically incorrect in those days.'

It goes without saying that other politics, infinitely more reprehensible than that surrounding animal welfare, pressed themselves on Thomas' consciousness, and the grand old Welsh flanker wrestled with the ethics of playing rugby in apartheid South Africa far more than many of those who would subsequently visit the country on so-called 'rebel' tours, organised by the desperate on behalf of the greedy. Thomas took the view that the vast majority of rugby folk 'wanted us to ignore the bad element and love them for themselves, their country and their hospitality, which has been the hallmark of the Afrikaner since his trekking days,' and concluded that it was 'not surprising that so many rugby people were beguiled by them and became so ambivalent over their racial policies'.

Rose-tinted naivety? At this distance, it is the description that most readily springs to mind. Certainly, another fine chronicler of rugby touring in this country, the New Zealand scribe Terry McLean, painted his pictures in darker, more disconcerting hues. And it is true to say that until recently, a trip to South Africa could still have its grim moments. When Clive Woodward took England there in 2000 for a five-match visit confined to the highveld – Tests in Bloemfontein and Pretoria, midweek fixtures in Kimberley and Potchefstroom – the final fixture in Brakpan might have been played 30 years previously, so malevolent was the atmosphere in the stadium that night.

But for the most part, the transformative effects of the World Cup production in 1995, followed by the many and varied splendours of the Lions tour two years later,

---

continue to make a difference. The '97 Lions had their trials and tribulations out there in the up-country badlands – none of those who witnessed the brutal game in Witbank counts it among their fondest memories – but at least the unpleasantness was confined to the field and the after-match reception, at which some buffoon of an Mpumalanga official dismissed the sickening assault on poor Doddie Weir with a wave of the hand and a spellbindingly ill-judged 'these things happen in rugby' comment. Virtually everywhere else, not least in a Johannesburg whose demonic reputation went before it, there were good times to be had.

Ian McGeechan, many of whose greatest moments as a player and a coach are rooted in South African soil, intends to do everything in his power to recapture the spirit of the '97 tour. This will not be easy, despite his good intentions. To begin with, the fixture schedule is three matches shorter, and therefore significantly more concentrated. Also, only one game will be played outside the traditional rugby showcase cities: the opener, in Rustenburg. Twelve years ago, the Lions visited Wellington and Welkom, as well as dear old Witbank. But most importantly, this party will be populated almost entirely by career professionals, the one exception being the venerable Shaw, who, at 35, knows what it was to play in the amateur era.

Tom Smith, the knee-high-to-a-grasshopper Scottish prop who was one of the beneficiaries of the Mpumalanga and Gauteng matches, said a few weeks ago that while the '97ers played like the professionals they had only recently become, they enjoyed themselves like the amateurs they had been hitherto. Of course, these latest Lions will 'get on it' with a vengeance at the end of the tour, especially if they sneak the series 2-1, but it is scarcely conceivable that they will knock back as much of the amber fluid as the hardened party animals of 12 years ago. Players learn a good deal about rugby in modern-day academy systems, but they don't learn après-rugby as understood by the likes of Lawrence Dallaglio and Jason Leonard, and they certainly aren't taught to celebrate like those particular sons of London town.

Some of the toughest rugby communities in Christendom – Pretoria springs to mind, as does Bloemfontein – have, in this writer's experience, been among the friendliest. Discussion and debate about the Springboks and their opponents runs freely like water and is as natural as air. In New Zealand, everyone knows everything about the union game: it's possible to buy a packet of gum at a corner shop in Invercargill and be told by a 14-year-old female shop assistant: 'That will be 50 cents, sir, and, by the way, your halfbacks are crap.' South Africans are similarly knowledgeable, and every bit as willing to tell a visitor his fortune, whether he asks for it or not. The difference? Somehow, it is more palatable to be written off to your face when the sun is shining.

A dozen years ago, the Lions were written off by everyone, including the newspapermen who travelled with them. But no one – certainly not McGeechan or his gruff coaching sidekick Jim Telfer – foresaw the Springbok selection for the first two Tests. The tourists had no fullback, but they had a kicker in Neil Jenkins; the Boks had a fullback to die for in Joubert, but no kicker. When you think of all the great South African victories in which dead-eyed marksmanship played a central part, some of the choices made by Carel du Plessis are mysteries that passeth all understanding.

Will the Boks make this mistake again? Surely not. Then again, it is hard to imagine them being as good as they were at the last World Cup, while the Lions will not be as bad as they were in All Blacks country four years ago, when they travelled with so many players, they had to hire Thunderbird II to get them there. This is a smaller, tighter, more logically selected unit, and they will make a decent fist of it. And so they should, for this is no rehearsal. The British & Irish Lions in South Africa? As Gerald Davies, the tour manager, said a couple of weeks ago: 'It is the last great adventure left in rugby.'

The British & Irish Lions were about to return to South Africa for the first time since winning the series 12 years previously, in 1997. The author had been on that tour and reflected that while the rugby landscape had changed considerably in the professional era, some things had stayed the same. One of them was a tour of the country by the Lions.

Chris Hewett has been rugby correspondent of The Independent **since 1996, covering four Lions tours and three World Cups for the paper, and has twice been named Rugby Journalist of the Year. Previously, he covered a wide range of subjects for the** Bristol Evening Post: **crime, the arts and local politics, as well as rugby and cricket. Born and bred in Bath, he captained the successful local club Walcot Old Boys and was the first player in more than a century to be sent off during his term of office. He also had the pleasure of dropping a scoring pass from the club's most illustrious player, Jeremy Guscott.**

THE NEW ORDER
By James Lawton

WHEN BARCELONA BEAT MANCHESTER UNITED TO WIN THE EUROPEAN Champions League final in Rome there was a charge in the air that could not have been created by just one exceptional performance. There was more than a whiff of mere certainty about the work of the winners. It seemed as much as anything the accumulation of belief and a certain passion, as though Barcelona were in possession of not just a winning game plan but the very spirit of the world's most popular game.

Yes, that seemed to be it. They were possessed by some higher calling, some ultimate means of expression.

For 10 minutes United inflicted heavy pressure – even to the point where panic seemed to be gripping the hearts of Barcelona. Then Samuel Eto'o scored a goal of brilliant conviction and skill and suddenly a team of ravishing promise had become a constellation. Even United loyalists, stunned by the measure of their team's defeat, conceded that they had seen something they would never forget and so it was hardly surprising the euphoria stretched further than the Trevi fountain where, in the small hours of the following morning, exultant Barca fans were still splashing happily. Indeed, it did not seem extravagant to believe that the ripple effect might reach out for more than a year and all the way to Johannesburg and the 2010 World Cup final.

Barca were crowned champions of Europe and, some said, also football itself – they were the foundation and the inspiration of a new empire, one on whose behalf Spain – driven by two key midfielders who had dominated the Roman night, Andres Iniesta and Xavi Hernandez – had made the first significant conquest in Vienna a year earlier with the European Championships title.

Now, Johannesburg represents the last hurdle to an unprecedented annexation of football success. In the late night cafes in the piazzas of Rome there was, surely, a most legitimate question. It asked simply if football's El Dorado, a true and desperately needed golden age, was all but achieved.

Yes, perhaps it was – the possibility had to be conceded when you thought of how marvellously Xavi and Iniesta had come to control the game, and how brilliantly Lionel Messi had surpassed – both in technique and competitive personality – his arch-rival of United, Cristiano Ronaldo.

Yet there had to be caution because we have known some false dawns down the years and one is still too recent to permit wholesale hubris. When you thought of such failed promise you couldn't avoid Gelsenkirchen, Germany, World Cup, 16 June 2006. It is just another old football dateline now but for a little while on that humid day in the Ruhr Valley there was some reason to believe it could prove one for the ages, just as in Rome there was that overpowering sense of new horizons to be conquered.

The excitement in Gelsenkirchen came with the spurt of belief that we might just be heralding a golden age of the world game, a brilliant intrusion into the growing idea that modern football was sinking, quite irrevocably, into a morass of diving and assorted cheating in which genuine beauty was all but extinguished. You surely remember the game and the scoreline – Argentina 6, Serbia and Montenegro 0 – and if some of the details are lost in that fading summer haze, the second goal, scored by Esteban Cambiasso, is still conjured as easily as a first kiss.

The Argentines, with Messi recovered, we were told, from injury sitting on the bench, made 24 successive passes, beautifully accurate, some penetrative, some made principally to gain a little time, a little edge in space, and then Hernan Crespo back-heeled a return ball into the path of Cambiasso. Ecstasy swept beyond national boundaries as the ball billowed into the back of the Serbian net. Here was something of quite dazzling promise. Here was a team gliding in the footsteps of the great innovative teams like the Hungary of the early-50s and the Brazil of '58 and '70.

The wider world of football yearns for such moments because it explains and confirms its status as humanity's favourite sport. It is, we are sometimes required to forget in the course of some turgid, over-hyped showpiece game, its *reason d'etre*, this ability to transcend the normal parameters of win and loss.

The Argentines, for all their innate ability, had never before presented themselves so encouragingly as potential saviours of the game's best values. Their reputation for bleak cynicism had always walked stride for stride with the outbreaks of marvellous virtuosity expressed down the years by such as Alfredo di Stefano, Diego Maradona, and, most recently, the extraordinary little Messi.

Going back to the 1966 World Cup in England, when a team of much ability led by Antonio Rattin betrayed themselves with shameful gamesmanship, the dark side of Argentina was both a mystery and a scandal of the game. In his recent autobiography, Sir Bobby Charlton declared, 'When the anger had dissipated I felt an over-riding sadness and regret that the team who had dragged football into the dirt, you could tell almost at full glance, clearly had the capacity to take it to the stars. They had beautiful skill, displayed in sudden bursts of speed, breaking a rhythm that a second before might have lulled you towards a little nap. But almost from the first whistle they spat out their phlegm and their hate, induced by what I could only believe was a terrible inferiority complex.'

But in Gelsenkirchen three years ago it was a different Argentina. This was a team that finally recognised its greatest strength, which was not mean gamesmanship, brutal tackling, but a touch on the ball which seemed to grow a little more luminous with every passing minute.

Of course, soon enough, and with much bitter disappointment we were mourning another example of a misplaced dream. Argentina were not, we had to accept, what we thought they might have been. Part of the problem, no doubt, was the failure of the coach, Jose Pekerman. He chained Messi to the bench, he watched, apparently passively, his team lapse into disbelief in the strength of their impact. They lost in the quarter-finals, in a shoot-out against Germany and with savage irony it was Cambiasso, the flag-bearer, who missed the vital kick.

Argentina, the team of brilliance and hope, were just another football memory when Zinedine Zidane mutilated what might have been the supreme moment of his sublime career by head-butting the baiting Italian defender Marco Materazzi in the final in Berlin. Inevitably coach Pekerman paid the price and now Argentina are in the hands of the iconic Maradona and the genius of Messi. They remain erratic contenders.

It is to Spain and the growing impetus supplied to them by Barcelona that South African football fans must look with the greatest confidence. Now there are two foundation stones for such optimism that in Johannesburg may well produce something that might just rival the peak of the game achieved by Brazil in 1970, when Pele announced himself once again as the greatest, most rounded player the world had ever seen and a fine Italian team featuring such major players as Giacinto Facchetti and Sandro Mazzola, were not so much beaten as engulfed.

There was the triumph in Vienna last summer, when the Spain of veteran coach Luis Aragones proved themselves on a different dimension to all rivals, including, most dramatically, the superbly revived Russians under master strategist Guus Hiddink. There was the eruption in Rome, orchestrated by Barca's 38-year-old coach and former midfielder Pep Guardiola, who in his opening season as a first-team coach delivered the historic treble of Champions League, La Liga and the Spanish Cup – and in Johannesburg it is Vicente del Bosque who carries the baton.

Del Bosque, 58, is not likely to be negligent in his duties. He is from Salamanca, the austere Castilian city which was a bulwark of the Inquisition and even today tends to see itself as the guardian of the Spanish soul. Certainly Del Bosque is a man of classic football instincts. He twice led Real Madrid to Champions League titles, but, scarcely believably, was still fired after the second success when Real president Florentino Perez instituted the age of the Galacticos, when the most successful club in Europe became something close to football's equivalent of the Harlem Globetrotters – a circus act rather than a beautifully drilled team.

'It is a great honour to be in charge of this Spanish team,' says Del Bosque. 'Wherever you look there is extraordinary talent, and of course this gives a coach responsibilities as well as great opportunity.' So far Del Bosque is guiding the Spanish juggernaut with an easy touch. They comfortably lead their World Cup qualifying group with maximum points and in February the impressive progress of England under Fabio Capello was thrown into sharp perspective in a friendly match in Seville. England were scarcely permitted a touch of the ball as Xavi took control of the game so profoundly he left to a standing ovation worthy of one of the great matadors.

Said Xavi, 'It didn't matter that this was a friendly. When you play for this Spanish team every moment is a pleasure. It is wonderful to develop such understanding.'

It also helps if you achieve almost 100% passing accuracy. The stern Italian Capello said that in one way he was pleased that the Spaniards had put in such a performance. 'It showed our players,' said Il Capo, 'how much work they still have to do. They have done well in qualifying games but tonight they came up against a team of great skill and discipline. It is the level we have to achieve if we hope to do well in South Africa. Everyone who goes to the World Cup finals cannot forget for a second the standards the Spanish team has set. They are technically brilliant – and they play with such strength and feeling.'

In Vienna last summer there was some remarkable evidence of a fierce unity in the dressing room, a willingness to put the success of the team before the individual. Arsenal's precocious midfielder Cesc Fabregas, who put in some exquisite performances when called off the bench to augment the efforts of Xavi and Iniesta, eventually won a starting place in the final – but he was hauled off the field at the climactic moments of a great triumph.

Fernando Torres, another vital performer who had established himself at Liverpool as arguably the world's most potent striker, was also back on the bench when Spain celebrated their proudest moment since their only other major tournament success in the same championships in 1964. Yet at the end of the game both Fabregas and Torres were at the heart of the celebrations, helping to toss the 70-year-old Aragones into the air – and making sure that he returned safely.

Will the Spanish football crusade conclude so happily in the World Cup final?

In Rome certainly there was a powerful sense of a nation's football destiny. Before the game Guardiola called for his players to end their warm-up early and return to the dressing room. He wanted to make an emotional tribute. He spoke of all they had already achieved. It was, some of those present reported, so moving that players were wiping away tears of pride when they returned to the field for the start of the game.

Guardiola talked of 'strikers who defend, defenders who attack ... we are speed, we are strength, we are effort, we are precision, we are one ...'

Whether or not Del Bosque achieves quite such eloquence in a year's time may not be as relevant as the reality already proclaimed in the historic cities of Vienna and Rome by the likes of Xavi and Iniesta, Fabregas and Torres. It is that Spanish football has compelling reasons to believe that indeed they are just a footstep away from El Dorado.

Spain were the European champions from 2008 and they ruled at club level, after Barcelona beat Manchester United to win the European Champions League in 2009. All the signs and structures were there to suggest that Spain had become the new rulers of football, and that the country would be the team to beat at the World Cup in South Africa the following year. Prophetic words, because Spain won the 2010 tournament, beating the Netherlands in the final.

EATING CHERRIES WITH THE CHAMP
By Mark Kram Jnr

SET OUT ON THE DINING ROOM TABLE IS A BOWL OF CHERRIES, WHICH JOE Frazier picks at casually as he remembers his old R&B group, Smokin' Joe and The Knockouts. In occasional gigs back in the '70s, during which he terrorised the heavyweight division with his lethal left hook, Joe was the lead vocalist for the The Knockouts and even had a contract with Capitol Records. While the fortunes of the ensemble more or less fizzled, the songbird in Joe is still apt to soar with unbidden spontaneity, given the presence of even an audience of one.

The Champ croons:

'And now, the time is near

'To domineer ...'

'Remember that one – "My Way?"' says Joe with a gravelly chuckle. 'Paul Anka rewrote some of the words to it just for me.'

Joe is 65 years old now, full of easy cheer that belies the public profile he has carved out as the unforgiving soul so incapable of letting go of the seething anger he has harboured for Muhammad Ali. That Joe is elsewhere today, even if he does get a few jabs at his old arch-rival between forays into the cherry bowl. Generally, Joe is in a contented mood, happy with his new crib on the 20th floor of a downtown Philadelphia hotel even if it has caused him some upheaval. For years he used to live on the top floor of his old gym on North Broad Street, a hideaway he had to abandon in the wake of six operations he has had since a 2002 car wreck left him unable to climb the stairs. With the property up for sale now, the gym has stood empty for close to a year, except for when Joe himself unlocks the door, dons an old boxing robe and taps out a few rounds on the speed bag.

Seeing Joe again reminds me of just how hard it is to unlink him from Ali, who used him as a verbal battering ram during their epic trilogy in the ring back in the

'70s. Of their three fights, Joe won one of them – the first by decision, a chilling duel at Madison Square Garden in March 1971 that saw Frazier send Ali sprawling to the canvas in the 15th round. Four years later in January 1975, Ali avenged that loss with an uneventful 12-round decision in New York, a bout during which Ali leaned on Frazier as if he were a light pole. Act III in October 1975 in Manila ended when the battered Frazier was stopped by his corner from coming out for the 15th round. No rivalry between individuals has ever surpassed it. Well beyond the pedal-to-the-floor action they gave us, it is the personal feud that has simmered between them that has elevated it to an operatic pitch. Vile utterances that Ali looked upon as showmanship designed to build the gate stung Frazier, even if Joe understood why Ali went off the way he did.

Joe chuckles as he expels a cherry pit into his hand. 'The "Butterfly" did that stuff whenever he was afraid,' Frazier says of Ali, who assailed Frazier as 'ugly', 'ignorant' and an 'Uncle Tom' in the days leading up to 'Thrilla in Manila'. 'He did it to get himself revved up. Remember, he did it with Sonny Liston before and some of those other cats. He knew I would put a whipping on his ass.'

Catch him under the spell of a foul wind and chances are Joe will be less charitable. Example: When the trembling Ali lit the Olympic flame in Atlanta in 1996, Frazier said he would have pushed him into the engulfing fire if he had the chance. Give it up, Joe – the press scolded. Even his old friends winced. But there is a part of Frazier that remains anchored in 1975, even as he sits at his dining room table 34 years later with the aroma of ribs baking in the oven and counts the blessings that have been bestowed on him: 11 children, 25 grandchildren and six great-grandchildren. While he has not seen Ali for years now – and gets few updates on how he is doing – he remembers how Ali once leaned in close and told him in a hoarse whisper: 'Joe Frazier, we were baaaaaad scam boogies'.

Joe sucks on another cherry and says, 'He said once I would have been nothing without him. But what would he have been without me?'

The sun has set on the Philadelphia skyline as Joe Frazier shuffles in to the apartment with a pack of paper towels large enough to clean up an oil spill. He hands them off to his friend, Denise Menz, who explains that Joe still thinks he is living back in the vast building that housed his gym. Space in his current dwelling is scarce, but that does not stop Joe from bringing in four cases of soda or whatever else happens to look like a deal during his peregrinations through the city. Denise says, 'Sometimes a hand truck follows him off the elevator. And I say to him, "Joe, what are you going to do with this stuff?"'

The grip of his handshake is still firm, scarcely the greeting of a man in declining health. But he has battled diabetes and high blood pressure for years and has very poor vision despite the fact that he has had surgery performed on his eyes. (He revealed in his autobiography that he was blind in one eye during his career.) Four operations have been performed on his back and he has had two more on his neck since the car accident. Concerned that he could take a spill and perhaps break a hip, doctors have told him that he should walk with a cane. Cognitively, he still seems to be doing fairly well, despite the fact that his speech is slurred and that he can be apt to wander off point. Grinning, Joe says: 'Conditioning helps out. Gotta keep your timing together. Cause you never know when somebody is going to try to push you around.'

But the gravitational pull of ageing has not kept Joe from living an active life. While Ali at age 67 has scaled back his public appearances due to his ordeal with Parkinson's disease, Frazier has become a hot property, according to his adviser, Les Wolff. In fact, just two days after I chatted with him at his apartment, Joe was scheduled to hop on a plane and fly to the United Kingdom for a series of appearances. It was a trip that he was at once looking forward to and dreading, the latter due to the fact that Frazier is a confirmed white-knuckled flyer. Planes have spooked him ever since 14 American amateur boxers died in a crash in Poland in 1980. One of them could have been his son Marvis, then an aspiring Olympic heavyweight who had been scheduled to be on the trip.

'I told him not to go,' says Frazier. 'Two weeks before that plane crash, I had a dream of a big fire. My whole family was burned up. All of them – gone. It was a house, not a plane, but I just had a bad feeling.'

Sheepishly, he says of his impending journey to the UK: 'If there was only a way I could just snap my fingers and be there.'

How Frazier has re-emerged in the public eye can be traced to the publication of the 2001 book, *Ghosts of Manila*. Authored by my late father, Mark Kram, the former *Sports Illustrated* boxing writer who covered each of the Ali-Frazier bouts, the book waged a vigorous defence of Frazier, who had been devalued in the elevation of Ali to sainthood by 'an increasingly uninformed generation of media that was barely born at the height of his career'. While *Ghosts of Manila* was assailed by a certain quarter of that media as an anti-Ali polemic, a piece of angry writing that aimed to settle old scores with influential figures of the day such as Norman Mailer, Howard Cosell and others, the more discerning understood it as an incisive deconstruction of the myth in which Ali had been embedded. While my father yielded to no one in his admiration for Ali as a fighter (and spoke privately of him with warmth), he just could not accept the fact that Ali was of profound social significance, given in part to his lockstep adherence to the racially separatist agenda of the Black Muslims. My father wrote in the introduction of the book: 'Ali was no more of a social force than Frank Sinatra.'

Whatever you happen to think of that statement, and there were more than a few people who howled at it, even ardent Ali supporters began to look upon Frazier with a degree of pity: yeah, Ali had been brutal on him. The book spawned a renewed interest in Joe that eventually led to a documentary this year by a British filmmaker called *Thrilla in Manila*, which cribbed the thesis of *Ghosts of Manila* without even a cursory acknowledgement. But whatever the filmmaker lacked in manners, he did assemble some compelling footage of the period and included an interview with former Ali aide Dr Ferdie Pacheco that betrayed even a loose definition of the word decency. The inexpressibly graceless 'Fight Doctor' looked the camera in the eye and called Joe Frazier dumb.

'He said that?' asks Frazier, his eyes lighting up with interest. 'Ah, they rip me so Muhammad can come out smelling like a rose. Guys who were on his payroll, they would be saying anything. And Muhammad, we were friends back in the beginning. When he was out of boxing for dodging the draft, I went down to see President Nixon to help him get his licence back. He said, "Smoke, we gonna cut up some money when I get back." I went along with him because he seemed sincere. But whenever a crowd was around, he would go off on me and shout: "Joe Frazier is no champion!"'

So what did Frazier think of the documentary?

He pauses and says with a shrug, 'Well, the truth is I never looked at it'.

Joe has been living with the spectre of Manila since it ended on his stool in capitulation. Had he come out for the 15th round and prevailed over Ali in that tropical heat, he would have beaten him in two of their three encounters. Chances are it would have changed to some extent how we look at Ali, even though he burnished his legend with victories over Sonny Liston, George Foreman and others, and has evolved into a cultural symbol for his evasion of the Vietnam War. In so far as Frazier is concerned, there would not have been this palpable sense of unfinished business that has pervaded him since his trainer Eddie Futch threw in the towel and told him: 'Sit down, son. No one will ever forget what you did here today'. For years Joe held a grudge against wise old Eddie, but years later he told me: 'Eddie stopped it out of love'.

I asked Joe 'what if ... ?'

'What if I had come out for the final round?' asks Frazier, whose eyes were swollen to the size of coin slots by the 15th round. Good question. 'What I have always wondered is if Ali would have come for that round. He was on his stool and he was going to stay there. But Ed was experienced and he thought I had enough.'

A photograph of a far better outcome hangs on the wall above the sofa, of Ali buckling to the canvas in the 15th round of their first bout. Joe looks up at it and says with a laugh, 'There he goes!' Of their second meeting, Frazier says: 'The referee let him mug me'. By the end of the third bout, Joe says, 'it was time for both of us to get out'. While Ali fought 10 more times, and in doing so absorbed some fierce beatings even in victory, Joe called it quits after two more fights and focused his attention on helping his son Marvis climb the heavyweight ladder to some handsome paydays. Of the relationship he has with Marvis, who checks in with him by telephone each day, Joe says: 'Every man should have a son like him'.

Joe yawns and says, 'Come on and stay for ribs'.

Cheerfully, he says his days are full, that the Lord has blessed him in abundance. Someone is always calling with an opportunity, such as the forthcoming Stephen King-John Mellencamp project *Ghost Brothers of Darkland County*. Says Denise: 'Joe plays a good spirit in it and does some singing.' Joe still enjoys belting out the old favourites and has even spoken of reuniting The Knockouts, which he says he would do in a second if he could get up on stage without fear of falling down. Somewhere packed away are copies of an old .45 he cut for Capitol.

He begins singing again:

'I faced the man'

'I had a plan'

'And I fought them my way ...'

It remains unclear at this point what will happen to the gym. Some have talked of tearing it down and building a hotel or a club. Joe is saddened by these possibilities, if only because the gym is so full of memories for him: Of his own days there in the days leading up to Ali-Frazier I, but also of aimless young men who came in off the dodgy North Philadelphia streets and learned how to box. Joe could see himself in them in the early arc of his own life, which began in the low country of South Carolina and included a period in New York where he 'borrowed cars without giving them back'. He came to Philadelphia, secured a job in a slaughterhouse and found a sanctuary under the wing of his old trainer Yank Durham, who would warn him in his grave baritone: 'I want to see you in that gym today!'

'I was born into animosity, bigotry, hatred and white-water/coloured-water,' says Frazier, who received word while in the UK that his 25-year-old step-grandson was gunned in a North Philadelphia bar. 'I look back on those days and think: "Well, you are a better man because of them". The world has changed to the point where we now have a black president. But young kids still have to have a place to go.'

Scattered across a napkin on the dining room table are a few cherry pits, which he arranges in a row as he speaks of how calls still come in from people asking if he gives boxing lessons. But the sport he so honoured is no longer the same as he remembers it, back when he and Ali stood astride a heavyweight division that included such stellar talents as Floyd Patterson, George Chuvalo, Jerry Quarry and an array of others. Heck, Joe says he was watching television not long ago and happened to catch a few rounds of 'Ultimate Fighting', which he says 'looked like two men having sex'. No, it is a far cry from how it used to be, so long ago when Ali and Joe were young, tough and 'two baaaaaad scam boogies'.

It took 34 years after his final heavyweight title fight in Manila with the champion, Muhammad Ali, for Joe Frazier to come to appreciate that life is more than the pits. For over three decades the man they called Smokin' Joe had allowed himself to fester over his two defeats in three fights to The Greatest. Boxing as he knew it has moved on, and now so has he. Finally, he had closure.

ERNIE'S HEIRS

By James Corrigan

SUCH IS THE STAGGERING RECORD OF ERNIE ELS IN THE BRITISH OPEN THAT nobody would have dared write him off for this year's Championship. Yet it is fair to comment that when he arrived in Turnberry he was not commanding the centre of the radar like so often before. In short, the Big Easy had been experiencing too many blips. The fear was, that with his 40th birthday approaching in October, he was inexorably fading from the screen.

Of course, the Big Easy will always have his fans and they will inevitably always include the punters who recognised that seven top 10s in his previous nine Opens was a form-line of which not even Tiger Woods could boast. Naturally, the hero-worship of this particular section of humanity is based on what he has earned them over the years. In truth, however, the whole of golf has a debt to pay to Els and South African golf in particular. For the Ernie heirs are everywhere.

They are there making side-bets on the practice greens before they venture out on to the professional fairways; they are there collecting trophies they had long dreamed of winning and receiving cheques their older relatives could never have dreamed of cashing; they are there representing South Africa. Els led the way and they followed. Soon it will be up to this next generation to do the leading.

Of course, it has not just been Els flying the Rainbow Nation flag these past few decades. Indeed, the merest suggestion that it has been would understandably have Retief Goosen spitting flames of indignation. Except even the Ice Man would admit what he owes to the gentle giant. Goosen grew up with Els and so too did his game, and so too did his belief. In truth, the US Open would not have been nearly so easy to win for Retief if his old sparring partner had not been there and done so first.

And then there is Trevor Immelman, that great hope of the new age. In the wake of last year's Masters victory much was made of his association with Gary Player and indeed, the influence of the Godfather of South African golf should not be underestimated. But the young champion was keen to stress that there had been another professional role model in his formation. It is one thing hearing about past glories and reading about the legends; it is an entirely different thing watching it on television for yourself. More real, more inspiring, more to come.

'What Ernie did, not only for me but for all the other young South Africans on the professional tours now, is show us what was possible,' Immelman told me last year. 'Of course, Mr Player had done it before, but in the modern age Ernie established himself as the ultimate global golfer. He set such an example by getting out there and winning all over the world. He showed the commitment a South African professional has to have to make it on the very big stage. He can look down the range and be so proud of not only what he achieved for himself, but also for his country. His impact will be felt for a very long time.'

They will all line up to say Amen to that sentiment. Charl Schwartzel, Richard Sterne, Louis Oosthuizen, James Kingston, Anton Haig and, more recently, Thomas Aiken and Branden Grace. Not only do they share a patriotism with Els but also a manager. Chubby Chandler, a larger-than-life character from the north of England, is quite clearly excited about the new Bokke on his books. 'They're almost like a rat pack,' says Chandler, who also represents the England cricketer, Andrew Flintoff. 'One steps up and wins and then another one steps up and wins and then another and then another. They're growing up together and going up together. And they're enjoying it together. They're a right bunch of characters.'

Sterne is the mischievous one, tempting the rest into laying wagers on their finishing scores. 'Yeah, we're all close,' says the 26-year-old, who has won four times on the European Tour in the past two years. 'You know, we travel quite a lot together. But we don't really help each other. There's more competition. But it's good competition. The guys have been playing really well, Louis, Charl, myself. We push each other on.'

It is obviously a tough school and a vibrant one. Says Chandler: 'You don't see many European events nowadays in which at least one of these are not competing.' Yet it is not just in Europe where the young South Africans are making a splash, as Chandler himself knows only too well. Another player on his roster is James Kamte. At the US Open at Bethpage in June, Kamte caused a stir across America.

True, it may only have been a practice round and Kamte may have only played nine holes with Woods. But here were two black men walking up the fairways of that New York course. And one of them just happened to be from South Africa. The rush to discover his story was only rivalled by the clamour to pass it on.

Kamte's tale is well-known throughout his own country. The labourer's son from the Eastern Cape town of St Francis Bay, who did not take up golf until he was 14, who gave up a promising football career to caddie at a local course and who all too soon made his remarkable and rather unprecedented graduation from bag-carrier. But in the desperation to emphasise the Tiger connection, the American press were too quick to pass over the contribution to Kamte's rise made by another golfing superstar. It was with some justification that Els called Kamte's qualifying for the 109th US Open 'one of the proudest moments of my life'.

Kamte is a product of the Ernie Els Foundation, set up in 1999 to help talented youngsters from underprivileged backgrounds. He could be the product for which Els has been waiting.

'Coming from an apartheid nation to being a democratic nation, this means so much to me,' said Els. 'He has unbelievable potential. This kid hits the ball as well as I've seen anybody hit it. He just has to learn now. Our mission was to find a black kid who would be our next Tiger Woods. Who knows? Maybe it could be James.'

As Els pointed out, Kamte certainly has the ball-striking ability and it really does not need saying just what it would mean if he could emerge as a big-time performer. Yet Player, as is that wonderful way of his, decided to say it anyway: 'We need a Tiger Woods of South Africa,' commented the golden veteran. 'Everybody is dying to see a black champion from South Africa. All our champions in the past have been white. I told him, if you become a champion, you will have all the white and black businessmen pouring money into your pockets.'

Kamte would be the first to concede that this would be about way more than the greenback. Talking to him and Oosthuizen in Malaysia earlier this year it was easy to sense the responsibility he feels. The previous week Kamte had won on the Asian Tour and success was now written ever larger on his résumé. He thought back and remembered the time he and Louis first enrolled with the foundation. They trained for 10 hours a day with only Mondays off. It was intensive, formative, and very expensive. The big man footed the bill.

'Ernie did everything for us,' said Kamte. 'He was flying us around, paying our accommodation, giving us pocket money, paying for food, caddies and giving us golf clubs. When I was leaving the foundation they had to drag me out because I didn't want to leave. If it wasn't for him I wouldn't be sitting here now.

'You know, a while ago we couldn't play golf but when everything was sorted out it became pretty good because we could start playing golf and there are now a lot of young kids who want to play. For me it's important to play well all the time because the kids back home can look at Louis and look at me and say: "If those two guys can do it, so can we when we grow up". So, it means a lot for us to compete out here to give those kids some hope.

'When I started out I was a caddie at a little golf course and it was expensive to get golf clubs. You had to work for five years to afford them, but things got easier as time went by. I grew up in a very small area – as did Louis – and we were very lucky to be in that situation because it is the type of area where no one is spoilt and you have to work hard to achieve something.

'I am grateful to have come from that kind of environment because it teaches you to get back on your feet when you are down. Some kids grow up with everything and know how to achieve nothing. I am grateful to have had that kind of life as a kid because I know what it takes to get up when you are down. I also know all about the need to be helped. Ernie was one of the people who picked me up and was unbelievable to me. I always said if I won a big tournament he would be the first person I would thank, and I did. I thank him every time I see him. He gave me opportunities when nobody else would.'

As legacies go, that is not a bad one for Els to leave behind. But the man is not yet planning on leaving anything behind. He is still a passionate player and things have gone on in his life – most notably his rebasing from Surrey to Florida so that his autistic seven-year-old son Ben can receive the best schooling – that have quite clearly affected his career. Els is not the type to make excuses. He just wants people to understand. Primarily his own people.

'There were a few times I would be sitting in press conferences and journalists would be asking questions and I would be thinking to myself, "I don't give a flying you-know-what about golf right now, I've got other things going on",' he said in an interview with the *Guardian* newspaper in May. 'It was particularly bad in South Africa. When I went back there they were saying all sorts of things – I've lost my drive, I'm not practising, I'm drinking too much – and I was like, "You have no idea".'

Considering all that he's done, all that he is doing, the very least Els deserves is a bit of slack as he tries to resurrect one of the most natural games golf has ever had the pleasure to witness. Who knows, maybe that would happen in the most stunning way imaginable at Turnberry. There were many of us praying it would. Schwartzel, Sterne, Kingston, Kamte. This is his Rat Pack and he is still their Pied Piper. Grateful does not begin to describe it.

ERNIE'S HEIRS

Ernie Els has been an inspiration to an exciting new generation of South African golfers. Trevor Immelman won The Masters in his late twenties, while the likes of Charl Schwartzel, Richard Sterne and James Kamte were all walking in the giant's shadow. Els was the Pied Piper. Another golfer, a product of the Ernie Els Foundation, stepped forward in 2010: Louis Oosthuizen won the British Open by a staggering seven shots at St Andrews.

BLACK GOLD
By Clinton van der Berg

EXACTLY 15 YEARS AGO ULI SCHMIDT UTTERED THE THROWAWAY REMARK that rugby wasn't in black peoples' culture. 'They should play soccer,' said the unreconstructed Afrikaner rugby hero, igniting a fuse of indignation and angry debate. It was a crass, insensitive thing to say, especially as Schmidt seemingly found it so easy to whitewash (the word is used intentionally) the history and deep passion for the game that courses through black rugby heartlands like the Eastern Cape.

A year later the Springboks ascended the throne as World Cup kings. There was a miserly single black player in the starting XV, but that didn't matter. When the party was at its height and the singing was at its loudest, those leading the band were blacks.

The Amabokoboko were born.

For once, the cheesy Castle Lager advert rang true: blacks and whites embraced, drank together, fell down together.

Not in their culture? That was an argument quickly killed off.

The win of 1995 may have demonstrated blacks' hearty appetite for the game, but it is to rugby's eternal discredit that such goodwill was never harnessed or repaid.

Ten years on from Schmidt's gaffe, Jake White opined that if the Springboks were so outstanding by drawing from a well of just five million white people, they would be near-invincible from the day team selection incorporated the millions of previously disenfranchised.

'How can we, with 40 million black people, justify a white team? If we are really being serious about making an effort, it's impossible.' It was sharply at odds with Schmidt's warped homespun theory and it went straight to the heart of South Africa's thorny transformation debate.

White grappled with the issues of transformation throughout his tenure, but history records that his efforts were hit and miss. Despite his best intentions, he never quite nailed down the challenge. Yet White's heart was in the right place and there's no doubt that he accelerated the careers of players like JP Pietersen, Bryan Habana, Ashwin Willemse and Jongi Nokwe. He forged them into black gold.

Rugby's transformation has nonetheless been fraught. On its own, the issue is massively difficult, but when meddling politicians are added to the mix it becomes combustible.

There have been 'quotas' and 'targets' and incentives, but change has been as slow and as clumsy as the New Zealand backline of recent times. Indeed, on the very afternoon that South Africa were making history by belting the All Blacks in a Tri-Nations fixture in Durban, senior Gauteng clubs Wanderers and Eldoronians were engaged in an appalling brawl thick with racial undertones. The police were called, but perhaps the greatest crime on the day was that Wanderers fielded an all-white XV. Given that Wanderers lies in Johannesburg's velvet belt and is known as one of the more enlightened clubs, who's to know what happens beyond the boerewors curtain on the east and west sides of the city?

You suspect that if you scratched away at the issue long enough, the thing to emerge among players would be fear: fear of black men, the forbidding *swart gevaar*; fear of their habits; fear of their methods. And blacks would be suspicious and fearful too: of being singled out, patronised and *moered*.

These fears are natural consequences of the human condition and aren't to be denied or embarrassed about. The broad challenge for rugby is, to use a front-row analogy, to take them on, to smash them. Confront the fear. Deal with it. The Springboks have.

It wasn't too long ago that the black wave was considered by some to be the certain death knell of South African rugby. The whites will leave – some did – and the blacks wouldn't be able to handle the rough, physical stuff. So went the argument.

And when players like Solly Tyibilika, Owen Nkumane and Hanyani Shimange couldn't breathe the rarefied air of Test rugby, the sad cynics punched the air. 'Told yooz!' But that's a disingenuous argument and conveniently ignores the game's many white failures. No one talks about them.

If black players haven't flooded the Springbok firmament, they have emphatically proved that they belong. Indeed, the sight last year of an all-black Springbok front row closing out the match against England at Twickenham would never have been countenanced a mere decade ago. England were crushed.

And now the 2009 Springboks arguably stand measure with any of the great South African teams of the past. Certainly, the team is among the most gifted of all time and three of their totems are men who would not have been allowed to play for their country in the old South Africa because of their pigmentation. The same holds true of the coach, a black man.

Bryan Habana is a former IRB Player of the Year and indisputably the finest Springbok wing to ever draw breath. JP Pietersen has won a World Cup and two years ago scored more tries than anyone in the Super 14. Beast Mtawarira is the broad-shouldered loosehead who last year turned in a performance rated by one New Zealand rugby writer as the 'greatest ever' by a prop forward.

Final proof that Mtawarira has been accepted is that he enjoys folk hero status the length and breadth of South Africa. Beeeeeasssst, indeed.

The point is made because when these three were selected, the Boks never suddenly lost their mojo or became soft. The sun even came up the next day.

The collective spirit and power within the Boks gave lie to former president Thabo Mbeki's claim that we may have to suck up a few defeats to advance transformation. It's easy to understand what he meant, but, done properly, transformation need not be a byword for defeat. It's not stretching a point to say that without a player like Habana, the Boks may not have won the 2007 World Cup. He was that good and for a while he strode the planet like a colossus. His colour was only an issue to those who wanted it to be. For the rest, like the black and white kids who adore him, he simply possessed the X-factor.

By comparison, Pietersen and Mtawarira are still fresh-faced rookies whose ambition and potential know no bounds. To miscast Mtawarira as a 'quota' selection is to forget the horrible pasting he inflicted on Phil Vickery during the British & Irish Lions series. And Vickery is a *meneer*.

It doesn't bear thinking that were it not for transformation, these three may well have been caught up in the jetsam and flotsam of everyday rugby, playing on the margins.

In a normal world, class will out, but in a world such as ours, struggling with the birth pains of a new South Africa, who's to say that Habana, Pietersen and Mtawarira would have been given their dues without the pressure on coaches to transform?

The really encouraging thing is that while De Villiers spoke of the 'pain' that transformation might bring, he has lent a certain dignity to the process. Speculation when he took the job that there would be 10 black players in the national team has proven to be hysterical nonsense. He has selected proven match-winners and nodded his head towards black players like Earl Rose and Morgan Newman without foolishly rushing them in.

The coach understands that sporting excellence springs from youth, not affirmative action, which is seldom an entirely happy business anyway. He may be smarter than we give him credit for.

Talk of quotas bubbles up every few months, as it did in June, but sports minister Makhenkesi Stofile articulated government's position well when he spoke with searing honesty in the wake of the 2007 World Cup.

'Let us put our resources into development,' he said. 'Quotas were only used as window dressing for international consumption.'

The experts call this gesture politics and it serves to confirm why sportsmen, rather than politicians, wield the power to inspire and encourage.

Yet another sign that rugby may finally be growing up came with the separate inclusion of the Protea symbol on the green and gold jersey ahead of the Lions tour. Rugby has never been a comfortable bedfellow with compromise, but on this occasion there was a happy coming together. The realisation from government is that, ever so slowly, a symbol once synonymous with Afrikaner domination is acquiring a different resonance among black people. It need not be killed off.

This is the view of Habana: 'I'm very proud to be called a Springbok and I'm proud to be called a South African. I grew up wearing the Bok on my chest.'

The consequence is that the hard line has been replaced by pragmatism, empathy even. The Springbok emblem sharing the Bok jersey with the Protea across the heart is symbolic of the merging of the old with the new, and was done seamlessly and without anger or distaste.

The world champion Springboks, who play with a swagger and a smile, are demonstrable proof of that.

As for Uli Schmidt, he lives in Australia now.

He isn't missed.

There was plenty to celebrate about South African rugby at the time of this feature. The Springboks, the reigning world champions, had beaten the British & Irish Lions in a series, won in New Zealand for the first time since returning from isolation, and lifted the Tri-Nations. The author reasoned there was an even bigger reason to celebrate: the Springboks had confronted the fear of transformation and dealt with it.

Clinton van der Berg is a published author, former sports editor of the Sunday Times **and was named SAB Sports Journalist of the Year in 2000. He is currently communications manager of SuperSport.**

BEST OF ENEMIES
By Richard Moore

WHILE ALBERTO CONTADOR CAN NOW BE SAID, WITHOUT ANY FEAR OF contradiction, to be the outstanding stage race rider of his generation, with his latest success following his Tour win in 2007, and his tours of Italy and Spain in 2008, he remains something of an enigma.

On the bike, the 26-year-old from Madrid is exuberant, expressive, exciting to watch. He dances up steep climbs with the same zip that the sprinter Mark Cavendish displayed to win six flat stages, and there is panache in Contador's trademark victory salute too – hands off the bars, he flashes a cheeky grin, pulls out an imaginary pistol, and aims and fires with a deft flick of the wrist.

But off the bike Contador comes across as taciturn, impenetrable – dare we say, even a little boring. He tends not to say much, and what he does say is usually unremarkable.

Or that used to be the case, at least. Which made the ructions that followed this year's victory all the more remarkable, while also confirming what those of us who followed the Tour half suspected – that for the three weeks of the actual race Contador was biting his tongue.

Who had been his toughest opponent, he was asked. Andy Schleck, the Luxembourgeois who placed second? Bradley Wiggins, the British rider who was fourth, behind Contador's team-mate, Lance Armstrong?

No, said Contador. 'The hotel.' He didn't have one hotel of the 20-odd that a Tour rider will stay in over the course of the race in mind, just the hotel in general. More particularly, the atmosphere – especially around the dinner table, you imagine – in whichever hotel his Astana team happened to be staying in.

The reason? Armstrong. The American, returning to the race he won seven times after an absence of four years, suggested in Monaco – where this year's Tour had its Grand Départ – that the question of who would lead the Astana team remained open. 'The race will decide,' he said, which seemed to contradict the official line that Contador, as the clear favourite for the yellow jersey, would be the undisputed leader.

Thus began the psychological war, or battle of wills, between the two nominal team-mates, which simmered just beneath the surface throughout the three weeks, and intermittently bubbled to the top. It was a sub-plot that proved as fascinating as the race itself; and at times even threatened to outshine it, due mainly to Contador's clear superiority.

In the opening week it seemed that Armstrong had the upper hand. The warrior was back and there were shades of the Armstrong of old – on stage three in particular – when crosswinds split the peloton asunder. When Cavendish's Columbia-HTC team massed at the front and drove a small group away, it was Armstrong – alone among all the overall contenders – who sneaked into the move.

If that was not a surprise, given that one of Armstrong's strengths was always his positional sense in the peloton, it was something of a shock to see two of his Astana team-mates join Columbia on the front, helping to distance the chasers, who included Contador. 'I was just trying to stay up front, out of trouble,' explained Armstrong. 'I've won the Tour de France seven times. Why wouldn't you ride at the front? It makes no sense that you wouldn't ride there. It's good positioning, experience, a little bit of luck.

'I'd prefer to stay out of the drama of who's the leader of the team,' he continued. 'I've won the Tour seven times, I think I deserve a little bit of credit. But Alberto's a great rider too and we've got to go with the two leaders, but that doesn't mean you can't take advantage of opportunities like today.'

Contador wasn't so sanguine, saying: 'I don't want to express an opinion on the tactics of the team. I'll let everyone draw their own conclusions. In any case, the Tour is not going to be decided by what happened today.' No, but it seemed to confirm that the pecking order in the Astana team hadn't been decided either. Armstrong, it seemed, remained very much in the frame.

For long-time Tour de France watchers there were echoes in the Armstrong-Contador feud of a similar rivalry in the 1986 race, when Bernard Hinault and Greg LeMond rode for the same La Vie Claire team. After LeMond had helped Hinault to his fifth Tour in 1985, the duo started the following year with the Frenchman vowing to help the American score a first ever victory for an English-speaking rider. That LeMond did finally achieve this in Paris owed everything to his strength and courage and absolutely nothing to Hinault, who, on the first day in the Pyrenees, attacked LeMond and gained four minutes. And then did so again the following day, though he cracked this time, allowing LeMond to fight his way back.

Like Armstrong, Hinault was as tough as they come on the bike, a master of mind games off it. His audacity knew no bounds. 'I'd given my word to Greg LeMond that I'd help him win, and that's what I did,' insisted Hinault in his autobiography, *Memories of the Peloton*. 'I tried to wear out rivals to help him, but I never attacked him personally; it wasn't my fault that he didn't understand this.'

Had LeMond been asked who his toughest opponent was during that 1986 race he may also have replied 'the hotel', since the atmosphere around the dinner table, with Hinault as dominant there as he was in the peloton, was quite poisonous at times.

Back to 2009, and the next act in the Astana drama came on the first mountain stage, to Arcalis in Andorra, when Contador put in one of his familiar attacks as the road steepened, sprinting away from all the main contenders to inch closer to the yellow jersey. At the finish, Armstrong was asked whether his team-mate's attack had been planned. 'That wasn't really to the plan,' he said, 'but I didn't expect him to go by the plan, so [it was] no surprise.'

Contador's progress towards the yellow jersey was gradual but inevitable, and when he did finally relinquish the unheralded Italian Rinaldo Nocentini, in the Alps, there was a sense that that was it: it would remain on the slender Spaniard's shoulders until Paris, despite the third week being one that the organisers fancied would keep the drama and suspense going all the way to the French capital. Three days in the Alps were followed by the only long individual time trial, 40.5km around Lake Annecy, and then, on the penultimate day, the most talked-about stage in years, finishing at the summit of Mont Ventoux.

But as Contador rode away from the field to win at Verbier on the first day in the Alps it was as good as over for the others, for all that Andy and Frank Schleck of the Saxo Bank team took it in turns to try and escape. The brothers' efforts were most effective on the final Alpine day, stage 17, when they dragged away Contador and another Astana rider, Andreas Kloden.

But what happened on the final climb, the Col de la Columbiere, ended any illusions of harmony in the Astana camp. Contador attacked towards the summit, the Schlecks chased, and Kloden was dropped, his hopes of a podium place disappearing as he lost ground.

'I spoke about attacking the Schleck brothers with Johan Bruyneel,' claimed Contador afterwards. 'The goal was to gain minutes. I also spoke with Kloden on the climb, and he told me to go for it. I thought I could go alone but the brothers managed to come back. When I saw that Andreas could not follow, it was too late. He was really struggling at that moment.'

But Johan Bruyneel, the Astana director, seemed to contradict this. 'I told [Contador], you don't have to attack today to win the Tour de France. The [time] difference was already there to Bradley Wiggins, who we were most worried about. It is a bit of a pity Andreas could not hang on, because I think we could have been first, second and third in the final classification.'

Armstrong, who came in more than two minutes down, was also asked about Contador's attack. 'I'm going to bite my tongue on that one,' he said. That didn't stop him tweeting: 'Getting lots of questions why AC attacked and dropped Kloden. I still haven't figured it out either.'

That night Contador was made to explain to his team-mates why he had attacked. And the next day – according to the French sports paper *L'Equipe* – he warmed up on the time trial course alone, with no team-mates for company, or even a car to accompany him. They were all otherwise engaged, collecting Armstrong's friends and family from the airport.

Twenty-four hours after the Tour finished on the Champs Elysees the gloves came off entirely. 'My relationship with Lance Armstrong is zero,' said Contador. 'He is a great rider and has completed a great race but it is another thing on a personal level, where I have never had great admiration for him and never will.'

Armstrong responded, via Twitter: 'Seeing these comments from AC. If I were him I'd drop this drivel and start thanking his team. W/out them, he doesn't win.' He added: 'Hey pistolero [a mocking reference to Contador's pistol-firing victory salute], there is no "I" in "team". What did I say in March? Lots to learn. Restated.'

While Armstrong will set up a new team, sponsored by RadioShack, and return to the 2010 Tour to try and win No 8, there is absolutely no chance of him ever racing by Contador's side again. 'On this Tour,' reflected Contador, 'the days in the hotel were harder than those on the road.'

Contador's off-the-bike travails make his performance on the bike all the more impressive. It also sets up a potentially explosive contest next year, when there will be no facade of co-operation or togetherness, but rather open and all-out war between the young Spaniard and veteran American. It should make for riveting viewing.

Despite riding for the same Astana team in the 2009 Tour de France, there was no love lost between Alberto Contador and Tour great Lance Armstrong. Contador was a clear winner of the Tour, that bald fact hardly began to convey what the Spanish rider endured on the 3 460km three-week journey.

Richard Moore is a freelance journalist and author. His first book, In Search of Robert Millar, *won Best Biography at the 2008 British Sports Book Awards. His second book,* Heroes, Villains & Velodromes, *was long-listed for the William Hill Sports Book of the Year. He writes on cycling and sport and is a regular contributor to the* Guardian, Sky Sports *and* The Scotsman. *He is also a former racing cyclist who represented Scotland at the 1998 Commonwealth Games in Kuala Lumpur.*

BUSINESSDAY

AUGUST 2008

SPORT

MONTHLY

GAMES OF TORTURE

ISSUE 1

AUGUST 2008

This was where the story began. The launch issue coincided with the 2008 Olympics in Beijing. The handcuffs symbolised the five Olympic rings but the coverline , 'Games of Torture', reflected the Chinese conflict with Tibet, while in South African terms it related to an inside feature that predicted the country would not do well in terms of winning medals. The prediction defied popular opinion – but was correct as South Africa returned with a paltry silver.

BUSINESSDAY

NOVEMBER 2008

SPORT

MONTHLY

THE INFERNAL THRONE

ISSUE 4

NOVEMBER 2008

The Kaizer Chiefs coaching position is probably the hottest seat in South African sport. This issue featured a story on Chiefs and it also had a piece on Sir Alex Ferguson, who is the longest-serving manager in English football. The burning chair, set alight as an original concept, captured that hot seat, and while it could be too hot for a Chiefs manager, it could be argued that Ferguson had done a 'Hell of a Job' with Manchester United over the years.

BUSINESSDAY

DECEMBER 2008

SPORT

MONTHLY

THE AUSSIES

ISSUE 5

DECEMBER 2008

South Africa were heading to Australia to attempt to win a cricket Test series
Down Under for the first time. We made a call that it would happen on this
tour at the end of 2008. Rather cheekily, and in keeping with the confident
nature of the prediction, we took the colours and the logo from an Australian
beer and simply ran with the coverline under the beer's logo, 'The Aussies'.
After a thrilling series, the Proteas returned having created history

BUSINESSDAY

FEBRUARY 2009

SPORT

MONTHLY

A STAR IS BORN

ISSUE 7

FEBRUARY 2009

JP Duminy had emerged as a new superstar of cricket after a sequence of stunning and mature batting displays in helping the Proteas beat Australia away in a Test series for the first time. The cover was a picture taken with permission from the family album of JP at the age of six months. The coverline simply said, 'A Star is Born'. We felt it was an original way of honouring the brightest emerging talent in world cricket

SPORT

THE WORLD HAS VOTED

RSA 2009

The Who's Who of the global game will converge on South Africa for the latest big thing to light up the world of cricket. All the movers and shakers from Bollywood will be in the country for the 2009 version of the Indian Premier League (IPL), the highlight of the

Twenty20 calendar. From the opening ceremony of world-famous firebrands on 18 April to the final five weeks later at the Wanderers in Johannesburg, the tournament promises to provide unrivalled action. Rajasthan Royals are the defending champions

RAJASTHAN ROYALS		✓
KOLKATA KNIGHT RIDERS		✓
KINGS XI PUNJAB		✓
MUMBAI INDIANS		✓
BANGALORE ROYAL CHALLENGERS		
DELHI DAREDEVILS		
CHENNAI SUPER KINGS		
DECCAN CHARGERS		

RSA 2009

ISSUE 9

APRIL 2009

In the month of a South African general election, the Indian Premier League
(IPL) was moved from the subcontinent due to security issues and South
Africa stepped in. The cover replicated an election voting form, ticking the
boxes of the teams playing in the IPL. Everyone was a winner. The coverline,
'The World has Voted', implied the cricketing world had voted to hold the
IPL in South Africa and given a ringing endorsement of the country

MAY 2009

SPORT

MONTHLY

Princess Diana is killed in a car accident in Paris
South African president Nelson Mandela turns 79
Winnie Madikizela-Mandela is back as ANC president
Labour leader Tony Blair is elected British PM
Mother Teresa of Calcutta, 87, has passed away
Titanic wins a record 11 Oscars, and best picture
Hong Kong returns to Chinese rule after 156 years
Hansie Cronjé's Proteas win in Pakistan
Pete Sampras wins his fourth Wimbledon singles
Mike Tyson chews off Evander Holyfield's ear
Martina Hingis is female athlete of the year
The Auckland Blues claim the Super 12 title
Jacques Villeneuve is crowned F1 world champion
Manning Rangers lift inaugural PSL title
Future World Cup-winner Francois Steyn turns 10
Natal No 8 Gary Teichmann is Springbok captain
The British & Irish Lions come to South Africa
and beat Carel du Plessis' Springboks 2-1

THE RIGHTING OF HISTORY

LIONS SPECIAL
ISSUE 10

MAY 2009

We settled on a powerful words-driven cover in the month before the British & Irish Lions were to tour South Africa. The last time they were in the country, 12 years previously, they had won the series. The words all related to that year they last toured, 1997, and its many landmarks in history. The coverline, 'The Righting of History', was again suitably ambiguous, while also saying that history would be corrected, with the Boks winning. They did.

SPORT

MONTHLY

MOVE OVER JENSON

ISSUE 13

AUGUST 2009

Michael Schumacher, long-retired legendary former F1 champion, was contemplating a comeback. We ridiculed his decision and photographed a red 'shopping scooter', put F1 Bridgestone tyres on it, and displayed the Ferrari logo. The coverline, 'Move over Jenson', referred to reigning world champion Jenson Button, and compared the Schumacher comeback to a pensioner taking on the youngsters. His subsequent return was disappointing.

WILTING MATILDAS

Beating the Australians on their home turf is easier said than done.
However, there is evidence that Graeme Smith's men have matured
to the point where it is their destiny

WORDS: NEIL MANTHORP

DECEMBER 2008

All too often a cricket tour to Australia would have a predictable outcome: Home side 1 Visitors 0. Few countries are able to go Down Under and come back with a winning result. But this was different and the signs were there for all to see that Graeme Smith's Proteas had a real shot at the prize. This opening spread, from a visual perspective, showed that the Aussies were down – and that's where we needed to keep them.

AUGUST 2009

Lance Armstrong had done wondrously well to finish third in his comeback Tour de France after a long absence and advancing years. He was an Astana team-mate of ultimate overall winner Alberto Contador, and the pair did not get along well. The image of Armstrong looking jealously as Contador milks the moment following victory tells the story of the conflict between the two cyclists.

BEST OF ENEMIES

Alberto Contador was a clear winner of the Tour de France, but that bald fact hardly begins to convey what the Spaniard endured on the 3 459.5km journey

WORDS: RICHARD MOORE. MAIN PHOTO: PATRICK HERTZOG

While Alberto Contador can now be said, without fear of contradiction, to be the outstanding stage race rider of his generation, with his latest success following his Tour win in 2007, and then his third and final stage win in 2008, he remains something of an enigma.

On the bike, the 26-year-old from Madrid is exuberant, expressive, exciting to watch. He dances up steep climbs with the same elan as the best. He sometimes attacks in stages, and there is panache in Contador's trademark victory salute too – hands off the bars, he flashes a cheeky grin, pulls out an imaginary pistol, and aims and fires with a deft flick of the wrist.

But off the bike Contador comes across as taciturn, impenetrable – dare we say, even a little boring. He tends not to say much, and what he does say is usually unremarkable.

Or that used to be the case, at least. Which made the tactics that followed this year's victory all the more remarkable, while also confirming what those of us who followed the Tour half suspected – that for the three weeks of the actual race Contador was biting his tongue.

Who had been his toughest opponent, he was asked, Andy Schleck, the Luxembourgeois who placed second? Bradley Wiggins, the British rider who was fourth, behind Contador's team-mate Lance Armstrong?

No, said Contador. 'The hotel.' He didn't have one hotel of the 20-odd that a Tour rider will stay in over the course of the race in mind, just the hotel in general. More particularly, the atmosphere – especially inside each hotel, now imagine – as whichever hotel his Astana team happened to be staying in.

The reason? Armstrong. The American, returning to the race he has so dominated, elbowed off his team, suggested to Monaco – where this year's Tour had its Grand Départ – that the race would decide,' he said, which seemed to contradict the official line that Contador was the clear favourite for the yellow jersey, would be the undisputed leader.

Thus began the psychological war, or battle of wills, between the two nominal team-mates, which simmered just beneath the surface throughout the three weeks, and intermittently bubbled to the top. It was a subtly plot that proved as fascinating as the race itself, and at times even threatened to outshine it, due mainly to Contador's clear superiority.

In the opening week it seemed that Armstrong had the upper hand. The warrior was back and there were shades of the Armstrong of old – on stage three in particular – when crosswinds split the peloton asunder. When Cavendish's Columbia-HTC team massed at the front and drove a wedge through it, it was Armstrong, alone among all the overall contenders – who sneaked into the move.

If that was no surprise, given that one of Armstrong's strengths was always his positional sense in the peloton, it was something of a shock to see two of his Astana team-mates join Columbia on the front, helping to distance the chasers, who included Contador. 'I was just trying to stay up front, out of trouble,' explained Armstrong. 'I've won the Tour de France seven times. Why wouldn't you ride at the front? It makes no sense that you wouldn't ride there. It's good positioning, experience, a little bit of luck.

'I'd prefer to stay out of the drama of who's the leader of the team,' he continued. 'I've won the Tour seven times. I think I deserve a little bit of credit. But Alberto's a great rider too and we've got to go with the two leaders, but that doesn't mean you can't take advantage of opportunities like today.'

Contador wasn't so sanguine, saying, 'I don't want to express an opinion on the tactics of the team. It let everyone draw their own conclusions in any case, the Tour's image up to be decided by what happened today. No, but it seemed to confirm that the pecking order in the Astana team hadn't been decided either. Armstrong, it seemed, remained very much in the picture.

For long-time Tour de France watchers there were echoes in the Armstrong-Contador feud of a similar rivalry in the 1986 race, when Bernard Hinault and Greg LeMond rode for the same La Vie Claire team. After LeMond had helped Hinault to his fifth Tour in 1985, the duo started the following year with the Frenchman vowing to help the American score a first ever victory for an English-speaking rider. That LeMond did finally achieve ▲

LITTLE GIRL LOST

Winning 800m gold at the World Championships in Berlin should have been the best moment of this teenage South African's life. Instead, she was left mentally exhausted, confused and close to trauma

WORDS: GARY LEMKE **MAIN PHOTO:** MICHAEL STEELE

We have seen this movie before – and it doesn't have a happy ending. Exactly 25 years ago we sat back and watched as Zola Budd was used and abused. We celebrated and championed her, not realising what internal turmoil she was going through. When the curtain came down on this fresh-faced teenager, she was content that her race was run, they spat her out like a piece of chewed biltong. The only consolation is that people who 'cared' were content that her race was run.

The world 800m champion should be basking in the glow of gold from Berlin. Instead, she has been cowering for weeks behind closed doors at the University of Pretoria, venturing out only when instructed at short notice by people who see her as a cash cow and a public billboard. Some 15 days elapsed after the final before she was prepared to begin training again.

Semenya is from the rural village of Masehlong in Limpopo. She did not pick up the phone and negotiate a fashion shoot deal for the cover of the country's biggest weekly magazines. YOU, Drum and Huisgenoot. Someone at Athletics South Africa (ASA) did so on her behalf, and asked for tens of thousands of rands.

Semenya doesn't fully understand the implications that people think she's a man, again, perhaps from speaking to her on the half. She has a Facebook account and is internet-savvy, but claims not to have seen the disgusting cyberspace discussions about her appearance, nor seen the gut-churning 'jokes' doing the rounds.

Twenty-five years on, if she is able to look back in life at the age of 43, like Budd (now Mrs Zola Pieterse) is doing in South Carolina, and say she's finally found peace, Semenya will be

fortunate. Because the first stones on the path of a tragic modern sports story have already been laid.

Semenya shocked the planet on athletics' biggest stage in Berlin, the 13th IAAF World Championships. She imperiously won the 800m gold in the fastest time of the year, in her first major event, and left the Olympic and world champions looking like they were treading wet cement. Afterwards she was asked to take a gender test to prove that her boyish appearance isn't something more sinister. Could she have mixed chromosomes, could she be a man trapped in a woman's body?

And then the politicians hijacked her. She was paraded at OR Tambo International Airport and taken by luxury vehicle back to Masehlong where she was treated like a hero by the Limpopo Government and a local property development company. She has been used to living in a hut for 18 years. Life has changed. The bandwagon was full. And, of course, there was the winning of the gold medal. And of course there was the magazine deal.

The similarities between Budd and Semenya are many. Both were teenage prodigies who took South African athletics by storm. Both had the smallest of backgrounds and were thrust onto the world stage. Both were asked to prove their female gender. Both were used for political gain, one by a conservative white government and the other by a black government.

Budd was barefoot and 17 when she broke the women's 5 000m world record in Stellenbosch. Because South Africa was banned from international competition, the time was never officially recognised, but that didn't mean others weren't watching. One of the Daily Mail newspaper, Sir David English, observed that the waif-like Bloemfontein Afrikaner had an ▼

SEPTEMBER 2009

The Caster Semenya gender testing saga was beginning to surface, amid a howl of denials. This opening image 'talked' perfectly to the story, a 'Little Girl Lost'. The picture was taken at the scene of her greatest triumph, the World Championships in Berlin. It suggested, though, that she was caught in her own world and perfectly captured the sentiment of the feature story.

FEBRUARY 2010

Tiger Woods was the talk of sport – not just the golfing world. He had even become a subject of ridicule following revelations of infidelity and turmoil in his private life.

The images in this opening spread perfectly complemented the words; it told the story of how ordinary Americans regarded Woods as something of a laughing stock – as they waited for news of other mistresses to come forward with their own sexual claims.

THE TAIL OF TIGER WOODS

When revelations poured forth of his serial infidelities, the legendary Tiger Woods suddenly found himself steeped in ignominy. Can he ever be the same player again?

WORDS: MARK KRAM JNR **MAIN PHOTO:** LUCAS DAWSON

B y now there can be no living soul on the planet who has not been exposed to the sordid unveiling of Tiger Woods. There can be no one who has not heard what happened initially or subsequently: How at 2am on 27 November he collided with a tree in his Cadillac Escalade, the rear window of which was shattered by his Swedish wife, Elin Nordegren. The stunningly attractive Elin did the job with a golf club, which some believed she also wrapped around the skull of her philandering husband. As each day passed, the story just got worse for the erstwhile prince of the links, whose sultry liaisons began popping up in the tabloids like some aggressive bacteria. The pokes that accompanied each revelation were plentiful and some were even funny in a juvenile way: What's the difference between Santa Claus and Tiger Woods? Santa stopped at three hos.

Oh … you heard that one.

At this writing, Tiger is ensconced in a treatment facility for his sex addiction in Hattiesburg, Mississippi. Having been to Mississippi (though not Hattiesburg), I can tell you that even stopping there for gas is punishment enough for any transgression that does not involve a jar of Vaseline and a cockatiel. But this is where we now find Tiger, at the Pine Grove Behavioral Health and Addiction Services, where photographs ▸

BusinessDay

SEPTEMBER 200*

MONTHLY

SPORT

IT'S IN THE GENES

ISSUE 14

SEPTEMBER 2009

This was the month in which women's 800m world champion Caster Semenya
returned to South Africa, but rumours were surfacing regarding her gender.
More specifically, there were suggestions she had undergone a gender test,
though it had been strongly denied by Athletics SA. This cover, a pair of jeans
behind a hospital screen, showed the secrecy, vagueness and confusion
around Semenya. The coverline, 'It's in the Genes', was suitably ambiguous

CRY FOR ME, I'M FROM ARGENTINA

ISSUE 21

APRIL 2010

The Argentinean Lionel Messi came to the 2010 Fifa World Cup as the best player on the planet. This cover showed him sitting on a globe, 'on top of the world' in his Argentinian kit. However, the coverline told the story in a masterly way. 'Cry for Me, I'm from Argentina', in a twist of the 1978 musical *Evita*. It was to say of Messi, 'I'm the best, but Argentina won't win the World Cup.' This bold statement was vindicated when they lost in the quarter-finals.

BusinessDay

JUNE 2010

SPORT

MONTHLY

ENOUGH TO BLOW YOUR SOCKS OFF

ISSUE 23

JUNE 2010

This issue appeared a week into the World Cup and with Bafana Bafana
having played two matches. The cover had to be conceptualised before the
event began – and therein lay the difficulty. However, we gauged the mood
in the weeks running up to '2010' and predicted that whatever happened on
the field, the event would blow the socks off the mirrors of the cars that wore
them with pride all over the country. It captured the mood perfectly.

SPORT

HE WALKS ON WATER

AND SURFING'S NEW GOD IS SOUTH AFRICAN P52

SILLY MONEY p10
Will more than £200 million
be enough for Man City to
buy the Premier League title?

KING LOUIS p34
The 2010 British Open
champion is all class – on
and off the golf course

THANKS A TON p46
John Smit's 100th Springbok
cap is an occasion to be
celebrated, not questioned

FINEST READS: Award-winning writers include Mark Keohane, Tom Eaton, Peter Roebuck,
Mark Gleeson, Clinton van der Berg, Gary Lemke, James Lawton, James Corrigan and Mark Kram Jnr

ISSUE 25

AUGUST 2010

This was the start of a new direction taken with the covers relating to the
magazine. For the first time it featured coverlines and wasn't confined to
concepts. This referred to the South African surfer Jordy Smith. The coverline
said, 'He Walks on Water' and 'Surfing's New God is South African'. It implies
that Smith is the future of the sport and that he is able to do anything. Time
will tell if we were correct with this statement but, so far, so good!

BusinessDay

SEPTEMBER 201

MONTHLY

SPORT

SHE CAN RUN BUT SHE CAN'T HIDE
WHY CONTROVERSY CHASES CASTER ALL THE WAY TO INDIA p32

SEMENYA

BERLIN

YOUR TIME'S UP p8
Keeping Zimbabwe isolated in
world cricket serves no purpose

UNHAPPY LANDINGS p26
Bafana's soft ride post the World
Cup sums up everything wrong
with the game in SA

COMEDY OF ERRORS p48
Peter de Villiers has played the
court jester for too long now

FINEST READS: Award-winning writers include Mark Keohane, Tom Eaton, Peter Roebuck,
Mark Gleeson, Gary Lemke, James Lawton, James Corrigan and Mark Kram Jnr

ISSUE 26

SEPTEMBER 2010
Caster Semenya was to compete in her first major international meet, the
Commonwealth Games, since an 11-month absence from the track following
confusion over her gender status. The cover showed her standing at the start of a
race, among some rivals. The coverline, 'She Can Run But She Can't Hide', related
to the fact that while the world 800m champion may win her races, she isn't yet
able to out-run controversy. The cover was moody and eye-catching.

LITTLE GIRL LOST
By Gary Lemke

WE HAVE SEEN THIS MOVIE BEFORE – AND IT DOESN'T HAVE A HAPPY ENDING. Exactly 25 years ago we sat back and watched as Zola Budd was used and abused. We celebrated and championed her, not realising what mental turmoil she was going through. When the politicians, media and those who 'cared', were content that her race was run, they spat her out like a piece of chewed biltong. The early signs are that the same thing is happening to Caster Semenya.

The world 800m champion should be basking in the glow of gold from Berlin. Instead, she has been cowering for weeks behind closed doors at the University of Pretoria, venturing out only when instructed at short notice by people who see her as a cash cow and a public billboard. Some 19 days elapsed after the final before she was prepared to begin training again.

Semenya is a humble 18-year-old from the rural village of Masehlong in Limpopo. She did not pick up the phone and negotiate a fashion shoot deal for the cover of the country's biggest weekly magazines, *YOU*, *Drum* and *Huisgenoot*. Someone at Athletics South Africa (ASA) did so on her behalf, and asked for tens of thousands of rands.

Semenya doesn't fully understand the implications that people think she's a man, apart from saying her accusers should 'go to hell'. She has a Facebook account and is internet-savvy, but claims not to have seen the disgusting cyberspace 'discussions' about her appearance, nor seen the gut-churning 'jokes' doing the rounds.

Twenty-five years on, if she is able to look back in life at the age of 43, like Budd (now Mrs Zola Pieterse) is doing in South Carolina, and say she's finally found peace, Semenya will be fortunate. Because the first stones on the path of a tragic modern sports story have already been laid.

Semenya shocked the planet on athletics' biggest stage in Berlin, the 13th IAAF World Championships. She imperiously won the 800m gold in the fastest time of the year, in her first major event, and left the Olympic and world champions looking like they were treading wet cement. Afterwards she was asked to take a gender test to prove that her boyish appearance isn't something more sinister. Could she have mixed chromosomes, could she be a man trapped in a woman's body?

And then the politicians hijacked her. She was paraded at OR Tambo International Airport and taken by luxury vehicle back to Masehlong where she was promised a house by the Limpopo government and a local property development company. She has been used to living in a hut for 18 years. Life has changed. The bankrupt ANC Youth League pledged R60 000 for her winning the gold medal. And, of course, there was the magazine deal.

The similarities between Budd and Semenya are many. Both were teenage prodigies who took South African athletics by storm. Both came from sheltered backgrounds and were thrust onto the world stage. Both were asked to prove their female gender. Both were used for political gain, one by a conservative white government, the other by militants within a black government.

Budd was barefoot and 17 when she broke the women's 5 000m world record in Stellenbosch. Because South Africa was banned from international competition, the time was never officially recognised, but that didn't mean that others weren't watching. The editor of the *Daily Mail* newspaper, Sir David English, observed that the waif-like Bloemfontein Afrikaner had an English grandfather. 'I can pick up the phone and get her a British passport in two days,' he bellowed. He did and it happened – at a time when passport applications took a year to process under Margaret Thatcher's watch. Within a week Budd was looking out of the windows from a rented house in Surrey at the pregnant grey clouds and an army of pressmen with their lenses trained on her.

Budd admitted that the *Daily Mail* paid £100 000 to take her to London and get the exclusive rights to her story. The money went into a trust fund – or was supposed to. 'My father got most of that money, and the little I got I had to pay 60% tax on,' she said years later. 'Out of the whole *Daily Mail* deal, I probably got £10 000.'

Resented and hounded by Sam Ramsamy's anti-apartheid campaigners, Budd nevertheless was fast-tracked into the 1984 Great Britain team that competed at the Los Angeles Olympics. During the 3 000m final, she had her calves spiked from behind by the American favourite Mary Decker-Slaney, who fell and left Budd to finish seventh. That is the image that she's still best remembered by.

Budd returned to South Africa, where she married Mike Pieterse in 1989, and competed for her home country in the 1992 Olympics in Barcelona. Despite having filed for divorce over her husband's alleged infidelity, the couple reconciled, have three children, and now live in the United States.

Zola has her share of cheers, but there have been more tears. Which brings us back to Semenya.

The most famous person in the tiny Limpopo village of Masehlong returned to a hero's welcome at OR Tambo following that women's 800m final in Berlin. In her first major event she had managed to upstage the great sprinter Usain Bolt. At the age of 18, she was granted audiences with South African presidents past and present, Nelson Mandela and Jacob Zuma, and some might even argue a future one in ANC Youth League motormouth Julius Malema. The self-proclaimed 'mother of the nation' Winnie Madikizela-Mandela chipped in with her own brand of rhetoric.

All over, Semenya clogged the blogs. Unwittingly, and unwillingly, she had been drawn into one of the sporting stories of 2009. The way in which Semenya had shot to the top of the world rankings in 1min 55.45sec in Berlin raised eyebrows.

But it was not all about her running exploits. Given her deep voice, stubbles of facial hair, flat chest, broad shoulders and boyish looks, suspicion surrounds Semenya. She has radically improved from finishing seventh in the heats at the 2008 World Juniors in 2:11.98, to becoming world senior champion.

The world's governing body, the IAAF, wants a closer look. They want a gender test, to see whether Semenya has a mixture of men's and women's genes. But they know it can have deep legal implications, costing both time and money. They would have to prove, with 100% conviction, that the South African who has female body parts, is not a female.

Whatever the outcome, it's a story that's set to run and run and – like the Paralympian Oscar Pistorius' efforts to compete against able-bodied runners – could find itself presented to the Court of Arbitration for Sport.

The IAAF's stance was offered by the English-speaking communications man Nick Davies, so there's no suggestion of anything lost in translation. 'The gender verification test is extremely complex and difficult. You need a medical evaluation. You need to involve gynaecologists, endocrinologists, psychologists and internal medical specialists and experts on gender. So we're talking about reports that are very long, very time-consuming, very expensive and that should be done under patient confidentiality.

'This is a health issue. We're dealing with someone who was born a woman and who has grown up as a woman and we now have this issue where that is being questioned. This is a natural condition. It's nothing that she has done. We have to wait till the process is complete, however long it takes. What could happen is that she might have to undergo surgery. She would have to have hormone treatment, etc. Theoretically, that is what can happen,' Davies continued.

'We're not talking about cheating, or doping. There's a sensitivity that has to be maintained. Legally, it's very complex. The athlete has always thought she was a woman and been a woman. So it's not exactly cheating is it?'

Semenya, it has to be underlined, is the world 800m champion. Which means that she has now entered the universe of the conspiracy theorists and the scientists. Drug testing comes with the territory. Lance Armstrong might lay claim to being the world's most tested cyclist, and he's been deeply resentful of the suspicion that he has been dabbling on the dark side. Still, in order to race he's had to appease the federations.

Which is something that Semenya, sooner or later, is going to have to do. No one knows for certain whether she was or wasn't gender tested in Berlin, not even the athlete. Calm heads are required. When South Africa's most successful Olympic sportswoman, Penny Heyns, was 17 – a year younger than Semenya is – she competed in her first of three Olympics.

'On arriving in Barcelona [1992], the girls were told to report for a gender test,' she said in the autobiography I co-wrote. 'This, we were informed, was standard procedure for females competing in their first Games [unless you happen to be British Royalty, with Princess Anne, in 1976, being exempt]. Zola [Budd] was the only member of the 1992 South African squad not to be tested, for in 1984 she had been confirmed as female on the IOC database.

'I had only just wrapped my head around the concept that we needed to provide a urine sample in front of strangers and now we had to prove our sex. That was some information for a 17-year-old to digest. The gender test involved a DNA check; a scraping of the inside of the cheek to check the epithelial cells for X and Y chromosomes. I received a laminated card, like a driver's licence, with my personal details and results going onto the IOC's master file. This is the first and last gender test an Olympic woman athlete has to have.'

Perhaps, the most damning statement is what followed. 'We had not been informed by our federation before the Games of this need to be tested in such a manner.' As much as things have changed in South Africa in the last 17 years, some sports administrations have remained internationally ignorant.

So, whatever the outcry over Semenya, a refusal to accept regular testing will see her banned from competing at the 2012 Olympics in London.

And it has been some outcry. South Africans have been deeply offended by the debate. That the IAAF's request to test Semenya came at the worst time is undeniable. It robbed a young, innocent teenager of the proudest moment of her life – a World Championships final victory – it publicly ridiculed her on the biggest stage and it has tainted her for the rest of her running days. It was not that she was asked to take a gender test, it was the botched way it was made public.

In the days following an arrival at OR Tambo that was choreographed by the politicians (parallels with Budd here), she was given a homecoming party in Masehlong. The politicians, however, are holding her up as a beacon of black South African talent and any IAAF interference is being regarded as both racist and insulting.

As August clicked into September, Semenya was only prepared to offer the tiniest of soundbites, and wait for instructions from individuals within Athletics SA who continue to milk the moment. I spoke with her and discovered a young girl, who should be a winner, feeling lost.

The IAAF and close followers of the sport – even her competitors – feel that passing a gender test will provide peace of mind. Then the athletics world can move on and Semenya can start living her life again and breaking more records.

The fuss is because Semenya was born with female body parts, was raised as a girl, but has long suffered ridicule. It's even said that when she arrived at a petrol station in Cape Town a couple of months back she went to the women's toilets and was confronted by an attendant who told her she should be going to the men's.

In her early teens she was an accomplished footballer at Try Again FC in Limpopo. One of the boys, it can be said. 'Caster looks like this, nothing will change it, she's a girl. But we had always let her change separately first before a game,' said 17-year-old goalkeeper Martin Mpati.

Initially, Semenya was prepared to tell the world to 'go to hell' over the furore. In the days and weeks after her homecoming, she was taken back into the bosom of those looking after her at the University of Pretoria, but that didn't prevent ASA from parading her in front of the magazine fashion photographers.

What should have been an uplifting experience as world champion has left her mentally exhausted, close to being traumatised. There is much sympathy for her overseas, but she is a marked woman. She has lost her naivety, her element of surprise on the track, now that she is the 800m world champion.

Despite the public barracking of the IAAF's insistence on a gender test as 'racist', ASA president Leonard Chuene, and the likes of Madikizela-Mandela and Malema, need to slip back into the shadows. 'I am not going to let that girl be humiliated in the manner that she was humiliated because she has not committed a crime whatsoever. Her crime was to be born the way she is born,' Chuene said last month. Female Olympic athletes have not since 2000 been asked to supply DNA for gender testing, but as head of the sport in this country, he should know that unannounced knocks on the door come with the territory.

At last count Semenya's official Facebook site had more than 3 000 fans. She also has a Facebook support group. But cyberspace can be a horrible place. The 'jokes' were crude. 'Caster Se-men, ya', read one as if bluntly 'proving' there was a veiled message in her name. And the anagram, 'Caster Semenya – Yes A Secret Man'.

Semenya is only 18, a world champion at an earlier age than even the uneducated heavyweight boxer 'Iron' Mike Tyson was. Look where he is now. Squandered more than $300 million in earnings and sucked dry by those who claim to have cared.

The hope is that Semenya is given professional guidance and counselling, she will need it in the coming years. As a sports science student at Tuks, she quietly admits that she likes to 'chill out with my friends, listen to hip-hop music [Akon being a favourite] and watch TV – mainly wrestling, and John Cena's a hero'.

She's a young girl with the world at her feet, but she needs proper mentoring and guidance, or she will fall apart.

In the townships a 'Zola Budd' is a taxi. Caster Semenya doesn't have a public transporter named after her just yet. When she does, it would be apt if it became a taxi synonymous with all those who have been given a rough ride early on, but whose journey was ultimately made memorable for all of the right reasons.

Caster Semenya arrived back from winning at the World Championships and was met at OR Tambo by a huge crowd and politicians quick to parade her. However, rumours started that Semenya had undergone a gender test. Politicians were threatening 'World War III' over the issue. The timing of the story was important. It was written before reports were leaked that she had taken the test, but her body language and other signs suggested things weren't as they seemed. This feature formed part of a winning 2010 SAB Sports Feature Writer of the Year submission by the author.

GUT BUSTERS
By Andy Capostagno

MY WIFE ONCE ASKED, 'IF TIGER WOODS IS SUCH A GREAT ATHLETE, HOW come he's got such a fat arse?' If it is true that inside every thin person there is a fat person trying to get out, then one of the things that may get in the way of Tiger beating Jack Nicklaus' record in the Majors will be unwanted weight gain.

Imagine a time, not too far in the future, when Tiger's finely tuned abs begin to sag and all that time spent crunching muscles in the gym is replaced by quality time with family and friends, crunching peanut brittle and drinking beer. Hard to imagine, isn't it, but Tiger is only human and one day he might join the ranks of the overweight and under-conditioned.

If that were to happen, a lot of us club golfers will celebrate, for it is we who prove on a daily basis that you don't have to be fit to enjoy golf. Take a wander through the average pro shop and you won't find too many Sergio Garcia retro slim-fit style golf shirts, but you'll have plenty to choose from in the XXL section.

Furthermore, if the increase in expertly manicured cart paths, electric trolleys and clubs designed to get the ball in the air quickly are anything to go by, the future of the game lies with us fat folk, not with Tiger and the Slim Jim 20-somethings chasing him. Apart from anything else, there's a lot more of us than there are of them.

Ironically, we have Tiger's idol to blame for feeling guilty about our lack of athleticism. When Nicklaus emerged as a gifted amateur at the beginning of the '60s he was a couple of decades away from being dubbed 'The Golden Bear'. Back then he was 'Ohio Fats' and 'Fat Jack', a chain-smoking lardball who became the target of abuse from 'Arnie's Army'. At the 1962 US Open at Oakmont, Nicklaus and Palmer were tied at the end of regulation play. During the 18-hole play-off the 'Army' did all they could to put Nicklaus off, but he won by three shots. Few recall today that the two men hardly spoke for a decade after that and only made up in the mid-70s when it had become clear that the fat kid from Ohio might be the best ever.

But the abuse Nicklaus received at Oakmont changed his life. He saw footage of himself smoking and thought it looked ugly. He gave up smoking and never went back, and also decided to do something about his weight. He trimmed down from about 90kg to about 77kg and made lots of money endorsing clothes.

Nowadays, of course, you don't have to be in shape to earn money endorsing clothes. Not if you're John Daly you don't. Is it just a coincidence that Daly's form has taken a step in the right direction since he started promoting Loudmouth golfing apparel? Or is it that he has had a stomach band surgically fitted?

The latter enabled him to lose 27kg between March and July this year, but the Loudmouth clothes meant that you always knew where Daly was on the Turnberry links at this year's Open Championship. Furthermore, playing in a Pro-Am with Daly before the Open, World Cup-winning England rugby player Will Greenwood said: 'He is not an Olympic athlete and I admit I was thinking what the hell he must have looked like before the band.'

Which brings to mind the thoughts of Lee Westwood back in 2000, when he said: 'If I wanted to be an athlete I would have taken up 400m running. I don't like to think of myself as an athlete, I'm a professional golfer.' At the time, Westwood was a podgy 95kg and his career was about to take a major downturn following the birth of his first child, Sam.

Westwood plummeted down the rankings and one of the suggestions from his 'team' was that he might reasonably lose some weight. So he went to the gym and shed the pounds, refashioned his swing with David Leadbetter and briefly returned to winning ways in 2003. But, once again, is it a coincidence that Westwood has begun to contend in the Majors again since forsaking his diet? He came agonisingly close at Turnberry and was in contention again at the USPGA, but anyone coming to him fresh might have wondered all over again, 'Who's the porky lad?' He admits to weighing 89kg these days, but his belt probably goes out a notch at Christmas and New Year and then he's not far off his fighting weight of 2000.

That was the year, incidentally, that Westwood won the European Tour Order of Merit, breaking the seven-year streak of another 'portly' campaigner, Colin Montgomerie. Is there any coincidence in Monty's run ending at about the same time as his first strenuous attempts to lose weight? Towards the end of the 2000 season Monty, Major-less again and beginning to slide down the world rankings, was asked what triggered the dieting and fitness regime.

He said, 'I saw a picture of myself in my study from 1995 when I won the Dunhill Cup with Sam Torrance and Andrew Coltart, and I was too heavy. Far too heavy.

I didn't look like a sportsman, if you like. I didn't like the way I looked.' Vanity caused Monty to join the fitness regime espoused by luminaries such as Madonna and Donatella Versace and the results were, predictably, disastrous. He trimmed down from 110kg to 82kg, but along the way he lost his swing. The fact is that the golf swing is a personal thing, built around the body that owns it. Muscle memory cannot be relied on if the muscles are different from what they used to be. Sensibly, Monty recognised the problem and without going to the dogs completely, allowed himself back up to around his current mark of 90kg.

Monty and Nicklaus had a shared reason for losing weight: they didn't like the way they looked. So is there a golfer out there who doesn't care about how he looks? Yes, there is, and his name is Craig Stadler. The Walrus, as he has been known for more than 30 years, is now 56 and tips the scales at around 110kg. To put that into perspective, 110kg is the fighting weight of your average provincial tighthead prop, and Stadler's height, 1.78m, is analagous too.

Twenty-seven years ago, when Stadler won The Masters at Augusta, he was a relatively trim 95kg, but already easily identifiable at a distance from the other Tour players. He won the last of his PGA Tour events, the 2003 BC Open, 21 years later. Stadler set two records on the day. His final round 63 made up an eight-shot deficit and, more pertinently, he was the first and so far the only Champions Tour player to win on the regular Tour.

The point being that Stadler is not just another pot-bellied slugger: he can seriously play the game. He tried losing weight a few years ago, but had the same issues as Monty. He said, 'I dropped from 230 to 195 pounds [104kg to 88kg] by dieting. I felt good, but I didn't feel comfortable. Especially putting. My arms kept trying to float away. I didn't have that gut in my way.'

Stadler plays the part of a mean *hombre* on the course, but off it he is jovial and popular. Last year he published the Craig Stadler calendar as a riposte to that of Natalie Gulbis. The latter is one of the more winsome members of the LPGA – a tall blonde beauty with blue-green eyes and 8% body fat. Stadler, one inch taller than Gulbis, boasts an 88% body fat count. He said, 'I want folk to see that you don't have to be in the gym all day and munching lettuce in order to be an athlete. I don't just play golf. When I'm in Japan I like to train a little with the sumo wrestlers – not wrestling, you understand, just the eight meals a day part of the training. And I like to go diving and swimming – but then I guess every walrus does.'

Now here's a funny thing. Right now several of the top 20 heaviest players on the USPGA Tour are household names. Not all are fat: Ernie Els (95kg) and Vijay

Singh (94kg) are just big people. But this year's Masters champion, Angel Cabrera, is a fully fledged member of the chubsters' union at 95kg, and Phil Mickelson is a not-at-all-athletic 91kg. Kenny Perry is a portly 100kg, but who is the heaviest golfer on the USPGA Tour right now? Kevin Stadler, a veritable chocolate chip off the old block, weighing in at 113kg for his modest 1.78m.

Stadler Jnr might not have as much talent with the clubs as his father, but he's obviously a knife-and-fork champion of note, and while he's not setting the world on fire, he's doing OK, thank you very much. So the next time someone tries to persuade you to slim down in order to improve your golf game, remind them of the importance of muscle memory, even if you don't have any muscles.

A light-hearted look at golfers who have managed to achieve success without spending hours in the gym. Craig Stadler, John Daly and even Colin Montgomerie all achieved significant success with a wide girth.

AN AGELESS ICON
By Gary Lemke

ERNIE ELS HITS 40 ON 17 OCTOBER, FOLLOWING HIS MATE RETIEF GOOSEN to that milestone and – judged on the leaderboards of golf's Majors in 2009 – is still the perennial tip for South African success each time a big one on the calendar comes around. His best days might be behind him, but he's not about to reach for the pipe and slippers.

If life was to offer Els a mulligan or two, the chances are that he wouldn't take any. Had you told him when he was a beanpole teenager representing his country at the 1988 British Amateur that he'd go on to become a world No 1, a three-time Major champion, a designer of golf courses, have his own successful international wine label, run a golfing foundation, own property around the globe, and buy Greg Norman's jet from the Australian, he'd have laughed in your face.

Few sportsmen have a sobriquet that fits as comfortably as 'The Big Easy'. Now that he's about to turn 40, he becomes one of the 'old farts' on the Tour. Tell the emerging Northern Irishman Rory McIlroy – all 20 years of him – that he's playing with someone twice his age and the chances are the kid will feel Ernie should be contemplating a future on the seniors circuit.

Els is hyped up before each Major, but there are so many good golfers out there that it's becoming harder and harder to win one. Even the mercurial Tiger Woods is starting to find that out, being caught and overtaken when in cruise control in the final round of the US PGA Championship, the last Major of 2009.

However, given the class of the player, the ridiculously smooth swing of his, and his experience, Els can never be written off. Sure, his three-year plan, announced in 2006 to overtake Woods as the world No 1, crashed before take-off.

Yet he remains our No 1 export, the biggest 'global name' that we have in sport. When people talk in terms of golfing generations, they will speak about Bobby Locke, Gary Player and Ernie Els. That's not to take anything away from Goosen, himself (like Els) a two-time US Open winner. It's just that Els is a once-in-a-generation golfer. And he has a magnetic personality.

Recently, Woods reckoned Els could 'have worked a bit harder' in his rehabilitation from knee surgery. In other words, our man was being accused of not waking up every day at 5am to visit the gym, wolf down some fruit and yoghurt for breakfast, and then tackle the cycling or rowing machines for another couple of hours. Call him human.

Besides, he has never had that training regime – and he hasn't done too badly at all, has he? If forced to take a mulligan from his life, he might want more Majors – in particular, the treasured green jacket of The Masters. That he hasn't won it is due in no small part to the rise of Woods.

'Tiger's also quite a lucky golfer,' Els once told me, and he meant no malice. Our own Gary Player might argue that 'the harder I practise the luckier I get', but when one actually has a look at the number of chip-ins that Woods has had over the years at big moments, or the number of 20-foot 'savers' for par, you do have sympathy for Els. After all, he might feel that both have the same ability from the bunker, and the same reading of a 20-foot putt. Woods though, will hole from the bunker, or drop the putt more times that Ernie. Is that luck, or simply fate?

Els though, has played well enough to win 64 professional tournaments, including the World Match Play seven times and the Nedbank Golf Challenge three times – that's apart from the three Majors, which included the 2002 Open.

However, as he glides up to the Big Four-O, he might regard his greatest achievements as those of someone who was a credit to the sport for more than two decades, and being a dedicated father and much-loved husband.

Ernie Els has long been the flag-bearer of South African golf on the world stage and over the period of this issue he was turning 40. We paid tribute to a man who has been a fantastic ambassador for not only the game, but for his country too.

WHAT LIES BENEATH
By Gary Lemke

PRESIDENT BILL CLINTON WAS IMPEACHED FOR LYING TO THE PEOPLE OF the United States over his affair with Monica Lewinsky. In Britain, politician and author Lord Jeffrey Archer was sent to prison for lying. Even the former golden girl of athletics, the USA sprinter Marion Jones, was jailed for lying to investigators about taking steroids.

So, how is it that Leonard Chuene still had a job, as president of Athletics SA, more than a month after admitting to lying to the world about Caster Semenya? He wasn't just economical with the truth – he lied about Semenya being subjected to humiliating gender tests that threaten to destroy not only her career, but her life.

You have to wonder how Chuene stayed in his position so long – and, with the facts at hand, other questions had to be asked: Who are Chuene's friends in high places? More importantly, why did they continue to protect him against an avalanche of evidence to take him down? Down from his job and perhaps even, d-o-w-n, period.

Most clear-thinking South Africans have stopped taking the ANC Youth League's Julius Malema seriously. But the cynical among us can wonder if it's not part of a bigger plan for him to publicly back Chuene; the old story of 'a good day to bury bad news'. Use Malema as the distraction and then quietly raise the petrol price by R2 a litre, or take the heat off another under-fire politician.

Based on Chuene's lies, Semenya, who won the women's 800m at the IAAF World Championships, but was subsequently reported to be less than 100% female, was given an audience with presidents past and present, Nelson Mandela and Jacob Zuma. Considering what Mandela has done for South Africa, Chuene should be washing Madiba's feet and apologising for misleading him. Instead, six weeks after lying over Castergate, which resulted in the 91-year-old congratulating Semenya on her victory, Chuene still had his job.

When rumours surfaced that Semenya might require gender testing, a defiant Chuene resigned from the IAAF, and our minister of sport, Makhenkesi Stofile, 'promised World War III'. These actions were based on a lie.

When Semenya was paraded to a nation, Chuene's ASA arranged for the athlete to have a cover fashion shoot makeover with the weekly magazines, *YOU*, *Huisgenoot* and *Drum*. This was based on a lie. *The Star* posters called her 'The First Lady of SA Sport' and *YOU* trumpeted its exclusive with the words 'We turn SA's Power Girl into a Glamour Girl'. The publicity was all based on Chuene's lie.

Before any of the explosive, damaging 'revelations' had broken, this magazine carried a story titled Little Girl Lost. Of course, we didn't know Chuene had been lying, but we suspected something was amiss and we swam against the tide of the time.

We discovered that, after being held up as a beacon of what impoverished black female talent could achieve, a broke Semenya returned to the High Performance Centre in Pretoria and asked friends for money for airtime. This was around the time of her magazine cover shoot and on the back of Malema promising her R60 000 for winning gold. He announced the payment on 25 August (and two months later was due to finally hand over the cheque – publicly).

Our feature ventured that Semenya was a mental mess and close to trauma, when the world heard the opposite. Hence the headline. We compared her to Zola Budd, who was also lied to in 1984, ironically also as an 18-year-old – for political and personal gain. History dare not be repeated, but it was.

Later, amid the breaking 'revelations', Chuene chaired an extraordinary ASA meeting. He told the media that the decision to retain him as president was unanimous. It was a lie; weeks later, three federations said they hadn't supported him. Chuene had repeatedly lied to the media, calling them racists. He even lied to the chief executive officer of South Africa's biggest sports body, Sascoc, when the governing association questioned him over Semenya's gender test. Then again, he had also lied to Madiba and Zuma, so who are Sascoc to rock his world?

Semenya is about to start serving a life sentence based on a lie. And what price will Leonard Chuene pay for that? His job as ASA president? If that is the sum extent, then he will have got off lightly.

The news that Caster Semenya had undergone a gender test was now public. This editorial laid the blame at the door of the ASA president Leonard Chuene and argued that he face criminal charges. A year later Chuene faced charges after an inquiry and forensic audit.

DINOSAUR KING
By Tom Eaton

THIS ESSAY IS ABOUT ADAPTING, ABOUT KEEPING UP WITH THE TIMES. I would suggest that it is anchored in modernity, but that is a dicey metaphor; firm anchors go against the mood of our age. Which is why, instead of quoting the papery patriarch *Wisden*, I will open with a quote from the new orthodoxy, cricinfo.com.

'In an era of fast scoring and high-octane entertainment, Jacques Kallis is a throwback – and an astonishingly effective one at that – to Test cricket's more sedate age, when one's wicket was a commodity to be guarded with one's life, and runs were but an accidental by-product of crease occupation.'

Thus spoke Cricinfo, and so it shall be forever and ever, or until there's a power surge and the servers in Mumbai explode. The official verdict on South Africa's greatest post-isolation batsman – and greatest-ever all-rounder – is that he is a 'throwback'.

It's not a kind word despite the apologetic 'astonishingly effective' bit stuck on afterwards. One could be charitable and suggest that it means Kallis harks back to the mythical golden age of cricket and stands shoulder to shoulder with all the other Great Batsmen Who Weren't As Good As Bradman. But we know what it means. What Cricinfo is telling the world and dictating to posterity is that Kallis is a relic, an anachronism – in short, a dinosaur.

It is a backhanded compliment that would resonate with many South Africans. For a variety of reasons many local fans have never warmed to Kallis. As his batting average steadily rose, so too did the volume of the accusations that he was a selfish batsman. His introverted and plain statements to the press were seen as signs that he was mentally deficient. An immense workload as a batsman sometimes translated into a tired effort as a bowler: Kallis, the chattering classes said, was lazy; would only bowl at full throttle when he was 'fired up'. Few international sports stars can have been so disliked for doing their job so well. The rib injury that kept him out of the recent ODI series against England was bemoaned by selectors and team-mates; from the public there was not a murmur.

But one blob of mud thrown at Kallis has always stuck; and that is that he is stodgy; that his approach to batting does not do justice to his immense ball-striking talent. Cricinfo says as much in his biography. Kallis, we now accept as common wisdom, has slotted into a very deep rut that allows him to score thousands of runs, keep his place in the team safe, but never adapt, never up the tempo except when it is safe to do so. He has been in an extremely classy comfort zone for 13 years, sleepwalking towards greatness but unable – or unwilling – to wake up and grab it.

That's the official version. But there's a problem with it. If Kallis is a dinosaur, he should be extinct. And yet this supposedly Jurassic cricketer is still with us despite his current layoff, stomping around in our rearview mirror and rapidly gaining on 150 Tests and 300 ODIs. Somehow he has survived, which can mean only one thing: Kallis has adapted. Contrary to the official version, he has evolved.

Of course, how much he has evolved remains a pertinent question. Some might argue that he has barely kept up with the game, while others would insist that he has proved his adaptability simply by sticking around for 13 years during an era of almost unprecedented change in the game.

This second, more charitable lobby has a point. The cricketing world Jacques Henry Kallis entered on 14 December 1995, was unrecognisably different from that of today. Indeed, the Test arena was positively primordial. Bats were twigs. Bouncers bounced off helmets rather than advertising boards, and the helmets they bounced off were life-saving devices instead of something you kissed after yet another inevitable century. This was the final age of the true dinosaurs, those thunder-lizards called fast bowlers. On the day of Kallis' debut, Shane Warne was officially the top-rated bowler in the Coopers & Lybrand ratings and Anil Kumble was fourth. But filling the other eight spots were an appalling array of exceptionally dangerous and cunning quicks: Ambrose, Akram, Bishop, Walsh, Donald, De Villiers, Younis and McDermott. Today's batters consider themselves thoroughly bloodied if they encounter Dale Steyn and Brett Lee in the course of one season.

If Tests were gladiatorial, ODIs were genteel, an affair of line and length and proper cricket shots nudged into gaps. In 1995 South Africa managed an average run rate of 4.6 – a statistic helped by their six-per-over slaughter of Zimbabwe (remember when six per over was a massacre?). If 4.6 sounds slow, it's probably because you've forgotten the game that year in which we were bowled out by Australia for 123 – in 46.2 overs. Yep, 2.6 an over. Way to put bums on seats, boys. Two months after Kallis made his debut Sanath Jayasuriya and Romesh Kaluwitharana reinvented cricket. The Sri Lankans' onslaught on opening bowlers at the Asian World Cup was a bolt from the blue, an unprecedented display of sustained aggression that set the cricketing world alight. Thirteen years later Jayasuriya's strike rate for that tournament – 91.3 – would get him dropped from any international T20 squad. We have come a very long way.

In his 14 years at the crease Kallis has seen the game speed up, dumb down, spread out. He has witnessed the death of swing bowling, although it seems unlikely that he will still be playing by the time the game gets around to a forensic verdict on why the most beautiful art of the fast bowler has vanished. He has no doubt felt the new pressure being exerted by broadcasters for batsmen to entertain audiences.

One cannot deny that during those 14 years Kallis developed into a superb batsman, perhaps even a great one. Those who say he falls short of greatness because he has never annihilated an attack like a Graeme Pollock fail to acknowledge the siege mentality that Kallis debuted into. They have forgotten the headlines throughout the summers of the early- and mid-90s bewailing South Africa's '90-for-5 syndrome', and the reams of copy wondering when we would produce a genuine No 3 who wasn't afraid of the short ball. Pollock was a jewel in South African cricket's crown in the '60s and '70s; but Kallis was the bedrock upon which we built our new castle after readmission. It is pointless to try to imagine how Kallis would have played had he debuted into the 2009 team; but it is tantalising.

His batting legacy is still open to debate, but his greatness as an all-rounder is beyond dispute. Some have suggested he is the equal of Garfield Sobers. He is not, and can never be until he reinvents the aesthetics, spirit and politics of South African life in general as Sobers did in the West Indies. But while there is plenty of daylight between Sobers and Kallis, the latter can at least console himself that he is fighting for second place with titans like Imran Khan and Ian Botham.

But am I describing the Kallis of 2009 or is this some gilded memory of him in the early-2000s, carving up the West Indians and English? We know Kallis has done great things but is he still doing them? The game has changed dramatically since his debut, and he has kept up, but just how well?

Again we return to the image of a dinosaur. Is Kallis a resurrected T-Rex, hopelessly out of his time but still stomping about and doing some damage? Is he a coelacanth, an unevolved freak that has nonetheless managed to survive and adapt just enough to stick around into the modern world? Or are both of these unfair? Has Kallis evolved into a modern cricketer? Does he deserve to be playing ODIs and T20Is in 2009 based on his contributions rather than his long history?

One answer could lie in those worse-than-damned lies that are statistics. If our main concern about Kallis is not the volume of runs but their rate, then let us look at historical run rates.

In 1996, his first full year of international cricket, the average run-rate in ODIs was 4.7. At the time of writing, in November 2009, the average ODI rate was 5.2 – a difference of 25 runs over the course of a 50-over innings, or a 10% increase. Interestingly the rise in the Test scoring rate has been 14%, from 2.93 per over when Kallis debuted, to 3.35 in 2009. That's good news for fans, who are now likely to see about 300 runs in an average day's play; but is it good news for Kallis?

Tracking Kallis' career strike rate against international scoring rates does not make for happy reading; he has always lagged behind the average rates in each format of the game, and even in his most free-flowing and prolific years never managed to catch the global average strike rate. To be sure, haste is not always a sign of progress: during Kallis' career plenty of international teams have thrashed along at 4s in Tests and 5s in ODIs, ending up, forgive the pun, at sixes and sevens. The diabolically bad West Indians of the early-2000s regularly achieved splendid run rates ... for the 20 or 30 overs they batted. But still, the lag does not look good when we review Kallis' development. Yes, one would rather have a slow 100 than a dashing 40; and no, we never expected Kallis to match dazzling attacking contemporaries like Brian Lara and Ricky Pointing; but is it unreasonable to have asked that he at least keep up with plodding New Zealanders or catatonic West Indians with a fraction of his talent?

The strike rate graphs don't look pretty. The global average zigzags up and down, but generally up; and there, a good few points below, is Kallis' graph, zigging and zagging more or less in tune, but always below. Not pretty at all.

Until, that is, you look a little closer. Is that last zag a fraction closer to the trend than his first zig? Is there just a hint of two trends converging?

More than a hint, in fact.

Call him a dinosaur, call him a throwback, but Jacques Kallis is gaining on the game. In 2008 and 2009 he has come closer to the global average run rate in ODIs that at any time in his career. As fast as global scoring rates are climbing, Kallis is going faster. He is evolving.

This is not to say that he should be triggering IPL bidding wars. He will never outscore the quickest. That has never been his job. But the fact that he is able to keep up with the game after 14 years, even to gain on it, is admirable enough.

If you think that this is stretching all kinds of truths to paint a rosy picture of the ageing star, that his creaking career is being held up by nostalgia and cherry-picked statistics, consider those batsmen who have failed to adapt to the modern game. Kallis' T20 career has been solid, as usual showing a preference for runs rather than fireworks, and his career strike rate leaves him languishing in the bottom third of the strike-rate charts. And yet below him are almost a team's worth of superb batsmen, each a class act, who have failed to adapt to the demands of the ultra-short game.

Some were never going to make the crossing: Ramnaresh Sarwan, Shivnarine Chanderpaul and Andrew Strauss are classical Test batsmen, and long may they remain so. And yet it seems freakish that Kallis should be comfortably outscoring a silky thoroughbred like Michael Clarke and clean-hitting destroyers like MS Dhoni, Shane Watson, Brad Haddin and Mark Boucher. Clearly this is not about hand-eye co-ordination or meatiness of bat; it is about adapting and evolving. Kallis has. Dhoni, exciting and charismatic as he is, has not.

This is not to deny that fortune has been kind to Kallis. The dinosaurs never got a chance to evolve, but Kallis has been spared the comet impacts that sporadically end the careers of international stars. Had Kallis been Australian he would have had cross-hairs on him since about 2004, and he would either have upped his game dramatically or gone the way of Matthew Hayden and other mighty thunder-lizards picked off by unnatural selection. South African conservatism and laager mentality has perhaps eased Kallis through situations where clearer, more pragmatic minds might have dropped him.

So, how much longer has Kallis got? How much more can he evolve? Perhaps a season or two. IPL riches are enough to put a spring in even the most exhausted step. His longevity depends on how often, and perhaps how, he bowls. Perhaps he has realised that the most difficult bowlers to get away in T20 are the slowest, and even now he is secretly working on his off-spin.

But one thing is for sure. Kallis has survived cricket's greatest changes because he is hugely talented and because he has defied his official biography and learnt to adapt. When he calls it quits we will see how far he came. We will look back at a modern South African superstar who nonetheless faced Waqar and Wasim, Walsh and Ambrose and who bowled at the Waughs and at Michael Atherton. He has spanned a generation. He has survived.

Over recent years, with the advent of Twenty20 cricket, the Indian Premier League and a flooding of the fixture list, cricket has evolved at an alarming pace. But amid all the breathtaking changes, one South African giant of a player has stood tall. Jacques Kallis, criticised as being 'too slow' as a batsman, has continued to thrive in all formats of the sport.

SMITH'S THE PRESENT AND FUTURE
By Mark Keohane

GIVE GRAEME SMITH SOME RESPECT. HE IS NOT THE PROBLEM IN SOUTH African cricket. He is the solution. Give him the power and let him give back the six-year investment of being thrust into one of the most demanding leadership roles in world cricket.

Our game is healthy with Smith at the helm, but those intimidated by him must get out or get on with him. And by that I mean selectors who pick a team but take no responsibility when it all goes wrong. In beating Australia in Australia there was a belief within the triumphant South African squad that the Test series win was the start – and not end – of a journey of world domination.

The disciples of that road trip got it wrong because what followed was too much looking in the rearview mirror and very little promise of sighting new land.

Smith's published captain's diary documenting the period 2007 to 2009 confirms that everything was geared to peaking in the Test series against Australia in 2009, and to the credit of Smith and coach Mickey Arthur, the South African side got it spot on in Perth and Melbourne to win the three-Test series.

The squad, tweaked and not overhauled since that momentous occasion, has never reproduced the highs of Perth and Melbourne. So what has to change?

I have heard arguments that the team is good enough but under Smith they have become stagnant and stale. Those holding this view suggest a change in captain, which allows Smith to focus on his batting. I disagree.

More pertinent is the role of Arthur, bowling coach Vincent Barnes and the selectors who felt comfortable in playing unfit bowlers, injured bowlers and a middle-order specialist as an opening batsman because they were not prepared to choose between Ashwell Prince and JP Duminy to bat at No 6.

The captain, more than the coach, is the influential figure in a cricket squad, but the coach still has to provide technical guidance and innovation, and Arthur has gone full circle with what he currently has to offer the current set-up. The same applies to Barnes, which doesn't mean there isn't a second opportunity and another cycle.

Smith, given his relative youth, is as much the future as he is the present and his assessment of who should be playing should be the most imposing in any selection. Unfortunately it isn't and Smith has to work with what he is given, which is never ideal in any cricketing situation.

South Africa's attack, especially against England, was never Test match fit enough to take 20 wickets in five days. The selectors and coaches have to take responsibility for this because the selections were inconsistent with the ruthless principles of what produced an away series win in Pakistan, England, Australia and a drawn series in India.

The preparation at home has always been poor in the past few years and one of the successes of the Proteas away from home is that come Test time there has been cricket played. Against Australia and England in South Africa, there were no warm-up matches and it is no coincidence that in both cases it took the Proteas three Tests to hit their straps and by that time the series could no longer be won.

Sentiment also played no part in the Proteas selections in the build-up to beating Pakistan, England and Australia in Australia. Two of South Africa's most gifted post-isolation cricketers, Herschelle Gibbs and Shaun Pollock, were dropped.

Smith felt the team had to move on because he needed two players who provided different qualities to the flamboyance (but uncertainty) of Gibbs the batsman and the solidity (but lack of strike power) of an ageing Pollock the bowler.

Smith wanted a Pollock-type cricketer to open the batting and a Gibbs-type tearaway to open the bowling. He got that with the introduction of Neil McKenzie and Morne Morkel. Smith was prepared to change to get a different result.

It is no secret that come the home series against Australia and against England, the captain did not get the team he wanted, especially in the case of McKenzie. Players were selected when out of form. Players were picked despite carrying injury and players were given the luxury of playing themselves into form during the early stages of the Test series against Australia and England. On both occasions it contributed to the team's undoing.

Some players are no longer good enough, yet there was the sentimental selection of Makhaya Ntini against England and the insistence to select a middle-order specialist as an opener. South Africa effectively played the first two Tests with an opening bowler and opening batsman handicap.

Ntini was dropped for the failure to bowl out England in Centurion and Durban, but what about the selectors who picked an attack unfit for Test cricket and a bowling coach who has been ineffective of late?

Barnes and Arthur's journey ended in Perth. They achieved their goals but in the past year have been incapable of adding a necessary dimension to sustain a winning culture. Neither Arthur nor Barnes have necessarily done too much wrong. It is rather a case that there is not much evidence that they have got it right during most of 2009 and in the early part of 2010.

Smith, in summarising South Africa's inability to beat England, said his team was not good enough, but it was more a case of the preparation and team selections not being good enough. The coaches need to be as honest and allow for the introduction of new faces, new ideas and a new broom because in this particular journey of meek surrender they too have not been good enough.

The Proteas are not wilting, but they are not blooming either. What was the highlight of the past must not be allowed to stifle further such highlights in the future. We all danced after Melbourne, but a failure to introduce change because of Melbourne is turning that dance into a stumble.

At the time the form of the Proteas started to dip, there were calls that their captain Graeme Smith had become too powerful within the set-up and that the team had become stale. This column argued that Smith was not the problem but in fact the solution to the Proteas' woes, and that perhaps the main problems lay with the coaching staff. Soon after this, the coach Mickey Arthur stepped down.

THE PLAYERS' CLUB
By James Corrigan

GOLFERS DON'T LIE. IT IS BURIED DEEP WITHIN THE GAME'S PROUD culture. They call penalties on themselves and they do so before their 'mistakes' are pointed out by others. Otherwise a stigma attaches itself that is impossible to shake off. Whichever fairway the guilty wanders so will follow the whisper: 'There goes the cheater.'

That only applies on the course, however. Off the course it is an entirely different matter. Walk into – or that should be 'break into' – any exclusive members golf club anywhere in the world and the rogues will soon become apparent. Perhaps as the so-called 'last male bastions' it is inevitable that what is now, somewhat ironically, known as 'laddish behaviour' would be accepted, if not celebrated. Tiger Woods may very well have believed he had not been 'true to my values' as he set out to rescue his marriage after the many mistresses began to come forward. But as far as golf goes, he is merely living up to the traditions of the dustier corners of the locker room.

Among the many opportunistic e-mails to hit the inbox in the midst of the scandal was a particularly shameless one from a British extramarital dating agency, which, it was keen to point out, 'creates a platform for married people to pursue affairs'. There was nothing clandestine about the subject box – 'Tiger Tips a Trend: Golfers are Biggest Cheaters'.

Apparently, more than 55% of its 380 000 members are golf fans.

'Golf is a sport often played by high-fliers, and we have already seen that go-getting ABC1 individuals are those most likely to cheat,' said a company spokesman. 'It's all about achievement; these people are relentless when it comes to getting what they want – the best car, the perfect home.

'But many don't stop at material possessions. When faced with an imperfect relationship, it is these individuals who will be most likely to pursue something extra. Opportunism plays a part too. If the rumours about Woods are true, he couldn't have picked a better sport. Golfing weekends and long afternoons on the range provide a perfect alibi for an affair.'

Some might believe achievement might be better measured in the quality and happiness of a family life, but perhaps this is not the time to be getting all moralistic; even for a father with two children under the age of three. Some of Woods' peers will certainly have no right to (not that any of his fellow professionals would dare to criticise the untouchable one who has always been Tiger).

Extramaritals are commonplace on Tour and some of the names of those who have strayed, and indeed the circumstances in which they have strayed, could fill the tabloids from now until New Zealand's next Major victory. When he returns to the players' lounge, Woods is more likely to garner a sly wink and a 'you old devil, you', than any looks of admonishment. Why? Because the history of their sport is replete with players who were considered to be great guys in the locker room – and absolute rotters in their home.

The tales of deceit are legendary on tour and are nearly always recounted with a gusto which implies admiration rather than castigation. Woods, as one of the main gossips on the circuit, will know all of the stories and for this reason may be feeling rather hard done by. He will also be aware of the roguish character traits of the two pioneers credited for preceding him in popularising the sport.

If Woods was the pioneer who so spectacularly showed that golf did not have to be the preserve of the white man, then Walter Hagen was the pioneer who showed that golf did not have to be the preserve of the upper classes and Arnold Palmer the pioneer who showed that golf did not have to be the preserve of the respectful, hip-flasked golf fan. All three had roving eyes, although only Woods witnessed the media brutally deconstruct his myth because of it.

Regardless of any of the arguments concerning Woods and his questionable right for privacy it is unarguable to comment that if Hagen and Palmer were playing in this age they, too, would have been exposed. Instead their legacy has had an easy ride and the lies they lived are actually viewed as a colourful part of their careers. They are not villains because of their bedroom antics – they happen to be even bigger heroes.

Let's start with Hagen, that delicious character from the Roaring Twenties known simply as The Haig who proved that blue-collar pros could make a healthy living from golf. The New Yorker is third on the all-time Major list behind Jack Nicklaus and Woods, but in terms of living the high life he made the pair seem like amateurs.

Hagen was the Great Gatsby of the fairways, a player who partied with as much consistency as he parred. As he raged against the amateur snobbiness of the sport, he made a great show of his ability to earn money without apparently giving a damn. The Haig would often turn up late for his tee times, swinging into the country club car park in a Rolls Royce still wearing the tuxedo from the night before. On one occasion he ambled up to the first tee in typically tardy fashion and the stuffy starter asked him: 'Been practising a few shots, Mr Hagen?' 'Nope,' replied Hagen. 'Downing a few.'

Such yarns furnish the folklore of the fun-loving pro who so memorably lived by the motto: 'Never hurry, never worry, always stop to smell the flowers along the way.' But then so do the whispers of what Tiger now famously refers to as 'my transgressions'. One only needs to flick through Tom Clavin's excellent biography *The Flamboyant Life of Walter Hagen* to realise how long-suffering his two wives were. The first, Margaret, would stay at home in Detroit with their baby son, while Hagen would travel the country playing in tournaments and exhibitions. It was not just work, however, as Henry Clune, a lifelong friend, conceded. 'I'm afraid Walter was as ill-suited for the restraints and ordinances of the conjugal state as a pirate,' he said. The anecdotes to evidence this claim are too numerous to print in full. Perhaps the most revealing one comes from the 1919 US Open in Boston. At least Woods kept his profession and 'transgressions' separate – Hagen had the temerity to chat up the girls even while in the heat of competition. It was on the 16th tee of the final round where he spotted an attractive blonde and by the 18th tee he had arranged a date. While Mike Brady, his opponent for the 18-hole play-off, headed straight for bed, Hagen had other ideas. 'We partied all night,' he was to say without a moment's shame. 'Champagne, a pretty girl and no sleep.' He was in no fit shape to compete the next day – 'Playing was not my only problem,' he said. 'I had a darned difficult time staying awake.' Yet he still managed to win by a stroke.

There were many more instances and many more girls. In 1923 for example, Hagen turned up in town and told Clune: 'Get me a pretty girl, get your wife and let's have a party.' It was only later, with the said pretty girl already wooed, that The Haig whispered to his friend: 'Don't tell her, but I'm getting married next week.' His second wife might have believed she had what it took to change him, but as he, himself, boasted in his autobiography years later, Edna did not have a chance. 'I met beautiful and charming women all over the world,' he wrote. 'A roving eye was my Geiger counter. My claim was staked with a devoted appreciation of their potential and ability to make my travels more enjoyable.'

Fast forward a few decades and there came Palmer, by no means as much as a showman as Hagen, but even more popular. It was the earthy quality which attracted Arnie's Army and which made him the first golfing hero of the common man. With his Popeye arms and his never-say-die attitude, Palmer transcended the comfy environs of the game and introduced a whole new audience to the sport. Golf could not only be entertaining to watch, but with Arnie it could be as entertaining to support. With Palmer arrived the raucous gallery.

But so, too, came the trappings of fame. Before her death in 1999, Arnold had been with Winnie for almost 50 years. It was depicted as the perfect marriage and who knows, perhaps it really was. But there were infidelities as revealed by Bob Rosburg, his friend and fellow pro. In their early days on the circuit the pair would often share rooms and on one occasion, Rosburg received a call in their hotel at 2am. It was a man asking if Palmer was there. 'No he isn't,' said Rosburg, checking the bed next to his. 'I damn well know he isn't,' came the furious voice down the line, 'because he's out with my wife. So tell him when he comes back I'm going to come over there and kill him.' 'Before you do that,' replied Rosburg, 'can I just say that my bed is the one by the window.'

Rosburg recalled this incident in a magazine interview in the late-80s and the Palmers were not happy to read it. 'It did disturb Arnie quite a bit that it came out,' revealed Rosburg. 'I shouldn't have said it. It was true, but when Winnie saw it I think it hurt her. You know, the women loved Arnie and he's the same as the rest of us.'

It is interesting that Rosburg received the flak for telling the tales. The attitude in professional golf is 'what goes on tour, stays on tour'. Rosburg had plainly broken this moral code. Of course, it is a strange moral code which sees the messenger slated more than the miscreant, but there you are – that's golf and they are the attitudes which pervade in the crusty clubhouses. It's why the true nature of the private lives of Hagen and Palmer remained out of the newspapers for so long and why, in the men's bars of this world, their status as womanisers is joked about and yes, still celebrated.

Yes, Woods can be accused of letting down his family, but surely he can never be accused of letting down his sport. He has grown up in this ridiculously macho playground, where women are often treated like second-class citizens and where the successful male can apparently do exactly how he pleases, regardless of the vows he has taken. It is not stunning that Woods, like so many of his colleagues, has 'played away' and neither is it stunning that his deceit eventually came to light. Perhaps golf can now grow up and move into the correct century. Cheating comes in many forms.

In the month after Tiger Woods' mistresses started coming forward to tell their stories, the revelations around his affairs created a stir everywhere. The stark truth, however, is that over the years extramarital relationships have been commonplace on the pro Tour. This was a controversial feature that produced a flurry of readers' responses.

EMBRACE AND ENJOY
By Gary Lemke

JAKE WHITE ONCE SUMMED IT UP PERFECTLY. HE WAS TALKING ABOUT the gamut of emotions a Springbok coach experiences during a Test. It could be a metaphor for South African sport. 'Everything might seem calm, like a duck gliding across a pond gracefully,' he said. 'But look under the surface and the legs are paddling frantically!'

Routinely, we wake up to headlines that jolt us out of our comfort zone. More often than not it's the chairman of the Parliamentary Sports Committee getting media space he doesn't deserve. To provide examples here would be giving credibility to him, but more importantly insulting your intelligence as a reader who appreciates and understands sport more than Butana Khompela ever will.

Yet even when that political motormouth isn't ranting, we make an art of the self-implosion. When Caster Semenya rose from the dusty streets of Limpopo to stand on top of the women's 800m podium in last year's World Championships in Berlin, we rightly celebrated another arrival of phenomenal talent. What we didn't know at the time was that Semenya had been subjected to a gender test and though 'World War III' was being promised by our defiant sports minister, evidence showed she was hung out to dry by Athletics SA.

Within a year of the Proteas reaching No 1 in the world in the Test and ODI formats, they hit troubled waters and coach Mickey Arthur and the entire selection panel was jettisoned only days before the tour of India. Thus, within the space of four months the country was coming to grips with two of its 'Big Three' codes replacing their coach.

There's ongoing corruption, racism and politics in our PSL soccer, while basketball is paying a high price for all-round poor administration and mismanagement.

The next sports crisis awaits. Even if Khompela doesn't threaten to send Beast Mtawarira back to Zimbabwe, or Imran Tahir to Pakistan, a firefight is looming over the Southern Kings and their Super Rugby status. If the subject is not addressed, it will all blow up in time to derail progress before the 2011 World Cup.

Then there's the permanent loaded gun around transformation and quotas. Swimming, currently the best performing of our Olympic codes, looks in rude health. But it's like the Jake White duck metaphor. Political interference is not far away, because questions will be asked about representivity in that sport. When more worryingly, the decaying facilities and lack of suitable pools is what should be addressed as a priority.

For now, though, we need to take a collective step back. Look what South Africa has achieved, as a country. Suck up the air and puff out the chest. This should be a time to banish all the doomsayers and the troublemakers and celebrate success.

Yet, less than four months away from hosting the 2010 World Cup and for every positive headline there are still two that are negative. We read and hear how Bafana Bafana are going to make a laughing stock of us. How prostitutes and druglords are going to make a killing, in all senses of the word. How our roads are making commuting a daily grind. How restaurants have spiked their prices. How air travel is going to be unaffordable in June-July. How guest houses are charging too much. How South Africans aren't buying up World Cup tickets. And so on.

But what about celebrating what we have achieved? This time last year, we came to the rescue of the Indian Premier League. Too dangerous to hold in India, South Africa stepped in at short notice.

We've hosted over a hundred global sports events since 1992, including rugby and cricket World Cups – and now the big daddy of them all. We had the British & Irish Lions, the Confederations Cup, the Barmy Army. We should bid for the 2020 Olympics. We've built transport networks; the Gautrain is a godsend. World Cup stadiums that stand up in every aspect to anything on the planet and the rand has stayed strong. Lance Armstrong even gave cycling a boost by announcing his intention to race 'the Argus'.

Next time you go into a supermarket or attend a sports event, look at the person to your left and to your right. You are the people who are making this country the envy of the sports world. Be proud and be on the same side. And embrace 2010 because it will be the time of our lives.

Many doubted whether SA was capable of hosting the 2010 World Cup. We highlighted what the country had achieved inside two decades and that it was time to put the negativity to one side and celebrate all that was good about the country.

THE TAIL OF TIGER WOODS

By Mark Kram Jnr

BY NOW THERE CAN BE NO LIVING SOUL ON THE PLANET WHO HAS NOT been exposed to the sordid unveiling of Tiger Woods. There can be no one who has not heard what happened initially or subsequently: How at 2am on 27 November he collided with a tree in his Cadillac Escalade, the rear window of which was shattered by his Swedish wife, Elin Nordegren. The stunningly attractive Elin did the job with a golf club, which some believed she also wrapped around the skull of her philandering husband. As each day passed, the story just got worse for the erstwhile prince of the links, whose sultry liaisons began popping up in the tabloids like some aggressive bacteria. The jokes that accompanied each revelation were plentiful and some were even funny in a juvenile way: 'What's the difference between Santa Claus and Tiger Woods? Santa stopped at three hos.'

Oh … you heard that one.

At this writing, Tiger is ensconced in a treatment facility for his sex addiction in Hattiesburg, Mississippi. Having been to Mississippi (though not Hattiesburg), I can tell you that even stopping there for gas is punishment enough for any transgression that does not involve a jar of Vaseline and a cockatiel. But this is where we now find Tiger, at the Pine Grove Behavioral Health and Addiction Services, where photographs of an unshaven Woods have emerged that look like him but only if he has been living in a cave for three years. In order to take care of his assorted 'issues' – which presumably at some point will include hammering out a divorce agreement with his estranged wife – he has taken a sabbatical from the PGA Tour, which without his once luminous presence resembles the clientele of a barbershop on a Saturday morning.

In the spitting inferno of fallen idols, it is hard to top the incineration of Eldrick Woods, who has won 14 professional Major golf championships and has accumulated $110 million in winnings and endorsements. In fact, he is equalled in his undoing in terms of sheer scope by only OJ Simpson, the former NFL running back-corporate pitchman who admittedly transcended the act of serial infidelity by allegedly murdering his ex-wife and the unlucky chap who happened to be dropping something off to her. As the once unassailable Woods now comes to terms with his new reality – which is to say, a place in society that looks upon him now as more sinner than saint – he has become a pariah in the eyes of the corporations that drew on his holy light to sell their wares to his adoring public. Given his updated status as a cheating husband and doer of unseemly deeds with women of questionable virtue, he found that the corporate world dropped him like an underperforming account executive. In so far as his suspended golf career is concerned … well, good question. At one point he seemed certain to eclipse the record 18 Majors held by Jack Nicklaus, which seemed to be what Arnold Palmer was thinking when he said a few years ago: 'Who knows what he is capable of doing. It may even go beyond what we thought.'

Way beyond, Arnie.

Way beyond …

Journalists across America have whipped themselves into a frenzy over the Tiger Woods story. In unison they've been asking themselves: 'How did we miss this?' For years Tiger has been portrayed through a lens of unbridled idolatry. Well apart from the fact that he was the perfect athlete, a prodigy who had been somehow born to greatness only a few can ever know, the thinking also seemed to be that he was impervious to the shortcomings found in lesser human beings (see the beer-swilling John Daly). Some of this has to do with the privacy in which Tiger shrouded himself, which allowed him to cordon off a part of his life that we now know was something less than exemplary.

Sometimes it just amazes me how perpetually naive the press is. It erects 'hero' upon 'hero' and stands in utter astonishment when evidence is produced that contradicts those agreed upon assumptions. Long before Tiger Woods became the scandal *du jour*, we had any number of tearful episodes that remind us that the innocence we think exists in sports is purely a hallucination – perhaps even the product of some part of the brain that compels us to create larger-than-life figures. We've seen this unfold in baseball during The Steroid Age, when the single season home run record was shattered by Mark McGwire and later Barry Bonds. Because it was such a compelling story, it seemed perfectly plausible to the press that a record that stood for years was suddenly not only challenged but obliterated. Incidentally, McGwire finally conceded in January that he used steroids, which is sort of like hearing Al Capone admit years later that he had once been a bootlegger.

So to the question: 'How did we miss this?' The answer is quite simple: By not looking. Or asking around – you know, the way reporters used to do in those old Hollywood B-pictures. But no one expended any shoe leather on Tiger, who gave nothing of himself in interviews other than that All-American smile and an unheated serving of canned quotes. It was enough that Tiger dazzled on the course, just as it had been enough for OJ to hurdle over tacklers and for Michael Jordan to fly through the air. Though it was generally known that OJ had been a wife beater and Jordan had been an inveterate gambler, womaniser, and unspeakable boor, both remained more or less steeped in myth until events overtook them or a few intrepid reporters let some of the untold tales loose in public. By the way, it should be pointed out that Jordan publicly revealed his inner creep at his induction last year into the Naismith Memorial Basketball Hall of Fame, where he enumerated an array of petty grievances he had compiled during his legendary career.

Countless explanations have been tossed out to explain how Woods got into the jam he is in, including the perennial favourite that he was pushed there by his parents: The late Earl Woods had Tiger swinging a golf club by the age of two, when he squared off in a putting match against the comedian Bob Hope on a popular TV talk show. The decidedly leaky reasoning seems to go: Of course Tiger grew up to be a less than trustworthy husband! Look at the abnormal childhood he had! But how convenient is it to blame old Earl, even if he did have aspirations of grandeur for his son that were to the extreme. I think Earl is getting something of an unfair hearing here, especially since Tiger was doing fairly well across the board until he checked his good sense into a bus locker and forgot where he left the key. Even Jordan understood that the privileges of celebrity require no small degree of discretion (albeit he did end up in compromising positions with Vanessa Williams, Vivica Fox and Janet Jackson). How did it happen that Tiger did not get the memo? Given the assortment of playmates that eventually surfaced, it appears that the only people who did not know that Tiger was carrying on like a canine in heat were the very people assigned to cover him (or his ass, whichever the case may be).

Exactly how many women Tiger bedded in his quest for sexual congress is still an unsettled point. But what we do know is that for a period of a few weeks in late November and early December an unending procession of women stepped forward to give a full account of their encounters with Tiger. Generally, they tended to be blonde or brunette, the average age of 30 and from the 'cocktail waitress' field. Reports have circulated that Tiger has spread thousands of dollars of 'hush money to his honeys', yet none of it seems to have kept any of them from yapping. Leggy Italian model Loredana Jolie Ferriolo is even shopping a 'tell-all' book in which, according to *The New York Daily News*, she plans to describe 'the healthy appetite [Woods has] for arranged sex, threesomes, girls next door [and] girl-girl'. Ferriolo even claims she had seen Tiger participate in gay sexual encounters. Tiger has no comment on any of this, except to issue an apology and flee to that sexual addiction clinic in Mississippi.

Now that the story is out in public, the shaming of Tiger Woods is fully under way in the press. In keeping with the old expression – 'if it bleeds, it leads' – Tiger has found himself splattered across the covers of tabloids. In fact, *The New York Post* featured a Tiger Woods story for some 20 consecutive days, including a 2010 calendar that depicted 12 of the buxom beauties in bikinis, lingerie and other revealing attire. Leading off that parade of pulchritude was one Rachel Uchitel – Miss January – who is rumoured to be eyeing the position of the second Mrs Woods (presuming the first Mrs Woods gets that divorce decree and takes the two young children she had with Tiger back to icy Sweden). The comely Ms Uchitel has been noisier than a newsboy hawking papers in the street. In an interview with *News of the World* back in January, she said that Tiger spent Christmas Day with her.

Here's some of her quotes: 'He took care of me really good. It was amazing and delicious.'

And: 'It is definitely over with his wife.'

And: 'He has been sorting things out. We are soul mates. I just want to get it done. I want to start over again with him.'

Tiger, welcome to your future.

I happened to follow Woods around one day at the 2006 US Open at Winged Foot Golf Club in New York. It was just after Earl died and Tiger was beginning his comeback, which only endeared him more deeply to the gallery of his fans that I stood among. As he walked up the fairway, exuding an air of unwavering concentration, a voice would occasionally pop up from the back of the crowd: 'Do it for Dad!' Tiger did not win that weekend, but he surely did not lose any fans, who I remember stood craning their necks for a better look at him.

'Think of how amazing this is,' said one of the fans, who had left his home in Pennsylvania at 3:30am to get to the course in time for play. 'That you can come here and stand within five feet of him.'

Standing not far away, another fan said: 'He is Tiger Woods. When we walked in here, [Dad] turned to me and said: "There he is: the finest athlete in the world."'

Still another fan said: 'Even just standing there by the tee, you cannot take your eyes off him. Somehow he just sucks you in. If he just stood there and hit 100 balls, you would want to stand there and watch him hit every one of them. But then I think: "This is just a person".'

I wonder what those fans are thinking now, if any of the adoration that they had for Tiger Woods has been coloured by his acts. Generally, as we have occasionally stated in this space, Americans are suckers for an apology, if it happens to come across with a convincing degree of sincerity. So far, Tiger has come up somewhat short in that department, if only in that he has addressed the public with vague pleas for understanding as his harem has torn off their veils and spilled out of the shadows into the light of day. One indication of how his apology has or has not been accepted is if his corporate sponsorship comes back, that if he could be viewed as safe enough to sell things again. But I wonder what kind of player he will be once he comes back.

Golf enthusiasts have assured me that this not going to be a problem, that Tiger is so talented that his superior skills will once again carry him to the pinnacle of his sport. They think once he gets back into it, he will once again challenge 'The Golden Bear' for that record 18 professional Major championships. But I am not sure of that. Whatever air of invincibility he once had will be gone when he comes back. I am certain of that, just as I am certain of this: Once someone has hit you in the head with a golf club, you can never look at it the same way again.

When revelations poured forth of his serial infidelities, the legendary golfer Tiger Woods suddenly found himself steeped in ignominy. We asked the question as to whether or not the prolific winner of 14 Major golf tournaments could ever be the same again. Woods, at the end of 2010, was still struggling for form, and only made the Ryder Cup team for the USA as a captain's wildcard pick.

THAT'S OUR BOY

By Gary Lemke

SURELY THERE MUST BE WORSE JOBS IN SPORT, THOUGH BACK IN 2005 THE influential *USA Today* newspaper couldn't find one in a national survey. One would have felt that being sparring partner to a prime Mike Tyson would be the pits. Imagine getting up to go to work, which constitutes being pounded to a pulp by one of the most fearsome heavyweight fighters ever. Then going home and not being able to smell supper because of blood-filled nostrils, let alone trying to eat through torn lips. And then waking up the next day to do it all again. All for a measly wage.

But no, the survey found that being a racehorse groom was top, or bottom, of the pile.

Boy Boy Jevu lives in a modest home in Cape Town's poor settlement of Du Noon, which lies near Killarney Gardens and the N7 highway that takes you up the West Coast. Daily, he gets up in the dark before he boards a taxi and makes the 5km trip to Milnerton, where he reports for duty at 5:30am.

The first thing Boy Boy does when he starts work at the Mike Bass Racing yard is pick up a bucket and broom and, in his wellington boots, makes his way to a stable door. He has long become accustomed to the pungent smell that is a mixture of manure and fresh overnight waste from a 750kg animal. In fact, Boy Boy does it with a smile on his face and a spring in his step.

Boy Boy is groom to the most successful racehorse South Africa has ever seen, Pocket Power. The two have an unbreakable bond. The words *Molo intshatsheli* (Morning champion) will cut through the crisp air, and the thoroughbred's ears prick in instant recognition. 'He understands Xhosa,' Boy Boy says. 'He's my friend.'

The groom is one of 60, tasked with handling the 120 horses at Mike Bass Racing stables. Each groom has two to care for. Boy Boy – his surname Jevu is hardly ever used – had the unique privilege of saddling both his in the recent glitzy J&B Met at Kenilworth, the social highlight on the South African racing calendar.

One of them was Pocket Power, the favourite and attempting a dizzying fourth successive win in the glamour event, having previously also made it four victories in the Queen's Plate, the 18th success of his illustrious career. The other was the 50-1 outsider, Fort Vogue, an improving younger colt who might yet succeed the older Pocket Power as the stable star.

In the final tense days to the Met, Boy Boy was probably the calmest person in the neighbourhood. 'I get more nervous when Pirates or Bafana play,' he said when I asked him whether the pressure of grooming the seven-year-old for the occasion was getting to him. And the married father of two boys aged 16 and five, was confident in the ability of his two charges to do the stable proud.

'I have already bet on them,' he said with a flashing grin. 'The swinger with my two. I'm telling you ... he [pointing to Pocket Power] is the winner but he [Fort Vogue] is Pocket's best friend. The two of them are like this [putting his extended two index fingers together]. They will be side by side but that one will be the winner.'

On race day itself Boy Boy didn't quite get the winner, nor did his swinger (two horses in the first three finishers) come home but there was a short head separating third-placed Pocket Power and fourth-placed Fort Vogue. Take the word of trainer Mike Bass' daughter, Candice Robinson, who felt before the race that Pocket Power's full sister River Jetez would be 'right there' and put them all in the quartet. Armed with that knowledge – some might prefer to call it supreme faith – and for a R360 bet you'd have collected upwards of R13 000 as River Jetez flashed past the post ahead of the field.

As it is, the groom has done well out of the most celebrated equine thoroughbred this country has produced. Sure, he might drink a bottle of beer while the owners crack open another magnum of Dom Perignon, toasting another Met victory, but he is a very satisfied man. 'Sometimes I have too much *phuza* when I'm celebrating at home, but I don't make trouble or fight. I am a family man, with my wife [Nosipha] and boys [Siphe and Awentu] very important.'

His job over the past few years has also taken him to Durban, where Bass launches an annual assault on KwaZulu-Natal's big seasonal highlight, the July. 'Maybe four or five months I'm away from home,' Boy Boy says. 'Then I miss my wife and children too.'

Boy Boy turned 40 last year and despite the association with a champion racehorse who is nearing a record R10 million in stake earnings – that after owners Marsh Shirtliff, and Arthur and Rina Webber had bought him for just R190 000 in 2004 – he is as modest as ever.

'My job is to clean the two stables. I make the horses feel good. I brush them, feed them, make sure they're calm. I look to see that they are not sick. Every morning after I have cleaned up I take them for a walk. And I do that again at half past two in the afternoon. Pocket Power and Fort Vogue listen to me. They are also friendly to one another. They like to see each other,' he says.

It's only for the past three years that Boy Boy has been assigned to tend to Pocket Power. 'I started with Mr Bass in 1986. I was born in 1969, so I was a young boy when I came here. I am very happy. Sometimes I sleep here on weekends if I must work but we all [grooms] get along together. There's more trouble in Du Noon. Sometimes if I go out to have some beer in the shebeen, the people watch you to see if you've got some money. It can be dangerous but I am alright. I enjoy my job, I like making Pocket Power happy. And he is happy. But he can also be very ...' and his voice tails off as he searches unsuccessfully for the right word.

'Temperamental?' I venture. Boy Boy doesn't say a thing, and I feel a little ashamed that I am not able to converse in Xhosa, his mother tongue. Why should he be talking to a writer in a mostly foreign language, where his answers will be exposed in print for the fullness of time.

'Very angry,' Boy Boy suddenly blurts, finding a way to describe the champion's moods. We are talking while the groom has a tight rein on Pocket Power and the photographer hunts for the elusive right shot. Boy Boy is clutching a handful of grass and the horse is content to chomp on it. 'Has he ever hurt you,' I ask? 'No, but he will bite if you come near him.' There was no chance of that.

But Boy Boy's luck ran out three days later. In the emotional moments after the Met was decided, he lost a back tooth when kicked in the mouth. Pocket Power had been badly cut into on his hind leg by flying hooves during the race and when being bandaged by the vet, he lashed out in pain and caught his groom flush. Fortunately, X-rays showed his jaw was bruised, not broken.

Boy Boy comes across as shy and humble, but there are moments when you can see that, perhaps when he's away from the job he loves and back in his community in impoverished Du Noon, there's more to him than meets the eye.

We start discussing soccer, the second of his great loves. I hand him a magazine. 'Katlego Mphela,' he says looking at the cover. The striker is one of the players who is going to have to fire at the 2010 World Cup if Bafana Bafana are to progress to the second round knockout stage of the big event in a few months' time.

'He's a good player, but ... he must deliver,' Boy Boy says, with deliberate play on the Sundowns hitman's nickname of 'Mr Delivery'.

In a manner that seems typical of his positive spin on life, Boy Boy is rather confident that Bafana Bafana will surprise many at the World Cup. 'We can beat Mexico, we can beat Uruguay, maybe not France ... second round is possible ... those guys have a strong coach, he doesn't take nonsense ... he's not a weak one like the last one.'

Soon enough, though, the topic is club soccer, not Bafana. 'Long time,' he replies to the years he's supported Orlando Pirates. 'I would like to meet Teko [Modise]. He's my favourite player. If I can ever meet him I will go up to him and shake his hand. But he must concentrate on the game, not on those other things,' he says with obvious reference to the midfielder's reputation for the bright lights and wild nights.

It is a collision of two worlds when one talks to a racehorse trainer of the stature of Mike Bass and a groom like Boy Boy Jevu. The glue that bonds them is an innate love for horses which confirms another aspect of that *USA Today* survey which asked 107 grooms to explain what the best part of their job was. 'Working with horses' was the response of 78 of them and this is no different. For Boy Boy, though, it must help that he handles Pocket Power – and now also Fort Vogue.

Boy Boy experienced a bittersweet Met, which the closeknit Mike Bass Racing stable and its followers shared. For Bass, who is a master at conditioning a horse for the big occasion and who has been churning out the winners for over three decades, it was a remarkable achievement to see three of his runners finish in the first four in a race of such magnitude and prestige.

Yet, while there was unbridled joy that River Jetez, the full sister to the champion, had finally picked up a major victory that is going to stick another couple of zeroes on to her value as a breeding mare, it's understandable that there were a few moist eyes after seeing Pocket Power finish third.

'The big boy got badly cut into, but he still ran great,' Robinson said in the hours immediately after the race. Following his record-breaking fourth win in the Queen's Plate a couple of weeks earlier she had called him 'a legend' and while superlatives are bandied about like cheap confetti in this day and age it's an accolade that sits well with Pocket Power. 'He is a blessing and I'll probably never work with another horse like this in my life.'

Nor will Boy Boy Jevu, but if Pocket Power could talk he might say the same thing of his groom.

Not everyone can be a caddie to a Major golf champion, or a Formula One commentator, travelling the world in six-star luxury.

Some people have to make a living from being a boxing champion's sparring partner. Others do it by being a racehorse groom, wearing an old T-shirt and taking a bucket and broom to start the 5:30am clean-up. It might not sound like the most pleasant job in the world, the best paid or most appreciated, but Boy Boy Jevu wouldn't have it any other away if he could do it all over.

So to him, and all the other unsung heroes of the sport of kings, we can only say a heartfelt *siyabulela kakhulu* (thank you very much).

Boy Boy Jevu is groom to South Africa's highest-ever racehorse earner, Pocket Power, who has won more than R10 million in stakes and prizes. Boy Boy lives in an informal settlement but mixes in a world of millionaires and thoroughbred horses. The divide between rich and poor is gigantic, but Boy Boy would not swap his lot for anything. This piece formed part of a winning 2010 SAB Sports Feature Writer of the Year submission by the author.

AGE OF DECADENCE

By James Lawton

FABIO CAPELLO MAY HAVE THOUGHT THE WORST WAS OVER. PERHAPS, HE could muse, his strong action had drawn a line against some of the worst effusions of the English football culture he had been charged with transforming quickly enough to produce a competitive showing in the World Cup finals in South Africa in a few months' time.

Then, moments before the start of a Premier League match between Chelsea and Manchester City at the end of last month, he found himself rolling his eyes once more. What he saw must have confirmed his most debilitating fear. It was that some of England's best rewarded football stars live in their own world, one so separated from the professional values he had always known as a successful player and coach in Italy, they might be inhabiting another planet.

In one way the latest incident was small and not unexpected.

John Terry, who was fired by Capello last month as England captain at the end of a squalid tide of controversy, offered his hand to his erstwhile Chelsea team-mate and best friend Wayne Bridge in the traditional pre-match opening rituals. Bridge, who earlier in the week announced that his detestation of Terry was so profound he could not contemplate spending a month or so in his company in South Africa, kept his hand by his side.

The cameras flashed and the headlines were written. In the most public way, Bridge was underlining his decision not to restore, however superficially, some sense that Capello's team could begin to concentrate on the basic imperative of attempting to be the best in the world.

For many it was the culminating evidence that English football, which once treated its professionals so meanly that one of the best of them, George Eastham of Newcastle United and England, went to court to win the right to work for whom he chose, was at the mercy of every celebrity whim.

Terry's whim was to conduct an affair with Bridge's former partner, and mother of his young son, Vanessa Perroncel, a French waitress and sometime glamour model. Bridge's reaction was more than a whim, at least according to those who argue that sexual emotion, and hurt, can disturb anyone's hold on pure logic, but it still begged several questions. One of them asked at what point a professional who collects wages of more than £100 000 a week sets aside personal feelings and gets on with his job.

If you think this is straightforward enough, you haven't been following the debate in England which has raged since Terry failed to impose silence on the media with a 'super' court injunction which was first granted, then rejected on appeal.

For some the issue facing Capello was plain enough. Did he go along with the theory that although Terry was a questionable character to carry the honour of leading his national team, and follow in the footsteps of someone as revered as the late Bobby Moore, there was no doubt about the intensity of his on-field leadership and that, in the end, this was all that really mattered?

This viewpoint, which pushed aside a series of unsavoury stories involving Terry's attempt to exploit privileges bestowed by the captaincy, was gaining ground rapidly right up to the point when Capello returned from convalescing in Switzerland after his knee surgery.

Indeed, one leading commentator advised the head coach to produce a philosophical Latin shrug and proceed with business as normal.

Irrelevant, apparently, was the fact that ever since he arrived in England at the end of a disastrous qualifying campaign for a place in the finals of the 2008 European Championships, Capello had been waging open war on what he found to be quite shocking indiscipline among squad members. 'Respect,' he said, 'is the proper basis for everything a team does. Respect not just for the coach but fellow players and, most of all, respect for your own status as a professional. Without that, there is no foundation for anything good.'

So if Capello railed against sloppy dressing, poor punctuality, constant use of mobile phones and the tendency to fill the team hotel with agents and assorted hangers-on, what was he really expected to do when confronted by the massive distraction of week-long headlines concerning Terry's extramarital adventure with a team-mate's partner?

Doubt lingered just as long as it took Capello to summon Terry to his office and tell him he was out of his job; that his conduct had been unbecoming of an England captain. The whole procedure took just 13 minutes. Terry, far from hinting that he was about to make a Tiger Woods-style *mea culpa*, apparently thought he could tough it out. This conclusion was enhanced, it was suggested, by his ability to buy the silence of Mademoiselle Perroncel. When a deal was apparently struck, Terry thought he was in the clear, despite Bridge's awkward insistence that he had been terribly betrayed by someone he had once trusted.

Terry was swiftly detached from his optimism by a coldly deliberate Capello. Afterwards, the head coach was emphatic that he would not elaborate on the reasons for his action beyond saying, 'It is for the good of the team.'

For some a deeper surprise was not that Terry had been axed but that he had lasted so long, despite the force of many of his performances for England. The charge sheet against Terry was, after all, formidably long.

It was opened nine years ago when he was fined by Chelsea, along with three team-mates, for drunkenly jeering at American tourists in a Heathrow airport hotel in the wake of 9/11.

He was left out of England's squad for the 2002 World Cup in Japan and South Korea because he was awaiting trial on charges of causing an affray. He was found not guilty but unsavoury stories of his private life began to accumulate so steadily he was forced to declare himself a changed man, saying, 'Discipline in your behaviour is as vital as it is out on the pitch – I've learned that the hard way.'

Not hard enough, though, to stop the drip-feed of adverse publicity. Two years ago he was fined £60 for parking his Bentley in a bay reserved for the disabled. The pattern appeared to be clear enough to many critics. Terry believed he could make his own rules and some of the results were dismaying to the ruling Football Association, whose upper echelon were particularly appalled by the news that a marketing company had been touting Terry's services as a spokesman for companies in the build-up to the World Cup. The FA was also shocked to hear that Terry had joined forces with his friend Tony Bruce, a ticket scalper, to sell conducted tours of the Chelsea training ground for hard cash. Terry, off-field earnings apart, picks up £150 000 a week from Chelsea.

Long before Capello reached his verdict on Terry, to many it seemed that the whole affair was not so much a crisis for the national team but a parable of the psychology of the modern English footballer. Until then, Terry's team-mate Ashley Cole seemed to occupy the front rank of those footballers most hell-bent on defining the extent of English football decadence.

He nudged to the front of the race when, after meeting secretly with Chelsea officials and deserting Arsenal, the club that had nurtured him since he was a boy, he published an autobiography of quite excruciating self-indulgence. He told of how stunned, and sickened, he was when his agent reported that contract talks with Arsenal were not going so well. He explained that he was on the pittance of £50 000 at the time and when he heard Arsenal's new offer – rather less than £100 000 a week – he was so enraged he almost drove his car off the road.

This was, however, merely by way of a warm-up. His disdain for referees became routine, on one occasion producing a gesture of contempt so profound he was forced to apologise. Chelsea's latest coach, Carlo Ancelotti, was just weeks into the job when he was obliged to deal with Cole's arrest for verbally abusing a police officer and, just a few days before Bridge's snub of Terry, the fullback was again forging ahead in the notoriety race.

It was announced that Cole and his pop star wife Cheryl were separating after the latest reports of his infidelities, which were additionally complicated by the charge that he had used Chelsea staff to smuggle female company into the team hotel.

Having shown hard-nosed support of Terry through all his transgressions, it seemed that even Chelsea were having a few reflections on the extent the celebrity culture could run before it made absolute nonsense of the concept of a professional football club. The word came down from owner Roman Abramovich, not always saintly in his own private life, that Chelsea players would face new disciplinary measures if they continued to damage the image of the club.

Beyond Stamford Bridge, the big question continued to centre on Capello's ability to hold a perilous line between his demand for discipline and a track record among his leading players that did not exactly make the choice of Terry's replacement a formality.

It came down to a shortlist of three players, none of whom could boast of unblemished credentials. Rio Ferdinand was given the job – over Steven Gerrard and Wayne Rooney – despite the fact that in 2003 he was suspended from club and international football for eight months for failing to attend a drugs test. At the time that had seemed something of a classic demonstration of failed responsibility by a player who less than a year earlier had joined Manchester United from Leeds United at a cost of £30 million. Ferdinand's explanation was that he had forgotten to attend the test because of the sheer pressure of his circumstances. He was moving into a new house, of mansion proportions it need hardly be said, and had to do some urgent shopping.

Gerrard's candidacy wasn't helped by the fact that much of last season was overshadowed by his trial on a charge of causing an affray. He was found not guilty, though not before admitting he had thrown punches at a disc jockey in a bar in the early hours of the morning.

Despite clear signs of Rooney maturing on the field, and being in quite luminous form for his club and country, it was still true that he ended the last World Cup with a red card for stamping on the prone Portuguese defender Ricardo Carvalho.

So Capello made an act of faith in Ferdinand, perhaps because of all the England players he had been most publicly enthusiastic about the coach's demands for new levels of discipline. 'Deep down,' said Ferdinand, 'I think we all believe it is time for people to look at themselves and develop a new attitude.'

England's superb qualifying record on the road to South Africa, the sense that on the field, at least, Capello has brought new levels of coherence, persuades some that he may still produce an impressive campaign in the finals. Sir Bobby Charlton, a hero of England's only World Cup success in 1966, insists that Capello remains the best candidate for such glory since his old boss Sir Alf Ramsey.

'No doubt these have been difficult days for him,' says Charlton, 'but once again he has displayed a lot of strength and good values. He has done what he believes to be right and no one is going to push him away from that position. Alf was like that. On the big issues, you just couldn't budge him.'

On one occasion Ramsey ordered the passports of key players, including Charlton and the captain Moore, to be returned to their empty pillows on the eve of a foreign tour. The threat was that they had one more chance to redeem themselves. Their crime had been to miss curfew by barely an hour.

No doubt Capello's challenge is rather more daunting. It has certainly gone beyond a call for punctuality. Indeed, right now it seems not much less than a need to change a whole way of life.

Another month, another lurid tabloid tale. This time the England captain John Terry had been exposed as a love cheat – with a former team-mate and friend's partner. However, this was no one-off. Modern professional footballers were now living in a world where 'playing away' and out of control private lives were simply 'normal' behaviour.

SHADOWY BOXER
By Clinton van der Berg

TEN YEARS AGO PAUL FOURIE* AND A FRIEND PULLED UP AT A SET OF traffic lights outside the Storyville nightclub in Johannesburg. The lights weren't working. His friend, the driver, hooted at the car in front of them, beckoning him to drive on. Gathered outside Storyville were six onlookers, who told them to shut up. According to Fourie, the group then advanced on the vehicle. One of them was allegedly Mikey Schultz, who punched the car visor. Four heavies pounced on Fourie's friend, beating him horribly.

Fourie claims Schultz pummelled him and walked off. Dazed and hurt, Fourie staggered to Catch 21 next door, pleading for the bouncers' help. On his way out, a woman told Fourie his friend was dead. He wasn't. But he was unconscious, bleeding and in a terrible state. Fourie dragged him off to hospital. Years later, it remains a disturbing memory; a memory not blurred by Schultz frequently dipping into public view.

Schultz is a professional boxer. He is also the alleged assassin of Brett Kebble, having secured a generous plea bargain that allows him his freedom provided he is truthful during the ongoing murder trial, which resumes in July.

It's an extraordinary set of circumstances, but in law the pursuit of the greater good often takes account of the lesser evil. As former Springbok Ray Mordt, a Schultz confidant, is said to have told him: 'You're bloody lucky, if this was America you would be in jail with no second chance.'

More than perhaps any other man in Johannesburg, Schultz enjoys a fearsome notoriety. Everyone knows Mikey, or at least his frightening reputation. There are stories of him tearing up bars, slicing people up and ruling ganglands with an iron fist. The urban legend is that he's a six-foot brute with bulging muscles. The truth is different. But for his elaborate tattoo work, he wouldn't stand out in a crowd. Lean and fit, he weighed just 76kg for his last fight.

One of his friends tells the story of a bloke once arriving at a Johannesburg nightclub demanding to be let in. 'I'm on Mikey's guest list,' he insisted. When the doorman objected, the man became stroppy, threatening to get Schultz on the phone. The doorman then went to the private area where Schultz was seated. 'Don't know him,' insisted Schultz, who wandered through.

'Who are you,' asked Schultz, 'and how do you know Mikey?'

'He's my mate. Let me in!'

'What's he look like?' asked Schultz.

'Huge, well built, big oke,' said the chancer.

'I'm Mikey Schultz – fuck off!'

The dichotomy is that those close to Schultz, or at least those who don't rub him up the wrong way, describe him in a way that makes you almost want to like him. He's deeply respectful of older people (addressing older men as 'uncle'), is known to be extremely generous and even kisses close friends on the cheek.

One of the few insiders prepared to be quoted is Branco Milenkovic, his promoter. 'He likes boxing, he's a fighter,' says Milenkovic. 'He's one of the most respectful boxers I've worked with. I've heard the stories, but can't believe it's the same person.'

Adding another bizarre veneer to the Schultz legend is his brazen friendship with police and former members of the Scorpions, some of whom openly embraced him before and after his last fight in Johannesburg's south.

Thin blue line indeed.

Schultz was born 34 years ago and grew up on Johannesburg's mean streets, the southern suburbs. He had an absent father and was brought up by his mum and sister Kathy, who later married Brian Mitchell.

He grew up tough, but wasn't a street fighter. Brother Donny used to carry Mitchell's bag to gym and it was the world champion-in-waiting who inspired Donny and Mikey to try boxing.

Donny later became a professional boxer and sparring partner to many of South Africa's best fighters. Inevitably, he also drifted into the world of bouncing, earning his keep as the main man at Presleys nightclub on the East Rand. He later shot and killed himself, something Mikey is said to have found difficult to forgive. Even now, years later, he still takes care of Donny's son, Brandon. The memory of Donny is honoured with a tattoo.

If Schultz has a reputation for being untouchable and fearless, there is one exception. While he's rumbled with gangsters and bouncers and angry bikers, the one person he fears is Kathy. His mates tease him. 'I'll call sis,' they warn, at which point Mikey pleads for them not to. He's terrified of sis.

Like many wayward boys, Schultz took up boxing to keep off the streets. He was 12 when he joined the Malvern Boxing Club, where Mitchell himself began his career. More stylist than slugger, he was handy with his fists and won a Southern Transvaal title.

Awarded his professional licence in 1995, Schultz asked Mitchell to train him.

'He wasn't aggressive and never brought trouble to the gym,' recalls Mitchell, who oversaw him gain a dozen wins in his first 13 bouts.

Not a devastating puncher, it was Schultz's fitness and workrate that saw him mow down almost all local opposition. After a draw with well-regarded Elvis Adonisi in 1998, he walked away, still unbeaten but apparently yearning for other thrills.

Soon after, Donny was dead.

The world of bouncing appealed to Mikey. Soon he was king of the pile, running his own company and cleaning up the streets – his way.

He got into fights, there were court cases and the Schultz legend grew. He was charged (and acquitted) for storming into a Boksburg bar and beating up patrons with a baseball bat.

In 2005, the Kebble killing went down. Evidence in court was that Schultz pumped six bullets into the high-flyer.

In 2006 he was questioned by police about the killings of Hazel Crane and Shai Avassar.

Two separate sources tell the story of how a hit was put on Schultz's life by the Hell's Angels. A man named 'Red' (real name Boris) was given the job. Schultz is said to have put word out on where he would be. He then contacted friends among the police who joined him at a restaurant at The Glen shopping centre in Johannesburg's south. Schultz knew the score, so he waited. With a loaded gun.

Depending which story you believe, the tale has one of two endings. The first has it that Red pointed his gun directly at Schultz, at which point Schultz shoved his finger down the barrel and dared Red to shoot him. Badly spooked, Red dashed off.

The other alleges that Schultz simply shot him through the menu and a mate finished the job off. The police, who were there, allegedly backed up Schultz's self-defence plea.

Schultz shot to broader prominence when he was linked to Kebble's assassination. Presumably the case was a wake-up call: the deal he thrashed out with the state demands that he stay out of trouble.

Tired of simply training fighters, chief among them local fireman Anthony van Niekerk, Schultz took up the gloves himself, determined to fill the void in his life. Now a father of four and older and smarter, he sought a sense of validation.

He turned to Mixed Martial Arts, a gory mix of fighting styles, and promptly reeled off five quick wins. Then he teamed up with his old friend, brassy boxing trainer Nick Durandt. He yearned to win a boxing belt. Any belt.

Eleven years on from his last fight, Schultz knocked out journeyman Oupa Mahlangu inside two rounds. Samuel Mathebula, another trialhorse, was whacked out in three.

Somehow, Milenkovic engineered a 'title' fight last November: Schultz against unthreatening Zimbabwean Tineyi Maridzo for the low-rent WBO Africa super-middleweight title. All Schultz wanted was that shiny bauble. With six defeats in nine fights, Maridzo was as safe as they come. Schultz never saw the punch, a booming right cross that caught him high on the temple. Schultz's world turned black. After just 87 seconds, it was all over. The screams of his many supporters, among them the biker gang Satan's Saints, turned to wails and groans. Women, including his wife, burst into tears. The men became aggressive, the mood nasty.

Schultz took his defeat manfully. He was gracious, honourable even, respecting the nature (and natural justice) of the most brutal of sports. In boxing, unlike the streets, boasting counts for nothing. When the knives, guns and baseball bats are stripped away and it's you against another man, naked save for gloves and trunks, the fight is fairer. Almost always, the best man, the best fighter, wins.

Durandt defends him against allcomers.

'I love working with him. He's my friend and has been for years. I know what's gone on in his life, it's not a secret. If I can help change his perspective, I'll be there for him. This is a guy who turned his life around with boxing. I'm proud to be part of his rebuilding.'

The exuberant trainer cares little about his fighter's dark past. 'Away from the bright lights, he works bloody hard in the gym, gets on with everyone and is a pleasure to deal with. I'm not saying he's an angel and didn't get mixed up in bullshit, but I'll do anything for him.'

Ex-footballer Mark Batchelor is another of Schultz's allies, notwithstanding his quiet withdrawal from Schultz's inner circle.

He says he once saw Schultz confront two drug dealers on a street corner in Turffontein because they were selling to a friend's son. Rather than beat them up, he had a quiet, firm word. 'Which Mikey is that?' asked a bemused woman nearby.

'He's loyal, and has a huge heart,' says Batchelor. 'He'll be the first to hold his hand up and admit to mistakes. He was the guy who guided me when I was going down the wrong way, fighting and stuff. He told me to pull myself together and it was he who asked Ray Mordt to help me along.'

What Schultz probably doesn't realise is that his life and his behaviour holds appeal by virtue of its dark undercurrent. People are drawn to him not for his warmth or personality, but for the same reason they are drawn to car accidents or reality television – they are fascinated by the ghoulish, the link with society's bleak underbelly.

Schultz's ambitions for a rematch were placed on hold due to the trial. The fight may now happen later this month.

Two or three more bouts and the boxing will be over for Mikey Schultz. The world of Mixed Martial Arts, the dream of seeing action in Las Vegas, then beckons the hard man.

The fight goes on.

*Name has been changed

One of the most feared figures in South Africa continued a boxing career while wreaking destruction out of the ring. This feature was particularly relevant because Mikey Schultz was the man who admitted pulling the trigger in a shooting that killed the mining magnate Brett Kebble, and the case in the Johannesburg High Court was being widely followed both in the country and abroad.

RISE AFTER THE FALL
By Peter Roebuck

IN A TRICE HASHIM AMLA HAS BECOME A MIGHTY BATSMAN AND A significant figure in the development of the game and much else around the country. With all due respect to various politicians, freedom fighters, businessmen, philanthropists, gurus, scandalmongers, writers, artists and so forth, he is probably the second most famous Indian associated with this land. The previous one was tossed off a train in Pietermaritzburg. Amla has previously been dropped from the national team but otherwise has suffered no such indignity. He can sit in whatever carriage he pleases and is admired by all sections of society. His story is the story of a community and country that have changed and matured together.

He is a Muslim, too, and therefore a representative of a second force and a wider world. Sport is hard and competitive enough on its own and it is too much to ask a young cricketer to carry one extra flag. Suffice it to say Amla has carried his loads lightly. At all times he has spoken softly but firmly, defending his position but never lowering himself to point scoring. Finding the middle path, he has refused to wear alcohol logos on his shirt but joined the raucous celebrations that marked South Africa's first Test series victory in Australia. He has obeyed the tenets of his faith and met the requirements of his game, has been adaptable and steadfast. Certainly he has not allowed his various disciplines to come into conflict. Off the field he has been mild but never meek. On it he has become monumental. He has charted the path not only for Indians and Muslims and young cricketers, but in no small degree for a nation too.

Although not that far apart in years, Amla and Makhaya Ntini belong to different generations. The speedster was a freakish figure produced by nature, nurture and outrageous fortune; Amla is the product of a society more at ease with itself. Ntini was alone, a reassurance, something to put in the shop window. By so spectacularly surpassing expectations, he made the future not so much possible as plausible. Ntini served as an advance guard creating the impression that a hundred followed in his wake and that a lot of work had been done. In fact, of course, the entire thing hung by a thread. His cheerful brilliance saved South African cricket.

Amla belongs to the second wave – the first was a mere ripple – of brown and black cricketers. Alongside players of similar hue, calibre and conviction, he is playing his part in fulfilling the game's and the country's cosmopolitan dream. It's a lot to ask from a young man also called upon to bat at first wicket down – the most difficult position on the list – but it is well within his capability. He is a thoughtful, unruffled fellow. Even a past master like Dean Jones could not rile him.

South Africa's recent history has been somewhat fraught. Contrastingly Amla's story has been a typical tale of a talented young batsman trying to make the grade. Take away apartheid and Durban and bloodless revolutions and symbolism and Indian cricketers of yesteryear and all the rest of it and what remains is a gifted cricketer working his way through the ranks. Of course it is a tale of rise and fall and struggle and setback and triumph and discovery and so forth, but that is sport, its very purpose, the man pitted against himself and also an opponent.

In Amla's case, and putting history aside, the main difference has been the extent of the ups and downs. After his first few matches in the colours of his colourful country he was not so much doubted as scorned. It is no small thing for a newcomer to be told that he is an impostor. Some never recover from the scrutiny that comes with high honours. Mark Lathwell was a case in point. The Devonian was a dazzling batsman until he played for his country whereupon he shrank back into a shy country boy. Exposure can make men yearn for the womb. Amla, though, took it all in his stride. Like Ntini, he has an equanimity about him that is not so easily shifted. In Ntini's case it was a matter of temperament. With Amla it tells of family, philosophy and faith. He is grounded by forces mightier than himself.

Amla's cricketing career began, like so many others in this country, at a strong cricketing school. Every country has its traditional sources of players, and the trick has been to keep the supply chain working or else to find alternatives. The West Indies have suffered because, cursed by modernity, the informal street games no longer produce players. No replacement has been created. England went through a bad patch after the aristocracy and coal mines fell into decline but are bouncing back because alternatives have been found in, well, South African schools and Ireland. South African cricket still depends on its top 20 schools, all the more reason to ensure that they are on the right track.

Amla attended Durban High School and emerged with a good reputation as a scholar and batsman. Already his qualities had been observed and his card had been marked. South Africa was looking for young batsmen of pedigree and young cricketers from the previously frustrated communities. Amla fitted both categories. Hereabouts he might have been spoilt, as so many plucked from their peers and pushed along are, but remained intact. Before long he was captaining the national U19 team and also scoring runs. Responsibility did not scare him. He has an unusual balance of character that enables him to keep everything in its rightful place. He was rushed along but not in a rush.

All too soon he was captaining his province, a lad of 21 called upon to lead a diverse group of men, fearful of their places, fearful of the future. At first it went well, four hundreds in a few weeks, another promotion taken in his stride. Perhaps, though, even for Amla, it was all happening too quickly. Somewhere along the way he had to learn about the finer points of batsmanship.

Next the South African selectors noticed his scoring, liked the look of him and included him in their Test team. Finally he came unstuck. Finally he had been promoted beyond his capabilities. Facing England on his home pitches, the youngster looked loose, flashy, and inept. And he was all of those things. An exotic backlift was followed by numerous speculations outside off-stump. Bemused English seamers pounced on his failings. Team-mates thought he was out of his depth and blamed political interference. Tensions were high, not so much between Amla and comrades as between a dismayed old guard and radicals persuaded that cricket had to be shaken from its complacency. No one blamed Amla but inescapably he was involved. To some he was part of the problem, to others he was part of the cure. Meanwhile his humanity was overlooked. The same happened to Justin Ontong and he never fully recovered. Cricketers cannot be microwaved.

After three fraught matches, Amla was dropped. It was the right move. Far better to admit a mistake than to persist with it. Amla's response was critical and telling. He did not panic or pander, but instead concentrated on correcting. He did not seek the unreliable counsel of miracle cures or listen to the agitated words of the frenzied but instead went back into the nets and back to the basics. He had learnt many lessons, knowing that his game was built on sand. Accordingly he set about tightening his technique. It was a characteristically level-headed response to adversity.

Recognising that he had too much on his plate, accepting that he needed to focus on his own batting, Amla stepped down as captain of the Dolphins. His next move was to shorten his backlift to give himself more control over his willow and more time to play his strokes. Before long the runs were flowing again. It has never been hard for him to remain at the crease. Some batsmen are obliged to furrow their brows. Amla has always been serene.

He was recalled to the Test team and responded with 149 against New Zealand in Cape Town. It was a vital innings. From that moment he knew that he belonged. No less importantly, his colleagues and community knew that he belonged. The deed had been done. He could walk into the dressing room as an equal, could sense the acceptance as he took guard. From then onwards he could look forwards, not over his shoulder. Black, green and blue, everyone has to pass the same test.

Amla started to put together the mammoth innings that have become his trademark. Organised, durable, composed, cerebral, he went to India and on another hot day in Chennai scored 159 not out. India were to become well acquainted with his skills. His grandparents had come from Gujarat so Tamil Nadu was not exactly his second home but he looked comfortable at the crease and in the country.

Before long the chance came to face the mighty Australians on their own patch. Already Amla sat high in the batting rankings. South Africa, too, were on the move. Suddenly the Aussies did not look unbeatable. A new generation of Proteas fancied their chances. It was a thrilling series, as good as any history has known. And the first drop played his part to the utmost. Putting the ball away with wristy strokes, subduing lifters with quick-handed parries, and standing his ground in his own modest way, Amla was consistent. All told he scored 259 runs at an average of 51. And it fell to him to stroke the winning runs in Melbourne as South Africa fought back magnificently to secure victory. Two days before he had watched with admiration as another darker skinned batsman, JP Duminy, defied the Australians for almost an entire day. Before that he had seen Duminy and AB de Villiers, a bright Afrikaner, bat superbly in Perth. A lot had happened in a few days. Of course it was years in the making, and a man who spent 27 years in prison had a bit to do with it.

Only one criticism could be made about Amla's performances Down Under. Repeatedly he had lost his wicket in the 40s and 50s. Hereabouts he looked capable but prone to inexplicable lapses. Perhaps he had concentrated so much of his energy on establishing himself that he had nothing left to complete the job. Still he had been a popular and effective member of a diverse team.

Naturally he was happy but not completely satisfied with his own performances. Amla wanted to play longer innings, wanted to hit hundreds. Test matches are won and names made by big scores. And so he went to India, another confronting cricketing country, and put it right. Undaunted, inexhaustible, he compiled nearly 500 runs in the series and lost his wicket only once. India could not find a way past him. He was an immoveable object. Only Walter Hammond has ended a series with a higher average.

India doffed its cap to its distant son, colleagues sang his praises, Muslims rejoiced and the game itself celebrated. In a short time Amla has learnt a lot of lessons and his rise has been instructive. Without flamboyance or ego, without compromising his faith or his background he has become a formidable batsman and a respected member of a team representing a nation striving for its identity. Throughout he has spoken quietly and practised hard, taking responsibility for his performances. It has been an impressive and reassuring contribution from a fine batsman and future leader. All things are possible.

Hashim Amla was often the yo-yo man of the Proteas top order. However, he produced a career-defining performance in India, where he scored 253 not out, 114 and 123 not out to pick up the Man of the Series award and up his batting average after 43 Tests to 47.26. Amla had returned stronger than ever following a scratchy start to his international career and the new batting rock had proved why he was finally here to stay.

SACHIN BETTER THAN HIS STATS
By Mark Keohane

VIRENDER SEHWAG WAS AWED, AND IF THE MOST EXPLOSIVE BATSMAN IN cricket appreciates the wonder of Sachin Tendulkar's 200 not out against South Africa in an ODI, there is no greater compliment that can be paid to Tendulkar.

'Just finish it. Finish it,' is what Sehwag was thinking as Tendulkar entered the 190s. It was only then that Sehwag believed it to be possible, but it was also then that he feared Tendulkar's body would not prove as strong as his mind.

He needn't have worried.

Afterwards Sehwag wrote: 'Importantly he had the hunger and the patience to last for the entire 50 overs. You need to bat out the entire innings to score a double. I knew if he had 150 balls he could do it and he did it in 147.

'Certain people have said I could have scored 200 in ODIs because of my strike rate in Tests, where I have got close to a hundred before lunch. But I have had the tendency to take risks once I reach the 120 or 130 mark in ODIs. That's the difference between me and Sachin.

'We have had chats about him scoring 200. I told him only he could do it. Last year in New Zealand, when he retired hurt because of torn stomach muscles on 163, I told him he had missed the opportunity but he said it would eventually happen if he was destined to do it. He said the same when he got 175 against Australia.

'On Wednesday he told me: "I got what was destined." You might say, this is 200 – a figure no batsman in the history of the game has crossed – but then we are talking about Tendulkar.'

Yet Tendulkar's mastery is still not universally acclaimed. There are those who refuse to accept that he is the best ever because at 36 he doesn't bat with the dash of the 17-year-old boy wonder who scored the first of what is now 93 international centuries. Cricket is an odd game, but nothing is odder than the often repeated opinion that some batsmen are better players than their statistics indicate and that when a player consistently succeeds the critique often is that the player is not as good as his statistics.

When it comes to Tendulkar he's better than his statistics indicate and they are unmatched in the past 30 years. Even comparing him to Don Bradman is unfair because they played the same game but in different eras and circumstances.

It is incredible how much purple prose is written on Bradman by those who never saw him bat, but whose writing continues to enforce the legend.

Yet those who have witnessed Tendulkar's incredible 20 years in international cricket look first for fault … not enough risk … not enough boundaries … not enough entertainment … Not enough … not enough … never enough!

In an age when cricket has been turned into little more than a run-a-ball-hit-and-giggle in Twenty20, Tendulkar scored 200 not out by playing an innings you would associate with Test cricket. He played cricket shots – the kind I'm told Bradman played. He didn't rely on baseball-style hitting to reach 200. He trusted his mind, his concentration, his technique and mostly his bat.

This is a batsman who has scored as many of his centuries away from India as at home and this is a man who averages more overseas than he does in India.

Still the critics question just how good he is.

I read a wonderful piece, written by an Indian contributor, S Balachandran, on Cricinfo. 'A successful man cannot have people simply singing praises about him. Ask his detractors,' Balachandran wrote. 'They would point out that the Roop Singh Stadium at Gwalior had short square boundaries, lightning fast outfields and an absolute marble-top of a wicket. And they would be absolutely right.

'But here is something they might consider. Give a top-class artist a canvas. Give him a room and give him a vista. See what he comes up with. For the art produced thereof we credit the artist himself; not the canvas for its whiteness and blankness. Not the room for the comfort it offered. Not even the vista for its having conveniently presented itself. They are all incidental. Art is transcendental. So too is Tendulkar's batting.'

It confirmed to me that describing Tendulkar as a run accumulator is like calling Picasso a prolific painter.

In the month that the Indian great Sachin Tendulkar became the first man to score 200 runs in a 50-over ODI, we reflected on what the batsman had achieved and came to the conclusion that he couldn't be judged solely on his impressive career stats. He was even better than they suggested.

THE GREAT MYTH
By James Lawton

OF ALL THE ACHIEVEMENTS OF DAVID BECKHAM, PERHAPS NONE OF them defined him quite so well – and perhaps in the way of his enduring celebrity quite so eerily – as the reaction that came over a few days last month when it appeared that for all practical purposes his playing career was finally over.

Unchallenged, he pulled up during Milan's game with Chievo and signalled that something was broken. It was an Achilles tendon and for a 34-year-old already desperate in his efforts to keep up with the pace of modern football at its highest level the news could hardly have been worse.

So of course he was in tears, as he was when he surrendered the captaincy of England, unilaterally, at the end of the 2006 World Cup, as the reality that his last great ambition was almost certainly in ruins swept through football. He had hoped, along with much of the English nation, that he would do something never accomplished by even the greatest of his football compatriots, not Sir Tom Finney or Sir Stanley Matthews or Sir Bobby Charlton, or the unknighted but unforgettable Bobby Moore, and play in four World Cups. For his millions of fans around the world it was his due. For his critics it was another distortion of England's football history, but as the possibility unravelled there was not much expression of the latter view.

The Times of London put a huge picture of Beckham on its front page, as it had a few days earlier after he played, as a substitute, at his old hunting ground of Old Trafford when his Milan team were not so much beaten as cut to pieces in a 4-0 Champions League defeat. On that first occasion the newspaper was responding to the fact that as he left the field Beckham stooped to pick up a green and gold scarf, the club's original colours and now a symbol of protest against the current American ownership. Later he strenuously denied that he had intended to intrude into the affairs of his old club. No, he didn't imagine he was offering a superb photo opportunity laden with news significance.

Whether he did or not, he had given another classic example of his ability to create an aura, and a separation from the reality of his current value as a football player, and perhaps even the one he had carried throughout his starry past, maybe unprecedented in the annals of the world's most popular game. It was as though the myth of Beckham was beyond assault by any circumstances, that even as he declined physically his ability to impose himself – at least in terms of personal publicity – on any situation grew only stronger.

There was the same sense when the severity of his injury was confirmed and he was flown to Finland for immediate surgery. Even then, there was an almost religious fervour behind the hope that Beckham would emerge from the hospital, miraculously restored and waving to the cameras. But, no, his chances of appearing in the England squad in South Africa were over, the surgeon announced. Or so it seemed.

What followed was especially surprising, some might say gut-wrenching, in that the creator of the new debate was not Beckham or one of his spokesmen or his wife Victoria, who has been known to get a little restive when her quota of front-page appearances is down, but the ultimate professional, the coach who is said to have expunged the last of his sentimentality early in a career suffused with success and a thousand examples of hard-headedness.

It was Fabio Capello, whose appointment as England coach at the end of 2007 and a dismal, failed campaign to qualify for the 2008 European Championships was welcomed not only for his football acumen but also the certainty that he would strip down the celebrity culture of a chronically under-performing team.

Beckham, said Capello, might still make the trip to South Africa as a member of the English party. No, perhaps he couldn't play but he could be an inspiration, a talisman, a symbol of all that was best in the English game. This was the Capello who in his first meeting with his new England players announced that everything was going to change.

There was, he made it clear, no possibility of a repeat of the grotesque pantomime which accompanied the England squad to Germany for the previous World Cup, when the notorious WAGS – wives and girlfriends – set up their alternative headquarters in the sedate spa town of Baden Baden just down the road from their husbands and boyfriends.

Players would dress smartly at all times. They would arrive punctually for team meals. They would not have cellphones permanently attached to their ears. Their agents would not infest the team hotel.

Earlier this year he showed this was more than mere talk when he brusquely sacked his captain John Terry after a stream of misadventures, including a hugely publicised affair with the girlfriend of his former team-mate at Chelsea, and best friend, Wayne Bridge. Terry went to Capello's office convinced that, after reportedly paying as much as £1 million for the silence of his former lover, he could survive in the lucrative role of team captain. Capello separated him from this illusion in just 13 icy minutes. There, even Beckham had to understand, was the evidence that even he would be obliged to accept that when the time came to select the squad for South Africa, Capello would defer to no one's reputation, not even one that had been constructed so carefully for the best part of 15 years.

With Beckham's name on the agenda, Capello suggested as much when he was introduced to some of the nation's leading sports writers and broadcasters shortly after his hiring as the £6 million-a-year man to resurrect the national team.

Over a few post-lunch digestives he volunteered some of his priorities. They included strong discipline – on and off the field – and a refusal to allow a team that had been described, for some mysterious reasons according to the hardest judges, as English football's golden generation, to live, even for a moment, off their reputations.

Inevitably, then, he was asked about the growing national obsession with the fact that Beckham was still one short of his 100th international cap. The question was quite elaborately, even cunningly, framed: 'Could it ever happen in Capello's native Italy, the winner, after all, of four World Cups and just one less than Brazil, that there would ever be such pressure for a player of even the greatest achievement – a Baresi or a Maldini or a Del Piero – to pass some ritual milestone with a selection that might be described as even faintly honorific?'

Il Capo, who was at the start of a crash course in English, frowned, consulted his interpreter, and said, finally, 'Not in a million years.'

But then when in England it seemed that the man who once played and coached for Roma, was persuaded to do as the English do. Or at least that part of what might be described as the deification of a football player.

Beckham didn't have to wait anything like a million years for his 100th cap. Capello gave him a walk-on part in an exhibition game at the Stade de France in Paris a few months later. England lost but Beckham, once again, grabbed most of the headlines. One by one, he picked off the men who headed him on the all-time list of caps won. He did so with cameo performances at the end of games, appearances which provoked at Wembley Stadium a reaction out of all proportion to what he achieved with his still fine ball-striking ability when he was given a little time and a little space. First he edged past Billy Wright, the centre half and captain of Wolves, a retiring, bushy-haired figure who was a foundation stone of the England team for 13 years until 1959, by which time he had won 105 caps. Then it was Bobby Charlton who was surpassed on the mark of 106 – and for some this was especially hard to mark down as anything other than a historical milestone which had been mocked by subsequent events.

You had a harder sense of this if you remembered how it was when Charlton's majestic career in an England shirt came to a close at the end of the 1970 World Cup in Mexico. Charlton was controversially replaced towards the end of a masterful performance against West Germany in a quarter-final match in Leon. England were leading 2-1 at the time and the England coach, Sir Alf Ramsey, was anxious to keep Charlton fresh for what seemed like a certain semi-final.

It was a strategic disaster. The Germans became much more assertive in Charlton's absence, Franz Beckenbauer pushed forward with a new freedom, and eventually they won 3-2. Ramsey admitted on the flight home to England that he had made a mistake and he apologised. He also told Charlton that it was the time to draw a close to his international career. He was 32, a year younger than Beckham when he launched his campaign to return to the England team despite decamping from Real Madrid for a contract reported to be worth £28 million to play American minor league football with Los Angeles Galaxy.

Bobby Moore, 108 caps, was the next faller as Beckham marched on along the margins of the England team. When he pulled up in pain in the San Siro stadium, Beckham had 115 England caps, the most of any outfield player, and just five short of the record-holder, goalkeeper Peter Shilton.

How had it happened? Capello deadpanned that Beckham was still a fine, influential player and that, who knew, he might be able to exert some influence while coming off the bench if things got critical in South Africa. As to the proposal that Beckham might join England in South Africa, as a kind of non-playing captain, and an inevitable magnet for publicity, Capello shrugged and said: 'David Beckham is a very good professional, a good example to his team-mates and very popular.'

Was he really? Or was he something more in the eyes of the ruling Football Association and its sponsors? Was he a worldwide celebrity who gave the English game a presence and an appeal – especially in the campaign to host the 2018 World Cup – that it might otherwise lack? And was Capello merely being pragmatic in his cultivation of the Beckham legend?

Some will always find it hard to be detached from such a suspicion, even as they brace themselves for what is widely believed to be an inevitable knighthood. For such sceptics, the trouble is that Beckham's achievements have simply never matched the scale of his fame.

In his first World Cup in 1998 he was sent off for a petulant kick at an Argentine player, Diego Simeone, obliging his team to play with 10 men at the vital phase of a round-of-16 game in which the teenaged Michael Owen had scored a brilliant goal to encourage English hopes.

The England coach, Glenn Hoddle, had left Beckham out of the first two group games – against Tunisia and Romania – because he believed he was unfocused. Beckham then appeared in the third game, against Colombia, and scored with a spectacular free-kick.

Two years later Beckham was ineffective in the European Championships from which England were ejected by Romania. At the 2002 World Cup in Japan he was plainly far from fit and was involved in another controversy when he jumped out of a tackle in the quarter-final against Brazil, a decision which led directly to an equaliser for the eventual champions.

In the next European Championships, in Portugal, Beckham was again nondescript, blaming his lack of impact on the training schedule at his new club Real Madrid. And then there was the World Cup in Germany in 2006, when Beckham wept first when he was replaced during the losing quarter-final against Portugal, then the following day when he called a press conference to announce that he was handing back the captaincy he had publicly campaigned for six years earlier.

If this sounds like a jaundiced view of the Beckham years it probably needs to be said that he has always displayed impressive dedication, and a superb ability to kick the ball, especially in dead-ball situations. He was an integral part of Manchester United's success through the '90s, including the winning of a Champions League medal in 1999, and right up to the point United manager Sir Alex Ferguson concluded that his celebrity lifestyle had become a circus far too damaging to the best interests of a professional football club.

Beckham's devotees passionately reject all such criticisms but they do have a certain difficulty when asked to offer the evidence of their hero's achievements, enough of them, anyway, to justify the astonishing late accumulation of international caps and the sense that whatever happens, and in whatever state of physical fitness he might find himself, he cannot be detached, even now, from any discussion about England's prospects.

Invariably, they point to the desperate afternoon at Old Trafford in 2001 when England laboured against an extremely modest Greek team to qualify for the World Cup finals. Beckham, no one can argue, was indeed England's saviour that day, scoring in the last minute with a beautifully struck free-kick.

It was a timely and valuable contribution from a player of impressive skill. But did it make him England's player of the ages? No it didn't, but be careful who you tell. Even Capello, the most stringent Il Capo English football has known since Ramsey, is unlikely to give you more than a shrug and an enigmatic smile.

The basis of Beckham's fame may be largely a myth but, if we didn't know before, we know now. It is beyond the limitations of mere facts – and any realistic challenge.

Two months out from the World Cup, the most-capped England outfield player of all time had built a career on milking opportunity and cashing in on his fame. Injury had derailed David Beckham's dreams of a record four World Cup appearances, but the author argued that the stark truth was that 'Becks' was never as good as he was cracked up to be.

MESSI WON'T WIN WORLD CUP
By Mark Keohane

THE BEST PLAYER IN THE WORLD WILL BE AMONG THE MOST ANONYMOUS in this year's soccer World Cup – and one of the best players in the last century will be central to Lionel Messi's spectator role.

Adjectives can't describe Messi's contribution to Barcelona in the past three seasons, but the man born in Argentina and groomed in Barcelona would have been a sensation had he been playing for Spain.

Messi will always have his critics because of his failure to transfer his club form internationally. He scores as a matter of course with Barcelona and fails with the same regularity for Argentina. In 43 international appearances he has scored just 13 times, but ineffectiveness has nothing to do with Messi's ability and everything to do with Argentinean manager Diego Maradona turning the world's most gifted footballer into a sprinter who always seems to be on the periphery of anything coherent in attack.

Maradona, unrivalled in his prime, has been the biggest disappointment as a manager. The natural instincts of Maradona the player are not reflected in the man who manages Argentina's World Cup aspirations. So poor has Maradona's Argentina been that their qualification was in doubt until the last weekend. How criminal that the world's best would not even have made it to South Africa.

Messi's life story is as fascinating as Argentina's failure to embrace the genius of the player and build their attack around him. He left Argentina when he was 12 years old because his club would not pay for the growth hormone treatment needed to give him a few more inches. Barcelona paid his medical bills and Messi has been a Catalan for the past 10 years.

It is one of the reasons Messi is not embraced in Argentina. The view is that Messi is Catalan, then Spanish and then Argentinean. Messi detests this theory and has always publicly committed himself to Argentina and being Argentinean.

But the Argentineans don't relate to him. He is a foreigner in his country of birth and the fact that he is media shy and avoids interactions with the Argentinean press further complicates his claims to being Argentinean first and Spanish second. He has been accused of not singing the national anthem and of not feeling pride at wearing the Argentina shirt and of not showing the same attitude he does in Barcelona.

Those sceptical of Messi's talent insist Messi can never be considered the world's greatest until he produces at the World Cup for Argentina. That's too simplistic a view. The demands of the European Cup are even more taxing than winning a World Cup.

Portugal's Ronaldo faces a similar predicament in South Africa because he fronts arguably the weakest Portuguese team in the past decade. Players of Messi and Ronaldo's class have to be judged on what they do weekly against the world's best players.

Messi, in 2004, inspired Argentina to the U20 World Cup in the Netherlands and in 2008 guided Argentina to Olympic gold in Beijing. His international debut in 2005 was less inspirational when he was introduced against Hungary in the 63rd minute and sent off 40 seconds later for elbowing defender Vilmos Vanezak. His international career has never got much better, although when Maradona surprisingly was asked to turn the madness into magic there was a belief that he would naturally resonate with the spirit of Messi.

The Argentinean press have never excused Messi for his international ineffectiveness, suggesting there 'is the one in Barcelona who plays outstandingly well, who dribbles and makes things happen; and one in the national side who can't develop his full potential, who seems to drag that magical left foot behind him and loses the ball, who shoots and scores only occasionally'.

One press report said that Maradona could do more with an orange than Messi can do with a football, but that Maradona, as a coach, was a disaster and Messi was the only player who could save Argentina – and Maradona – from embarrassment in South Africa.

The more astute, and less emotional, observers blame Maradona for an inability to give Messi the centre stage. Maradona could counter his critics by saying he does not have a strike partner to complement Messi.

That would be a cop out. There are enough gifted players in the Argentinean squad. It is the same strategy that will determine Messi's effectiveness and if the qualification is the barometer – when Argentina qualified in their last match – Messi will be more a passenger than pilot in South Africa.

Maradona has selected 94 squad members in 14 months, but never built his team around Messi. It is why one has to cry for Messi more than Argentina. The greatest player, on the world's greatest stage, will be undone by one of his own, more than by any defender.

Enjoy having Lionel Messi in South Africa, but don't expect to see the little general of Barcelona because the man who should be playing for Spain will be playing for Argentina ... which could explain why he doesn't sing the national anthem.

Typical of his direct approach, the columnist pulled no punches when it came to playing down the prospects of the fancied Argentinean football team that was coming to the World Cup. Lionel Messi was the best player in the world and expected to lead the Argentinean challenge. This column predicted it would all end in tears for the South Americans – which it did, as Messi failed to score at the World Cup, and the team fired their coach Diego Maradona after the tournament.

STILL LIVING A LIE
By James Corrigan

THE CONTRAST COULD NOT HAVE BEEN ANY MORE PRONOUNCED. TWO golfing superstars with 'family problems', but only one of them celebrating an emotional victory with which everyone could empathise. When Phil Mickelson won the most enthralling Masters in recent memory, America cried in delight. The sport at last had a positive story to monopolise the headlines.

A week which was supposed to be all about The Tiger Woods Scandal had ended with The Phil and Amy Love Story.

Here's how the weepie unfolded on that final day at Augusta. For the first time since she was diagnosed with breast cancer last year, Mickelson's wife went to the course to watch him play. Amy's timing happens to be as good as her husband's.

She saw him collect his fourth Major in spectacular style and so confirm himself as his generation's main challenger to Woods. Amy – whose treatment is ongoing – was in tears as he walked up to the final green. Within a few minutes, Phil's waterworks erupted too. By the side of the green they were in each other's arms, and with their three children completing the huddle an iconic image flashed around the world.

At that moment, Woods' public rehabilitation from the multiple mistress outrage became that much more forlorn. However 'good a person' the world No 1 had pledged to become, he would never challenge Mickelson in the family man department. At the start of his comeback event Woods had claimed that Major titles meant absolutely nothing compared to a happy home life. Fine words, but it was his rival who acted out the promise. Mickelson's victory was total; moral as much as sporting. Woods' disgrace had only been emphasised.

Of course, this comparison of karmas had not been helped by Woods' reaction when he had stepped off the 18th green. 'I finished fourth – it's not what I wanted,' he told the TV interviewer. 'I wanted to win this tournament. I only enter events to win.' When asked about his dour mood in that final round Woods became even more surly. 'People are making way too much of a big deal of this thing,' he snapped. 'I was not feeling good. I hit a big snipe off the first hole and I don't know how people can think I should be happy about that.'

What on earth had happened to the humble Tiger of six days previous? It is worth recounting the events of that manic Monday if only to assess the PR operation. He had played golf in front of the paying public and answered the questions of the baying media for the first time in five months. A sporting life had apparently been reborn. His re-emergence into the competitive arena had gone as well as he could possibly have hoped. Golf's No 1 was back. And the blessed reality was that he looked nothing like the world No 1 we once knew.

Inevitably, the brunt of the focus of a world led by the media would concentrate on the media conference, the first Woods had given since the sex scandal broke last November. The media was desperate for its time and at last Woods had obliged. This was no televised statement, no quick-fire five minutes. There were no restrictions on questions and there he sat for 35 minutes being fired at. Perhaps he wasn't as open as certain critics would have liked. But he was, unarguably, 'open' and ducked very little. With hindsight it was such a skilled performance. He let on very little but gave across so much.

'I missed my son's first birthday [while in rehab] and that hurts a lot,' he said with the day's killer quote. 'I vowed I would never miss another one. I can't go back to where I was ... it was something I regret and I probably will for the rest of my life.'

Where Woods happened to be was in the middle of the biggest controversy ever to hit golf. When his car crashed into a fire hydrant at the end of his driveway on 27 November last year his life began to unravel. His wife smashed out his windows with a golf club, he was rushed to hospital, he declined to be interviewed by police. Why? There was no implication of his wife's role in the bizarre scenario which will remain a mystery, but nobody really expected there to be. Woods was desperate to take each and every aspect of the blame himself. 'I lied to a lot of people, deceived a lot of people,' he told the packed room. 'I fooled myself as well. The full magnitude of it, it's pretty brutal.'

Woods claimed to 'totally understand' why some of his sponsors dropped him; just as he 'totally understands' the ridicule. The solution, he said, was to carry on his treatment as well as the Buddhist meditating on which he has re-embarked. 'It's not how many Major championships you win, it's how you live your life,' he said, outlining the fresh priorities. 'I need to be a better man going forward than I've been before. If I win Major championships along the way, so be it, but I want to help people along the way.'

Naturally, there were plenty who remained unconvinced of his sincerity and continued to hold up his participation in Georgia as evidence of a Machiavellian reintroduction to the world of big bucks and big kudos. When he delivered his emotional statement a few months before he appeared more likely to don a strait-jacket sooner than a green jacket. 'When I gave that speech in February I had no intentions of playing golf in the near future at all,' he said. 'But then I started hitting balls and started getting the itch to play again. And then Hank [Haney, his coach] came down and we started working again. It felt like old times. That's when I made the decision to play again.'

But there he was – playing again. Interestingly Woods believed he had crossed his Rubicon in his practice round and not the press conference. 'As far as getting out there, I was definitely more nervous,' he said. 'That first tee I didn't know what to expect, I really didn't. I've never been in that position before. To be out there in front of people when I have done some things that are just horrible and for the fans to really want to see me play golf again – that felt great. For them to cheer me after what has transpired in my life is incredible.'

The reception he received as he walked up to the final green was indeed incredible. Fred Couples, his playing partner, called it a 'standing ovation' and even allowing for the fact Augusta doesn't have grandstands to stand up in, it was hard to quibble. Golf fans in general may have yet to be won over, but these golf fans seemingly had been.

The noise had something to do with the growing galleries as the attendance increased towards the 50 000 mark; but more to do with the reaction of Woods, himself. In the past he would treat cheers like he would autograph hunters – with total ambivalence. There he tipped his hat and from the walk from the ninth to the 10th tee did the old ice hockey routine of high-fiving as he slid by. The Iceman had thawed.

'The encouragement I received just blew me away,' he said. 'I know the people here are extremely respectful, but today was something that really touched my heart. I'm going to try to be more respectful to the game and acknowledge the fans like I did today. I haven't done that in the past few years and that was wrong of me. I've made a conscious decision to try to tone my negative outbursts,' he added. 'But consequently I'm sure my positive outbursts will be calmed down as well.'

Fast forward to Sunday and the illusion had been shattered. He had cursed during the play on Saturday and the negative outbursts were fulsome. The American network CBS felt obliged to apologise for Woods' behaviour and so the myth unravelled. Had Woods changed at all? The grotesque advert aired on the eve of Thursday's first round added weight to the cynics' suspicions.

Anybody who saw the ill-timed, ill-considered, just plain ill spot could have been forgiven for thinking that Nike had a new ouija board to market. How else could they explain this macabre 30 seconds in which Woods' father, Earl, makes contact from beyond the grave?

'Tiger, I am prone to be inquisitive, to promote discussion,' came the voice as his son coldly stares into the camera, wearing a cap with the obligatory huge swoosh. 'I want to find out what your thinking was; I want to find out what your feelings are. Did you learn anything?'

So what had he learnt? To listen to advisers who assure him it is OK to use the scandal to flog his sponsors' equipment? To listen to advisers who insist there's nothing at all hypocritical in complaining about the intrusion into his family's privacy and then to parody a private discussion between himself and his dead dad? To listen to advisers who say it's not remotely distasteful to base a marketing campaign on an addict's rehabilitation and in the process borrow words from a dead dad's past and put them into his lifeless mouth?

Yep, Tiger had learnt all of that. Those personal advisers of his must know what they're doing.

But then, did they and do they? Woods had been presented that week as someone he could never be. He will never be some grinning fool interacting with the crowd like a ringmaster, or a desperate busker. We saw in the heat of the contest that while Woods the man might be intent on change, Woods the golfer wants to remain exactly how he was before (OK, minus the club throwing). If he can't put everything he has into all that matters on the golf course – ie winning – then what is the point? Is it possible for the most ferocious competitor the game has ever known to act like it doesn't matter? It was something Woods would have to consider as he drove back down Magnolia Lane 'to take a little time off and kind of re-evaluate things'.

From a purely sporting perspective his reflections should be positive. His words straight afterwards might have suggested a personal disaster but for everyone else this would have been a remarkable performance. Nobody should forget that the last time he had tapped in competitively was 15 November and during his period away he had been in rehab. Forget the whys and wherefores of his absence and consider the golfing aspect. Woods had more than three months off without practising. And he was still able to contend until the very late stages. He will shake off the rust and the ridicule did not appear to affect his self-belief. He will be winning tournaments again very soon and winning some of them quite spectacularly.

But where does he go with his PR game? There's nowhere he really can go now after Augusta. He can only carry on in this absurd charade of the reformed human being gaining his redemption as a reformed champion. No doubt he plans, if given the chance, to right the wrongs of his personal life. But in truth there were very few wrongs to right in his career. Fair enough it would be ideal to see him engaging with the fans, not chucking clubs, not screaming his frustrations. But that's not him. That's Phil Mickelson. Tiger should not be asked to 'live a lie'. There's been too much of that. Augusta proved it. Good guy wins. Bad guy loses. How ridiculous.

A carefully-constructed PR campaign with the intention of evolving Tiger Woods into the nice guy of golf, following his absence from the game over his private life, jarred with reality when it actually came to the world No 1's comeback. This feature coincided with the much-awaited return of the troubled American.

RETURN OF THE WHITE WINGER
By Mark Keohane

THE WHITE SCHOOLBOY WINGER, WITH EXCEPTIONAL TALENT, HAS A RUGBY future in South Africa, and that is the greatest compliment to the transformation of the game.

Transformation will always be an ugly word in South African rugby because of the botched attempts to find some form of equality in racial numbers, but it is this generation of South African players who can be the most content because from here on in the best will play on ability.

The emergence of white Bulls wingers Gerhard van den Heever and Francois Hougaard is also a blessing to the many wonderfully talented black wingers who can comfortably know that in the future they will make a team because they are the best in this country and not because they make up political numbers.

Rugby union for the good schoolboy white winger has been rugby league for the past decade in senior professional rugby because so few teams were prepared to pick white wingers. The easiest out in selecting black players was to find blokes with pace and ask them to catch the ball, run and hopefully score a few tries. White players felt they were competing for 13 places because the two wing options were an exclusive black club. How terrible, but how true of that tortured time in our rugby.

Inevitably when a black winger excelled the general view was there was a better white player somewhere and the black player was there on default. No more.

And bloody hell, it is long overdue.

Everyone associated with rugby underestimated South Africa's return to international rugby and some kind of normality. Mindsets were engrained, politicians made more decisions than coaches and because a coach invariably resorted to type when deciding between two players, the coaches (all of them white at the time) went with what gave them comfort, which was a white player.

This is changing and while the pace of the change will always be a debate, the right selection decisions are being made for the right reasons. It is about ability and not a compromise.

Van den Heever is the symbol that good enough is good enough. Hougaard is a scrumhalf converted to wing, and when Fourie du Preez heads for Japan at the end of the 2011 World Cup, Hougaard is the favourite to play scrumhalf for the Bulls and possibly the Springboks.

But it is Van den Heever who gives every white kid belief that he does not have to play another position if his pedigree is suited to numbers 11 and 14. And he also gives every black winger a similar comfort that wingers in South African rugby will finally be selected on potential and pedigree.

The Bulls, the leaders in South African rugby for the past five years, have to be applauded for embracing the concept of white wingers because it meant that their professional coaches and selectors had to embrace black players in other positions. This has happened and where the Bulls were once stereotyped as the conservatives and inherent racists of South African rugby, they are now the most progressive in their thinking and selections. Their feeder system was built with brick and cement, and not purple prose.

Others must learn from this because the future and health of the game in this country won't be determined by white and black, but in the right identification of talent.

When last have you heard a young white South African player say he is going overseas because he is prejudiced by the quota system? It does not happen and that is testimony to a changing generation and a natural shift in thinking.

Former Springbok Ollie le Roux shares the story of Mark Andrews telling a few All Blacks (over a few beers during a week with the Barbarians) that South African players and New Zealand players were similar in that they were so passionate about their rugby. Le Roux's story, told to me and many others, was that New Zealander Greg Sommerville countered Andrews' view as such: 'No mate, we are not similar. We are passionate. You guys are just plain angry.'

South African players, for a good 10 years, were angry. And I am talking about the white players. They didn't know what they should think, what value system they should embrace. Rugby, when the world detested apartheid South Africa, was a bastion for the white player to fight for something he did not necessarily believe in but was supposed to believe in. Rugby was for whites and soccer for blacks. Not this generation.

Rugby, in the past few years, has become a game for South Africa's new generation and not a crutch by which to determine an identity from an abnormal past.

South Africa's new generation hurt when they lose but they don't take it as an affront on the psyche of this country. They have not failed a system in which the colour of their skin determined superiority. When they lose they have failed their own ability or not been good enough to win. And they move on to the next week.

This generation is privileged because of the normality it enjoys. The previous generation must delight at this change and not resent that they could not experience a similar sporting experience. The turbulence of the past decade was a necessary evil in the quest for Nirvana.

South African rugby is not there yet, but it is headed to a place where there is more sunshine than rain. Van den Heever is proof of this. What a talent. What a joy to watch. Similarly Hougaard and the Cheetahs' Lionel Mapoe.

Bryan Habana and JP Pietersen remain the premier wingers in South Africa and are among the best in the world. But no country has three youngsters in the class of Van der Heever, Hougaard and Mapoe that close to national recognition.

These three jewels have to be polished because they inspire the 10-year-old newcomers to the game to know that if you are South African and you are good enough you will be picked for the Springboks.

A good white player does not have to seek comfort in the jersey of another country. The player who leaves because of this belief does not distrust the system; his anxiety is self-inflicted and a reflection on doubt that he is good enough. Similarly the good black player.

It feels good to be South African, but it must feel even better to be a South African rugby player turning 20. They play sport in a country when historically sport was too often a political statement and a misguided tool to reinforce stereotypes.

Thank you Gerhard van den Heever, Francois Hougaard and Lionel Mapoe, and thank you to those coaches who pick the best because they are the best. It is a greater gift than the 1995 and 2007 World Cups because this game's well-being must be built on integrity and not on silverware.

There was a difficult time in recent South African rugby history when wingers were the obligatory 'quota' selection. That in itself led to talented white wingers turning to another position, or another sport. Finally, though, the writer argued that the current generation of youngsters is privileged because there is now normality when it comes to selecting players.

FALL OF AN UNTOUCHABLE
By Peter Roebuck

LALIT MODI IS A MIXED BAG. IN HIS TIME HE HAS BEEN BEHIND BARS AND high on the rich list, and indeed might appear in both places again. A maverick in the mainstream, a wild card in the pack, a mover and shaker, an opportunist, a rascal and probably a scoundrel, he surrounds himself with sycophants, takes risks and always doubles the bet.

In a few years he has presided over a massive revolution in the game, tapped into India's newfound confidence and cricket's newfound daring and cut so many corners and favoured so many friends and made so much money that now he totters and may fall. At times Modi resembles a media baron of the old school, riding roughshod over the rules. Along the way he has been accused of nepotism, corruption, rigging tenders, promoting heavy gambling and sundry other offences, and all of it in a day's work.

Ego, ambition, calculation and audacity were all wrapped up in a character that knows no modesty and little restraint. Modi believes he belongs in the highest realms and yet also on their fringes for he is immature and wants power without responsibility, money without accountability, fun without consequences.

Not that he is alone in his disdain for correct custom, for the grave elders, too, have had their snouts in the trough. Indeed he can be viewed as a man of his time, cynical of propriety, scorning the old guard. Modi's problem is that he yearns for power and respectability and at the same time wants to fly by his own lights. It does not work. Outsiders, chancers, are not protected. They live and die by their wits.

As Bob Dylan once put it, 'to live outside the law you must be honest'. Serious politicians will not forget that in the past month he has brought down a minister and in part caused the Indian government to endure a vote of no-confidence in parliament.

Modi has not kept his sheet clean. Indeed he has shown no inclination to play by the rules. Now the state itself is set against him. A brash interloper has pushed his luck too far. Whatever largesse Modi has bestowed, however many praise singers he has hired (and the television commentators have not spared themselves), he cannot escape the forthcoming examination. He runs the Indian Premier League, not India. He is an entrepreneur, not a power broker.

Hitherto little attention has been paid to Modi's past, yet his present can be found in it. No one wants to be a spoilsport. Nor has much attention been paid to the present, anyhow until he ruffled the wrong feathers. Till then he kept rising, kept pushing, kept pressing, riding a populist wave, ignoring protocols and practices.

However, a man cannot so easily escape his own shadow. Biographies have been written but while his sun was at its zenith they were ignored. They reveal a chequered past and forecast the current shenanigans. As a young man Modi was convicted of abduction and possessing cocaine by the courts in Florida, that sunniest and most unscrupulous of locations. Ever wilful, he had gone to study at an American university after dropping out of high school in India. Presumably the brashness of the new order appealed to him. Certainly the freedom of a university campus suited him better than the cramping of boarding school life in his own country. A picture forms of a spoilt boy with a sense of adventure and a high opinion of himself.

After plea bargaining, Modi was put on probation for five years and given a hundred hours of community service. Complaining of ill health, exploiting wealth and contacts, he was swiftly allowed to go back to India. The details about the abduction are unclear but it was a bad business. His exasperated parents expected him to join the firm in the traditional manner. His father and grandfather had made their fortune in industry, and had built a town for that purpose, named naturally enough Modinagar. But Lalit was not to be restrained by old Indian conservatism. He did not want to follow in anyone's footsteps, he wanted to mix with the mighty, make his fortune, secure influence and dominate the scene. His IPL parties are notoriously flashy and fleshy. They start an hour after the match and finish at 4am, with Russian girls laid on and gawkers paying the equivalent of R9 000 for the privilege of joining the inner sanctum. The old ways could not compete with that. Modi wanted it all, and he wanted it now.

Far from returned to the bosom of his household, Modi pursued his own interests. Far from letting his parents choose his partner as tradition dictated or even seeking their permission to marry his own nomination, he met a woman nine years his senior, whose first husband had been convicted of a scam in Saudi Arabia, and promptly decided to wed her. Modi convinced his grandmother and duly defied his parents.

His wife had moved in high circles and came with contacts of her own. Indeed her family has become embroiled in the nepotism that has put Modi's position in peril. Her husband's next move was to shift from bustling Mumbai to the quieter pastures of Rajasthan, a change of venue suggesting that business was slow. Undeterred, Modi soon forged alliances with the right wing party ruling the state and was often to be found at the elbow of its chief minister, a position that helped him considerably when the call for cricket started to ring in its ears. Hitherto cricket and Modi had been mere acquaintances, now they became close pals. Cricket provided the opening he craved. What is an empire builder till he has an empire?

Nothing was allowed to block his path. Thwarted in his attempts to secure election to the Rajasthan Cricket Board, Modi applied under an alias and with the help of sweeping rule changes introduced by his chum the chief minister, took his place at the high table. He was underway. Before long he had teamed up with Sharad Pawar, a senior figure in cricket and government, and had played a big part in bringing down the previously indestructible Jagmohan Dalmiya. Pawar took office at the Board of Control for Cricket in India (BCCI). Modi's star was rising.

Till now he had not been much of a businessman. Although considerable, his wealth had been inherited or was a by-product of marriage. At first he lived in a house owned by his wife's father. Cricket changed all that. Within a few years he was able to occupy a suite of rooms at the Rambagh Palace, the most luxurious hotel in the state, and could summon ministers to his side.

Twenty20 was his making as it could be his undoing. The BCCI disliked the format and did not want to take part in the initial World Twenty20 played in South Africa. Modi saw its possibilities. When India unexpectedly won that first event, he saw the ferment that followed and knew his time had come.

The IPL, his greatest creation apart from his own career, captures Modi's character. Along the way it has become a hotbed of intrigue, murky cash, dubious tenders, tax dodges, tax raids, wild parties, political rows, match-fixing allegations, film stars, gooey-eyed girls, rigged bidding and manifest nepotism. It might be possible to find a member of Modi's family who has not reaped the rewards but it's not easy. In any case he could console them by giving them a lift on his private jet or aboard his yacht. Modi's lavish lifestyle has been observed by detectives, sleuths as they are called in India, with its relish for rich text and felicitous phrases, operating at the behest of the revenue service. The taxmen cometh. Those not directly involved in the froth and bubble of the product are surprised that the IPL enjoys the tax breaks permitted to the BCCI on the grounds that it is a non-profit organisation. The IPL has no such role. Observers wanted to know why a bunch of cricketing profiteers were not required to contribute to the fiscus?

Why had the IPL been treated so generously? Why, for that matter, had Maharashtra (Pune) waved its entertainment tax for the IPL? It started to stink. To their frustration the hundreds of revenue officials studying the accounts cannot find numerous vital documents.

Modi's problems did not begin till he overplayed his hand. The IPL decided that the time had come to introduce two new franchises. Excitement was high and a bidding war began. Except that the process was not transparent; indeed it was rigged. Two years beforehand Modi had promised Pune that it'd be given a franchise. That begged the question – how did he know? Ahmedabad was guaranteed the second franchise, mostly because his brother ran the state. Family members were part owners of three other franchises: Rajasthan, Kolkata and Punjab. Another relation owned the online and digital rights to IPL. It smelt like rotten fish.

Modi could not control the final verdict but he could manipulate the bidding. His strategy was to limit those entitled to bid and then tried to fix the result by giving dud information to other tenders. Telling them that $300 million was enough when he knew his choices had bid higher. Unfortunately Cochin called his bluff and outbid his brother. Furious, Modi started to spread rumours about the ownership of Kochi and pointed out that a minister's girlfriend was involved, forcing the minister to resign due to a conflict of interest.

It was a mistake. Modi had made some powerful enemies. Politicians started to ask questions about the ownership of the other franchises, and to seek confirmation that Modi had offered the unwanted victors $50 million to withdraw. A hue and cry ensued. Modi had lost control of the game.

Unable to stop the focus on his own affairs, Modi raised the stakes, defied the BCCI and even Pawar, hitherto his lord and protector, and the next chairman of the International Cricket Council. Doubtless Modi reckons that the higher it goes the more it will be buried, and he might be right. But India has a vigorous democracy and a media, and the story is a corker.

Meanwhile, other sleuths are exploring the role in the IPL of various bookmakers, most of them based in Dubai, where most of jiggery pokery has its origins. Rumours persist that results have been fixed and that a few of the teams dance to the bookies' tune. While admitting the point is hard to substantiate, former Test captains of high reputation are convinced that the IPL has been corrupted.

Hitherto the prospects might seem bleak, but the IPL is not all bad, and nor is its founder. To the contrary, it has been a roaring success, with vibrant crowds, dancing guys and dolls, large television audiences, rising interest around the world, great players on the field, youngsters given a chance, big hitting, fast bowling, leg spin, close finishes and wild excitement. Hitherto regarded in some quarters as a staid game played in pristine whites, cricket has put on some garish clothes, shorn itself of solemnity and let down its hair.

It's not to every taste. Sometimes, though, revolutionaries are required. Kerry Packer took cricket into the night, turned it into a television spectacle. Modi has taken the next step, shortening its running time so that it could compete with soccer, rugby, hockey and the rest. Of course cricket has survived, confirming that it was merely pretending to be grave. Shakespeare and Mozart wrote farces so it'd be absurd for a game to be continually grim. Thanks to Packer, Modi and necessity, cricket has learnt to laugh as well as cry.

Modi, too, survives, for now. He stands before our eyes, beaming, unabashed, confident of his position, believing that he understands power and money and so destiny. Muhammad Ali said he was not so much conceited as convinced. Modi is both, and thinks he can ride out any storm.

Danger lies not so much in cricket as in the tax inspectors poring over his books. Are his tracks well enough covered or did hubris take its toll? Most likely a deal will be done, with Modi's wings clipped but not sufficiently to bring him crashing down to earth. After all, he did not travel alone.

Lalit Modi, the smiling face behind the Indian Premier League and the man who made millionaires of a whole breed of new professional cricketers, seemingly had it all. Then allegations of nepotism, match-fixing, tax dodging, murky cash and rigged bidding threatened to take down the IPL's most recognisable face.

IT'S NOT ABOUT THE GAME
By Mark Keohane

SOUTH AFRICA, WERE IT NOT FOR THE NOT-SO-SMALL MATTER OF HOSTING the Fifa World Cup, would not be at the tournament. Bafana Bafana, over the past decade, have not been good enough to be a factor in African football, let alone make an impression globally.

It is why the side, a month before the World Cup, was ranked 90th.

So why the absolute nonsense when it comes to expectation surrounding Bafana Bafana? If the side should make it to the second round it would be the equivalent of winning the tournament. By rights, they have no claims to a top-two pool finish. By rights, they have no claim to being at the World Cup.

A large portion of the soccer media in this country is culpable for creating an illusion that there should be some kind of hope for Bafana Bafana. These media types confuse the support of the national side with the national side winning against the best.

The support of Bafana Bafana by all South Africans has been incredible and my observation is of a nation supporting their team regardless of history or racial make-up.

Many in the white community are wearing the colours of Bafana Bafana even though they don't like soccer, be it the South African version or that played in Europe and by the likes of Manchester United, Chelsea, Real Madrid and Barcelona. I know it is difficult to believe there are those who don't enjoy the beautiful game, but in this country (like rugby-fixated New Zealand) they exist.

Despite this, every school has celebrated Bafana Bafana and the World Cup and every local sporting code has added its voice to the soccer community in this country.

For most South Africans the buzz is about the tournament and not the inability of Bafana Bafana to beat anyone of note. It is about having the best players and teams in the world here and it is about the opportunity it gives every South African to sell what is good about this country.

It is a chance to show off as South Africans and, having been in the international wilderness for much of the 1970s and '80s, it forces the world to focus on Africa's southern tip. It is about recognition that South Africa exists; not about Bafana Bafana's inability to score a goal.

The South African Football Association (Safa) has agreed to pay the squad R1 million for each goal scored. This was explained as wanting to reward the players should they not advance beyond the first round. Some have argued it is rewarding mediocrity and that there is more financial gain in losing 5-2 than winning 1-0. It is an argument difficult to fault, but those holding this view miss the point that the cash offer is as much an illusion as Bafana Bafana's prospects at the tournament.

Given Bafana Bafana's goal-scoring record against tier one nations, Safa could dangle a R1 billion-a-goal carrot to the country's strikers and still know the money is safe. Safa's only risk is that of an own goal from the opposition.

The significance of the World Cup in South Africa is not about how many goals Bafana Bafana scores or if the side manages the odd draw. Of greater importance is that it proves to a patronising Western world that South Africa, on behalf of Africa, has the capacity to entertain and produce a show the equal of any other continent.

The local focus in the countdown to kick-off should be at the sight of the magnificent new stadiums. Instead of wondering if Bafana can score a goal, know that South Africa does not have to stand back to any country when it comes to putting on a show. The clever caps should be applauded for their stadium designs and the hard hats for the manual hardship it takes to build a stadium.

We should be applauding Danny Jordaan for the job he has done and there should be further applause for the behind-the-scenes workings that have enabled South Africa to be seated and ready to sit soccer's greatest exam.

It is crucial we deal in reality at this time because there are too many column inches and advertising campaigns given to the romance of Bafana Bafana actually winning a game, and for that matter Matthew Booth actually getting a game.

On the subject of Booth, why all the media hype about him and why the prominence of his face on so many advertising campaigns? There are far better black players not enjoying the profile.

Is it because Booth is white and there's a feeling among sponsors that this will encourage white local support? If that is the case it is as misguided as the belief that Bafana Bafana has a hope in hell at the tournament.

Bafana Bafana does not need a white face to garner white support because this tournament is not about Bafana Bafana, but about South Africa's standing as a country.

If we can all see that, then we can all accept the limitations of Bafana Bafana and we can all drop the unrealistic goal-scoring and match-winning expectation.

The only ones feeling the pressure should be all of us local South Africans because it is our attitude that will dictate how this World Cup is remembered; not that of a national soccer squad not good enough to be at the World Cup.

The success of the 2010 Fifa World Cup was never going to be about how Bafana Bafana fared on the field. Much more significantly was that South Africa could prove to the sceptics that it had the ability to put on a tournament that would rank with any that had gone before. Which proved to be the case.

GOING TO THE EXTREME
By Gary Lemke

A DAY BEFORE ATTEMPTING THE MOST CHALLENGING SWIM ANYONE HAS yet undertaken – a one kilometre journey across the glacial waters of Lake Pumori, at an altitude of 5 200 metres and just below the summit of Mt Everest – Lewis Pugh thought of death. In his final dress rehearsal, wearing only a Speedo costume, cap and goggles in unimaginably cold 2°C melted ice, the 40-year-old very nearly became a postscript to another ambitious environmental campaign to highlight the effects of climate change on the Himalayan region.

Pugh dived into the near-freezing waters, as he did in being the first person to swim across the North Pole in 2007, but quickly found himself fearing for his life. 'I learnt there and then that you can't bully Mt Everest,' he said weeks later back in South Africa. 'As a former soldier in the elite British SAS, they used to talk about the initials standing for Speed, Aggression, Surprise. When I left the SAS and went into swimming I decided that the best way to tackle cold was with speed and aggression. You have to just dive in and commit to it 100%.'

Such tactics had worked everywhere before. But everywhere is not Everest. 'It had taken two hours to hike up to the lake across excruciating terrain and, at that altitude, it was utterly exhausting.' He then proceeds to re-enact the hike. Left foot placed in front of right and a small step is taken, then another, slowly. His breath quickens and there's a cough. 'There's a lot of coughing,' he says.

Once at the lake, he reverted to his SAS tried-and-tested training. 'I dived in and went as fast as I could. That had worked in swimming across the North Pole. But, after 300 metres I was terrified ... I couldn't breathe properly at this altitude. I felt like vomiting ... my heart was pounding [his heart rate monitor slipped down his chest, but he guesses it was around 190 beats per minute] and I had no stamina. For the first time in my life I had to swim breaststroke to survive. Twice I thought I would "go under". Just one lung full of water and that's it ...'

The next day was the swim itself. 'Everything I had learnt up to now I was going to have to unlearn. There had to be a radical tactical shift in approach. In extreme swim attempts such as this one, there are four ways I go about it. The first is working out how I'm going to do it, the second is to place as much emphasis on safety as possible – the army teaches you not to take undue risks – the third is to try mitigate those risks and the fourth is to delegate it all to someone else. In this case it was a major general [Tim Sewell of the British Army] leading the expedition.

'We undertook to do everything differently on the day itself. Where I always used to use crawl, I changed to breaststroke for the first time in my life. Where I had gone fast, now I was going slowly. Where I used to be psyched, now I was frightened.'

Breaking news of his achievement appeared on Sky on 23 May. 'A British endurance swimmer has summoned the peak of his powers to become the first person to swim under the summit of Mt Everest. Lewis Gordon Pugh battled freezing waters wearing only a pair of Speedos, a cap and goggles to cross the one kilometre glacial lake next to the Khumbu Glacier. He came close to drowning during test swims for the event amid bouts of altitude sickness on the Pumori Lake, which sits 17 000 feet [5 181 metres] above sea level. But an adapted approach saw him through to complete the swim in a time of 22 min 51 sec.'

Ah, the old, brave Brit battles to victory cliché? Sitting in a Cape Town office I asked him to nail his allegiance to a patriotic mast. 'I spent five years with the British SAS and it left an indelible mark on me. I have a deep fondness and a deep loyalty for Britain. But I buried my father in Simonstown and if I didn't feel South African why would I go as far as to bury my father here?'

And it was his father who sowed the environmental seed. 'He was at an atomic bomb test in 1952. He used to describe that moment when the bomb went off and afterwards when he had to go back to pick up all the dead animals. That left quite a mark on him. He really instilled in me the need to love and protect the environment.'

What had kept him going during those agonising 23-odd minutes? 'It's a strange thing what your mind does in extreme conditions. Actually, I imagined I was back at the Sea Point pavilion with my mother and Jack Russell dog. And I found myself talking to the Jack Russell.'

Pugh has no more extreme swims planned for the immediate future and likely nothing in the next two years, if at all. He plans to drop the 'swimming' part and become a global environmental campaigner, spreading his message as far afield as the United Nations.

He is adamant that those who don't believe that global warming is significantly changing the face of the planet are in denial. 'I wouldn't even call them climate change sceptics, they're climate change denialists. The same people who don't think the glaciers are melting – be it in the Arctic, the Alps, Central Africa, Antarctica or the Himalayas – probably think that Elvis Presley is still alive.'

Death only visits once, and Pugh has on many occasions had time to think and reflect.

On 12 May, some 11 days before the Pick n Pay-SAP Everest Challenge, Pugh was shocked into thinking, again, about the meaning of life. 'Just had a very sobering moment,' he tweeted. 'A body of a Nepalese sherpa has been carried past us, down hill. He died on Mt Everest five years ago.' A month later and the image remains vividly etched into Pugh's mind. 'You should have seen the size of him, so small. He was in a body bag, and he died trying to help some guys scale Everest.' There's a quiet anger in his voice.

The sherpas are skilled mountaineers who exist on the slopes of Everest but many have lost their lives helping those who want to get to the summit. They are the helpers who fetch and carry for their 'guests', but many pay the ultimate price for doing so. 'The nature of what they do really struck me,' says Pugh. 'There are memorials dedicated to those who have died up there. Why would anyone die to help some rich white guys get to the peak of Everest?'

He's even more outspoken when he discusses the impact of the BP oil spill in the Gulf of Mexico that cost $1.25 billion in a cleaning up operation in the first six weeks after erupting on the sea bed on 20 April. 'Criminal,' he interrupts. 'They [BP top executives] should be criminally prosecuted. They should go to jail. What I can't understand is why people haven't responded more vigorously, by boycotting BP.'

To help one imagine the size of the spill, there is a fascinating internet link where you can 'move the spill'. I typed in Johannesburg. Now think of Mafikeng, Rustenburg, up the N1 towards Polokwane, down to Middleburg and Secunda and through Vanderbijlpark and Potchefstroom. It's an environmental disaster.

'As are the melting ice caps,' Pugh says. 'Speaking to the sherpas on Everest, each one has a story. So much has changed in the past 20 years. Most glaciers are melting away. The glaciers in the Himalayas are not just ice. They are a lifeline and provide water to approximately two billion people.'

It's been two weeks since Pugh successfully swam one kilometre across Lake Pumori. But while he speaks coherently and with absolute authority, you get the impression the ordeal has taken a staggering toll on him, physically and mentally. He is humble, gentlemanly, professional. A law student product from the University of Cape Town and University of Cambridge, he became a maritime lawyer in London but has devoted his existence to public speaking and environmental campaigning.

He chose to deliver his message by swimming in extreme conditions, because he enjoys the sport. He reckons he clocks up around 2 000 metres a day in 'normal temperatures' but has chosen to be different. One can't comprehend what he has achieved, not only under Everest or the North Pole. 'You would die,' he says matter of factly, when asked what would happen to Joe Average if they were to dive into 2°C water.

Would he be prepared to die in the duty of environmental campaigning? 'No ... it would be a silly thing to do [die] in the process ...' and his voice fades, as if he's been there a million times before in frequent bouts of solitude.

South Africa's inspirational environmental campaigner, Lewis Pugh, had just arrived back in the country after undertaking what was probably his final harrowing challenge, a one kilometre journey across the near-freezing waters on Mt Everest. Afterwards, Pugh called the feature 'the most accurate account that had been written about him in 20 years'.

FOOD FOR THOUGHT
By Mark Keohane

THESE MEN AND WOMEN DON'T SAY MUCH. IT WOULD BE ILL-ADVISED AND it would be interpreted as ill-discipline. Here, in the uncompromising environment of the Infantry School in Oudtshoorn, the ethos is to listen, to obey and not to question. This is a soldier's world and only a few of those who have been seduced by the prospect of boxing in the next Olympics will get to London in 2012. Boxing may be their passion, but the military is a more probable end for most of them.

They arrived in Oudtshoorn in January – more than a hundred young men and women – with fists of fury, good intentions and ambitions of Olympic and Commonwealth gold. They came knowing they would be taught to box and schooled in military, with the allure of a fixed monthly income, a bed, and three guaranteed meals a day.

The best of the hundred is Siphamandla Natyandela, just 20 years old and a regular winner of medals among South Africa's elite flyweight amateur boxers.

Natyandela never wanted to be a soldier. He had no interest in rifles, armed combat and wearing a uniform. He is a boxer, he says. The boots of a boxer are different to those of a soldier. So are the steps the two take. A boxer is expected to dance; a military man to march. A boxer patrols the ring; a military man a border post. One uses hands to win; the other cannot rely on such innocence.

This kid is no soldier but he wants to be in Oudtshoorn. He wants to get up at 4am each day and run 10 kilometres. He wants to report to military training during the day because it gives him a pass to boxing training in the evening. He wants to dismantle an opponent's defence, even if it means he must first learn to dismantle rifles during the day. Natyandela lives for those night sessions, a combination of push-ups, weights, banging the heavy bag and working the speedball. If his fitness allows it, he gets to prove he can box. And his fitness is good because he came to box, all 51 kilograms of this South African Olympic hopeful.

Being in Delta Company allows him to box. It also ensures he eats every day.

'The food is good … very good,' he says. 'I have everything I need: Good training, medical assistance and the use of the best equipment. But the food … it is very good.'

Gideon Sam is president of Sascoc and the most influential sports administrator in South Africa. He was elected to fix South African Olympic sport after the dismal failure at the 2008 Beijing Olympics, when South Africa won just one medal.

'Never can that be acceptable,' said Sam at the time. 'Twelve medals by 2012 … that has to be our goal. If we don't think big we shouldn't be here.'

Cynics scoffed. A few of the more forgiving applauded Sam's boldness, while some questioned the man's sanity. South Africa's swimmers had medal potential but only a couple of athletes were ranked in the world's top 10. Where would South Africa find the dozen to dazzle us with their medals?

'Boxing,' said Sam. 'South Africa has won 19 Olympic medals in boxing, but since international readmission in 1992 we haven't won one. Don't tell me we don't have boxers in this country … what there hasn't been is a blueprint about how to maximise the natural talent by creating opportunities through institutions like the military.'

Sam, his roots in the boxing stronghold of the Eastern Cape, accepted there was a problem in talent identification but also in building Olympic and Commonwealth champions because the few good ones sacrificed Olympic glory for the more immediate demand of feeding their families. Many of the best amateur boxers are brought up on a diet of poverty and pity, so cash will always be the king decision-maker in determining when the amateur turns professional.

'Financial hardship means our boys can't be blamed for giving up a dream for money, so we at Sascoc, as the custodian of South African sport, had to find a way to negate this conflict, show these talented fighters we care, not just about their medal prospects, but also about their well-being,' says Sam. 'What we now have is a young boxer with a dream but also with a job. If he doesn't make it as a boxer, he still has a future in the military, with the security of a salary and the opportunity to further his education.'

Welterweight Bongani Mwelase won Commonwealth gold in 2006, turned professional and is fighting Lovemore Ndou for the IBO title in September. Hawk Makepula and Philip Ndou were Olympic fighters who won world championship belts. Two fighters from five Olympic Games over 18 years: the return is abysmal, but then so was the investment.

'I look at these young boxers in front of me [today] and I say to you that you are here because you had a dream. We are here to make sure you will always have the opportunity to try and live that dream,' said Sam in addressing the 100-plus fighters in Oudtshoorn. 'We care and we believe in you. Never stop believing in yourself. Never stop believing in your dream.'

SANDF General Aubrey Sedibe was equally emotional and passionate. 'The Delta Company [of the SANDF Infantry School in Oudtshoorn] has brought new life to the Western Cape boxing community. The synergy of military sport and civilian partnership we are experiencing in their region should be a catalyst of a chain reaction for other sporting codes. The drought of medals during world sporting events by SA teams can be terminated by strengthening the bond of all South African sports organisations. It starts here in Oudtshoorn.'

Natyandela recently went home to Ngangelizwe, Umtata. It was a rare occasion, he says, because he owes it to his family to be in Oudtshoorn realising the dream.

'It is always nice to be home, but they know I want to make it to London in 2012, and to do that I cannot be living and training in Umtata, because that way there is no guarantee about your safety, your income and how many times you eat.'

He doesn't want to be a soldier but he knows that to be a boxer he has to also be a solider. Also the food is good at the Infantry School. Natyandela mentions that more than once, but so are the grooming, the guidance and the discipline.

'When you send a soldier to war he has to be trained to be emotionally strong and his body has to be the strongest possible. Despite the natural talent of these intakes, many of them don't have that discipline because of circumstance and environment. We change that quickly here,' says Corporal Nneko Mokoena, the voice behind the commands to punch, swivel, bob and weave.

Mokoena's speciality is boxing so there is more enthusiasm than fear in his tone, but the boxers are no special cases in the day. They are treated as soldiers first and then boxers, and their schedule is that of a solider who can throw a punch and hopefully take one as well because only 12 of the 100 will make it to a training camp in Cuba, and of those 12 not all will be certain of Olympic selection.

'Delta Force is just one of the selection points,' says Sam. 'To make it you are going to have to be bloody good. We aren't sending anyone to London out of goodwill. This is no charity. It is a chance to box for your country, but even bigger than that it is a chance to have a career and to live better. We know only a small percentage can ultimately make it, and that is just where the system has failed the majority who don't. Projects like Delta Company are a starting point in fixing that.'

'Run solider run ... mark time ... company halt ... about turn ... shoulder arms ...' Uniforms, guns, lots of screaming or more appropriately controlled chaos. Oudtshoorn Infantry School is not a place for boxers, but one for soldiers with a few boxers among them.

'Punch, swivel ... left ... left ... right ... jab ... jab ... punch.'

Sam doesn't hold back his enthusiasm.

'Cuba, boys ... Cuba is the promised land.'

Cuba is where 12 of these boxers will go because no country does Olympic boxing better than Cuba.

'To be the best you learn from the best,' says Sam.

Boxing has given Cuba 32 of their 65 Olympic gold medals, and at the 2008 Beijing Olympics Jackson Chauke was South Africa's only representative.

'Unacceptable,' says Sam. 'We want at least three boxing medals in London in 2012. To get three medals we can't send one boxer.'

Natyandela dreams of owning one of those three medals. But for now, at three in the afternoon, he must first march before he can dance ... 'left, left, left right left ...'

He doesn't like the heavy boots. No boxer does. He wants to dance, but he knows to dance he first has to march.

'Soldier', screams the corporal. Only tonight will he be a boxer again. That is why he is here. To box. He can cope with being a soldier first because tonight he gets to box, to rest and to eat ... good food; very good food.

Amateur boxing had over the years been one of South Africa's most successful Olympic codes with 19 medals pre-isolation. Since 1992, there has been a drought. Radical new steps have been taken though to reap rewards in London 2012 and beyond. Finally there is a structure and proper planning.

AUGUST 2010

VOYAGE OF DISCOVERY
By Mark Gleeson

ON THE LAST FRIDAY OF AUGUST, VASCO DA GAMA WILL MARK THEIR ENTRY into the top flight of South African professional football in front of a potential crowd of 50 000 spectators at Cape Town's new World Cup stadium.

It is the most important match ever in the history of what started out as a social and sporting club for the Portuguese community in the Mother City and is now the most unlikely of professional sporting franchises.

Sceptics might suggest it is the biggest game they will ever play. Everything will go downhill after the heady heights of starting your first-ever Premiership season with a match against the mighty Orlando Pirates, at home and as part of a double-header attraction with neighbours Ajax Cape Town, that is hoped will fill the stadium to capacity, riding on a wave of post-World Cup euphoria. Vasco's ambitious crew has other ideas, though. Survival, they admit, would be top of the agenda but actually, almost conspiratorially, their sights are set on a top-eight place this season. If they achieve that, it will be a success that would rank among SA's best sporting fairytales. The club has long been a thriving amateur set-up, providing teams from U7 level upwards. Several South African internationals had their formative years in Vasco's set-up, two of them from the fabled 1996 African Nations Cup winning side – Andre Arendse and Shaun Bartlett – and the Cape Town Spurs side that won the league and cup 'Double' in 1995 drew its backbone from former Vasco players.

Vasco's first team made its own way over the years, right up to the second tier of South African football before selling the franchise. That became FC Cape Town, who in March beat Kaizer Chiefs in the Nedbank Cup.

Having lost their status, Vasco continued briefly as an amateur club until members decided they wanted to be competitive again. Four years ago, 31 of them clubbed together to buy the status of Strandfontein, a club in the Vodacom League, effectively the third tier of the domestic game. The purchase price was R225 000.

Two of the directors have since been bought out, leaving 29 controlling the club, dipping into their pockets and watching proudly as the club raced up the ranks again. All but one of these directors hails from the city's Portuguese-speaking community and are either entrepreneurial businessmen or professionals.

In four years, Vasco moved from the third tier on to the brink of promotion to the Absa Premiership. This they achieved on a dramatic March day at their own grounds in Parow, with some 5 000 spectators packed in on a sweltering afternoon, when the temperatures peaked in the mid-30s, by scoring a second-half penalty to conclude a two-legged victory over Black Leopards. 'It was one hell of a party that night,' says barman Tony de Andrade.

The club lies off Frans Conradie Drive in Cape Town's northern suburbs, its grounds busy from late afternoon with the enthusiastic noise of teams training. The evening traffic home provides an equally voluminous soundtrack as it whizzes by. On the other side, the Shoshozola Meyl suburban train, its puke purple and aqua signage almost necessitating sunglasses, creaks to a halt at the nearby station. Overhead, the club's grounds are directly on the flight path into Cape Town International Airport. A British Airways jet is low enough for its noise to catch the attention of the players, whose heads momentarily jerk skywards and then just as quickly back to their training game.

In recent years, Vasco have acquired a more glamorous neighbour. Directly across the road lies Ikamva, the headquarters of Ajax Cape Town, its fields greener, its livery livelier and with the all-together modern feel of a happening professional club. The signage for the Ajax fan shop stares directly at the Vasco ground, almost mockingly symbolising the gulf between the two. Ajax were always intended as a sleek professional outfit, to profit from their Dutch connection and breed potential world stars. Vasco find themselves now on the same level by happenstance. Vasco's pitch is worn through overuse and the clubhouse tatty, although the bonhomie sipping a Castle at the bar is full of the enthusiasm that surrounds these halcyon days. There is no pretence here; this is an old-fashioned football club. On a windswept, winter's night, coach Carlos das Neves is running his players through 90 minutes of training. As he's cajoling two groups in separate six-a-side scrimmages, the Ajax players are exiting their ground, heading home from training in a convoy of opulent vehicles. 'Our guys go home in a lift club,' jokes Kyle de Souza, the club's top supporter, also a director and who never misses a training session.

The transition from effectively an amateur side to professional outfit is going to be a dramatic one for Vasco in the next weeks. Less than a month before the start of the new campaign, Das Neves had yet to settle on a single new signing. Indeed, he had little idea what his squad would look like. 'Four-and-a-half weeks to go and we don't have a side, but we decided to be careful and not to rush into anything. We spent a lot of time looking. We've been very careful in our selection because we also don't want to lose the heart and soul of the club,' says the coach.

It was his signature style in his playing days, as a classy midfielder for Hellenic, that Das Neves always seemed to have so much time on the ball and so maybe in management too. Ahead of them, though, is potentially a most torrid time. 'What could we really do, some say we are not ready or we'll never be ready. We could have sold the club again but who has the money nowadays for a PSL franchise anyway? We've decided we've got to give it a go, give it our best shot. No one said it was going to be easy.'

The club's nominated home ground this season is the Bellville Stadium, just a few kilometres from their Parow training base. Cape Town clubs have turned their nose up at the athletics venue in the past, as it is rather unglamorously situated next to the Tygervalley shopping centre, while its open stands leave spectators exposed to the rain, wind or beating sun, whichever the Mother City throws at them.

But it is also a venue that visiting teams will not relish playing at. Teams from the rest of the country, be it Gauteng, KwaZulu-Natal or the Free State, have never enjoyed trips to Cape Town. Before they've even set foot off the plane, they are already expecting the wind to pump, their opponents to be physical and the supporters to be abusive.

This will work in Vasco's favour in the coming campaign, if they can make Cape Town a fortress, as Ajax and Santos have managed over the years, they stand a chance of some success. Away days will be difficult, but enough points at home could see them survive.

Last season, Vasco had a squad of 22 players – 'two for every position,' explains their coach. He has been in the job for the past 10 years. 'The longest-serving coach, except for Jomo Sono, and he hired himself,' he jokes as he sits in Vasco's version of Anfield's famous boot room, off to the side of their change rooms. This season, Vasco will aim for a squad size of 25. They have just more than a week before the transfer window closes at the end of August to finalise their make-up. Signings in the last weeks have included the 35-year-old Sibusiso Zuma, once the captain of Bafana Bafana but now in the autumn of his career, and Malawi international midfielder Joseph Kamwendo, who has arrived on loan from Orlando Pirates as he seeks more playing time.

There have been some 60 trialists who have come through Vasco over the past six weeks, eager for a platform to launch, or in the case of a considerable number re-launch, their careers in the PSL. 'We have become the dumping ground after all the other sides have dumped what they don't want,' Das Neves chuckles. Few of the trialists impressed. 'I will only sign players who are better than what I've got.'

But what Das Neves had last season, and with which he won the National First Division title, does not, even by his own admission, cut the mustard. So a major overhaul is on the cards.

Conventional wisdom will have it that Vasco will have to spend liberally to come even close to their goals. 'No,' says Mario das Neves, de facto managing director of the club. 'We are going to run to a tight budget.' He determinedly insists it can be done.

Vasco da Gama will live off the R1 million grant they will receive every month as a PSL club. It is the same money all 16 teams in the top flight get, a benefit of the R1.6 billion television deal that the league struck with SuperSport two years ago. Last season, Vasco won promotion on a quarter of the money and had no full-time staff. Das Neves juggled his job as the financial director of a sports marketing company with his coaching duties. National First Division clubs received R150 000 a month (an increase in the grant has just been announced) and the shareholders put in another R100 000 monthly. Now the directors won't be dipping into their pockets anymore.

Mario, one of three Das Neves brothers with professional playing experience, forms part of a five-man committee, delegated by the 29 shareholders, to run the team. Avelino de Oliveira will be the full-time operating officer and the working quintet is overseen by another four of the shareholders, a watchdog committee if you like. 'All guys who have been very successful in business,' adds Mario das Neves. Carlos says the shareholders are friends, they socialise together too. 'It's no normal football club. Most of the guys can't wait for the meetings to end so that they can get out the cards and play. There aren't the egos or people with anything to prove. Everyone is just so thrilled with how far we've got in such a short period of time.'

'It is not a club where you are going to come and make any money,' Carlos das Neves has told prospective signees. Zuma was earning an effective R500 000 a month during his brief, and spectacularly unsuccessful sojourn with Mamelodi Sundowns. He is likely on 10% of that now. 'We have to try and survive on the grant, we don't have a sugar daddy,' the coach adds. Brother Mario is confident a sponsor will be found soon to add to their income. 'We've got time, although we need a sponsor, we are not desperate to go out and sell at any price. We know the potential of the brand and the status we have now and we are keen to activate that.'

Spreading a million monthly across a full-time football team – salaries, expenses, travel – would seem a major challenge, but Vasco insist it is doable. 'The ball won't always run our way, but if we think out the box and do a few things differently, we can achieve,' says Mario. 'It doesn't have to end in a Bay United,' a reference to the Port Elizabeth club relegated from the Premiership last year and catapulting out of existence this year when they failed to win promotion back, with their benefactor running out of cash and leaving the club to die an ignominious death. 'We have no intention of going bankrupt, we are going for the ride and to give it our best shot.'

Vasco da Gama had been virtual amateurs only a few months back, but had earned promotion to the top-flight of the PSL on the back of hard work, a strong club ethos and they had overcome the odds. The poor neighbours of fellow Premiership side Ajax Cape Town, the newcomers were to play Orlando Pirates in their first league match of a baptism of fire, but whatever lay ahead, the club's staff and supporters were determined to enjoy the experience.

THE SILENT ASSASSIN
By Tom Eaton

HAD MUTTIAH MURALITHARAN BEEN AN AUSTRALIAN, THE CHAMPAGNE
would still be drying on the newly-renamed Muralitharan Harbour Bridge in Sydney.
But of course Murali is not Australian, and his final one-man play – beautifully
scripted by a master dramatist – played out on the fringe of the fringe to warm
but sparse reviews. Most were statistical eulogies, marvelling at the speed and
consistency with which he took his 800 Test wickets. Some were character sketches,
describing the man as modest and likeable, remarking with some surprise that he
should have waited until now to engage in some handbag-swinging with the endlessly
bitching Bishen Bedi. But very few cut to the heart of what Muralitharan meant to
cricket and why his exit has been as muted and humble as the man himself.

Some former batsmen held back their most effusive praise because Murali,
although the most successful bowler in history, was still just a bowler. But even
for those who give bowlers their dues, and who saw Murali clearly as the giant he
was, it was difficult to stand back and describe Murali as the champion of slow
bowlers. The Sri Lankan has cast a huge shadow over cricket, but that shadow has
always been and will always be diffused by another mighty light source, the twin
sun called Shane Warne.

It was a glorious race, surging from the 20th and into the 21st century, the two
finest spinners in the history of the world matching each other stride for stride into
the stratosphere, dragging the breathless game behind them. Like all great contests
it was made even more compelling by their difference. Where Murali's action was
a boa constrictor vomiting an apple, Warne's was the sweep of a Great White's tail.
Where the Sri Lankan was skinny and bug-eyed, the Australian was always one
crème caramel away from being lardy, his bleach-blue eyes almost porcine in that
sunburned face. And of course, where the off-spinner was soft-spoken, modest
and retiring, the leggy was strident.

For their respective camps of followers, the differences in their bowling records are just as stark. For the Murali acolytes, the Sri Lankan is the once and future king. For Warne's fans, there's Warne, daylight, and then Murali.

At this point I need to come clean. For me, the One True Spinner was and still is Warne. I could present my two strongest arguments – that leg breaks are far more difficult to bowl than off breaks, especially off breaks grooved by a deformed elbow; and that Warne played on helpful pitches in about 35% of his Tests, while Murali enjoyed sympathetic tracks in about 80% of his – but it won't help. If Murali is your man, such factoids will only sound like distant buzzing. If Warne is your bloke, who needs stats when you've got that barely contained aggression, that perfect action, that glorious loop and drift, and that tiny inferno of chaos when the ball lands and rips?

I do not believe Muralitharan is the greatest spinner of them all. But I do concede, as must anyone else interested in cricket's bigger picture, that his impact on the game far outweighs Warne's. For all his macho posturing, bad-boy tantrums and run-ins with authority, Warne was an insider: white, English-speaking, a natural in front of the camera. Despite 18 years of touring and beating the world, Murali always came across like a country hayseed seeing the Big Smoke for the first time. For him to have rocked the game to its core took some doing; but of course if anyone was going to do it, it had to be an outsider.

It is difficult to imagine, but in 1995, three years into his career, Muralitharan was nowhere. Completely overshadowed by the names dominating spin bowling – Warne, Anil Kumble, Mushtaq Ahmed – he might have been completely invisible had he not had the oddest action in the game. Sure, he was taking plenty of wickets, but with an average of 34 and a strike rate of 75 balls per wicket, it seemed that he was outlasting batsmen rather than outfoxing them: bowl 40% of your team's overs and you'll get four or five sticks per Test.

And then, in the Boxing Day Test in Melbourne, Murali collided with his destiny. Darrell Hair decided that the Sri Lankan was throwing, and no-balled him.

It was a brave act by a maverick umpire, and seemed to have shaken cricket awake from its geriatric reveries. But that raised arm did not come out of the blue. For many in the Anglo world, over-flexible elbows were just the latest incarnation of what they saw as Asian cricket's over-flexible ethics. Three years previously, Ian Botham had accused Imran Khan and Pakistan of getting reverse swing by tampering with the ball. In the subsequent lawsuit, Khan accused Botham of racism. It seemed an easy and somewhat lame retort, but by placing the accusations in a cultural or even political context, he had highlighted the fact that to many hundreds of millions, cricket is a clash of civilizations.

In 1995 you could have been excused for thinking that talk of such a clash was overblown. Cricket seemed firmly ensconced in the long rooms of London and Sydney. One Anglo cricketing superpower (the West Indies) was handing the mantle to another (Australia). But for those with their eyes on the horizon, the emergence of Asia was clear as the rising sun in the east. The battle for the soul and the wallet of cricket was about to begin. In less than a year the World Cup would sprawl interminably across the subcontinent. For some traditionalists (too often a euphemism for crusty racists mired in colonial fantasy worlds), Muralitharan embodied the first wave of a horde of ball-tampering, elbow-bending Fuzzy-Wuzzies hellbent on overrunning the playing fields of Eton. And as such, he needed to be taken down, and taken down fast.

Hair thought he saw a bowler straightening his elbow. I say he thought he saw a chuck, but more of that shortly. What he really saw was an alien cricket culture getting impossible results, turning the ball square, turning it the wrong way, turning it more than – shudders! – the spin god Warne. Hair was applying the laws of the game, and applying them with courage and vigour. But why he decided to apply them with such vigour when so many others are fudged, is the real issue. There is no evidence that Hair was a racist, but perhaps something else stirred in his subconscious; a call to arms; a sense that the Saracens were at the gate.

Indeed, when he repeated the dose, no-balling Muralitharan in a one-day series in 1999, he went so far as to describe Murali's action as 'diabolical'. It was a choice of adjective that betrayed far more than Hair would have liked: In 1995 he had been fighting the Saracens for Western hegemony. Now, by his own unconscious choice of words, he revealed that he was fighting Satan himself.

And so it was that the soft-spoken Sri Lankan became the major fault line as the cricket world's tectonic plates shifted and rattled the edifices of the old order. But he wasn't alone for long. By the early-2000s eyebrows had been raised at Saqlain Mushtaq's doosra, and Harbhajan Singh's wrong-un had been no-balled. Before you could say 'Cheatin' varmints!' six young spinners with suspect actions were sent home from the 2004 U19 World Cup. The establishment's worst nightmare was coming true. Acting with astonishing vigour for a body usually comatose, the International Cricket Council (ICC) banned Muralitharan's doosra.

Of course the problem with all of this was that Muralitharan, the vanguard of the chucking brigade, had never chucked a cricket ball in his life. Exhaustive studies had shown that a deformed elbow rendered him physically incapable of straightening his arm. Yes, there was some flexing going on at the point of delivery, but in the strictest interpretation of the law – the interpretation Hair had used – Murali could never be a chucker, no matter how hard he tried.

What was even more troubling to the establishment was the discovery, leaping out of the research that it had hoped would nail the Sri Lankan, that all bowlers flex their elbows at the moment of delivery. From Barnes and Tyson to Lillee, Marshall and McGrath, every technically perfect hero in the cricketing pantheon has had a little wobble thanks to basic human anatomy. Suddenly the fetish of the straight arm and the 13th Commandment – Thou Shalt Not Chuck – were starting to look a little silly.

It got much, much sillier when new research showed that it is impossible for umpires to see a throw when the bowler has a large carrying angle (the angle at which your forearms hang away from horizontal, up to 17° in the case of Murali and Johan Botha). To identify any jerk in the elbow, the umpire would need to remain at the same 90° angle to the elbow to monitor its movement; and given the extreme contortions of these bowlers, said umpire would have to magically whiz around the field, from square leg to third man to mid-off, etc. Without such superpowers, the only thing the umpire can see is a whirl of deformed angles and a highly convincing optical illusion of a straightening arm.

And so, a full 10 years after Murali was first called, a new law was introduced: bowlers could flex up to 15°. It seemed a pragmatic response (anything under 15° is not detectable by the human eye) but in truth it was the final rearguard action by the elite. The Saracens are going to chuck whatever we do, the thinking seemed to go, so we'll let them chuck but we'll be damned if we'll let them chuck big. Today 15° is cricket's equivalent of the 38th Parallel in Korea: a powerful ideological border. On this side of the line is fair play, blue skies, and a land in which batsmen can do whatever the hell they want. On the other side lies anarchy, rapine and cricketing communism. Bowl an off-break with a 16° flex, and the terrorists win. Muttiah, the son of a confectioner and the most destructive bowler in the history of cricket, can no longer be touched by such petty concerns. His record will never be touched. Nobody will take 801 Test wickets. It would seem that Murali has won. But has he?

In 1914 trade union leader Nicholas Klein beautifully outlined the four strategies used by any establishment to undermine and ultimately make their challengers go away. 'First they ignore you,' he said. 'Then they ridicule you. And then they attack you and want to burn you. And then they build monuments to you.'

We all ignored Murali at first. Then we saw his odd action and laughed. Then, in 1995, the establishment noticed him, and in 2004 tried to burn him. And then, magically, Murali became a superstar and simultaneously disappeared. Somewhere in the high 500s he suddenly became invisible. Brilliant Murali was hard at work, somewhere. We just weren't quite sure where. As he wheeled past 600, 700 and then on to 800 over the past five years, all but ignored by the establishment's media, he proved that praise can be the ultimate weapon.

By recasting Murali as an international treasure and appearing to reach a workable compromise around the 15° law, cricket's elite managed once again to disguise the elephant in the room: that throwing should not only be legalised for spinners but actively encouraged too. Had Murali and Harbhajan spent the past five years fighting for their right to bowl a doosra with as floppy an arm as they wanted, we might have forced the issue into the spotlight and seen that banning a spinner from bowling a doosra is exactly the same as banning a batsmen from playing a cover drive with a super-springy five-inch-thick bat.

We might have had a chance to get back to the fundamentals, the contest of bat and ball, and understood how monstrously one-sided – and therefore pointless – cricket has become. And perhaps we would have seen Muralitharan in a new light. Not as a Fifth Columnist for the forces of anarchy; not as a freak who had circumvented the laws of the game to come out on top; but rather as the finest off-spinner in history, and the man who smiled shyly, trotted in to bowl, performed magic, and whispered to a hundred million Asian children, 'Yes we can!'

The most successful bowler cricket has ever seen finally retired from the international arena after taking a world record 800 Test wickets, the last of them with the final ball he bowled. However, over the years he wasn't always widely applauded and given the recognition he should have. Records came at a cost for this likeable Sri Lankan and this feature paid tribute to the genius, giving him the credit he earned and deserved.

NEW WAVE GENERATION

By Clinton van der Berg

CHANCES ARE THAT ONE OF OUR FINEST SPORTSMEN COULD STROLL DOWN Cape Town's Long Street and not warrant so much as a second glance.

That's the reality of surfing's closeted subculture and its cultivated image of cool: beaches, babes and Bohemian revelry.

Jordy Smith may not be the name on everybody's lips just yet, but the 22-year-old is fast seeping into the public consciousness. The mainstream press have come calling, corporates are banging down his door, he's crossed over into movies and music and, importantly, he represents a generation that are doing it for themselves. Politics, angst and white guilt be damned.

We speak in the aftermath of him ascending to the No 1 position on the world surf rankings by winning the Jeffreys Bay leg of the ASP World Tour – the Billabong Pro J-Bay. His triumph confirmed a splendid trifecta: the same day Nelson Mandela celebrated his 92nd birthday and Louis Oosthuizen famously won the British Open. If Smith didn't quite hog the headlines, he earned his fair share. Besides, the celebrations were epic: with vuvuzelas blaring, he stumped up R50 000 at the local bar for him and his mates.

'The town was turned upside town,' he recalls. 'I wanted to celebrate with people who had been a part of my success, which seemed like everyone.'

Smith is one of those sportsmen, like so many other South Africans overseas, who operates largely on the fringes. There's the occasional dispatch from Hawaii or Bali, but his world is where he's at. And where he's at, to give it context, is huge.

Aged 14, he was saddled as a future great. Four years later he won the World Junior Surfing Championship. Today, he has million dollar endorsements, counts Hollywood stars among his friends and is credited with performing the most outrageous surfing manoeuvre of all time. 'Super Freak', they call him, which is as good an endorsement as any.

Smith grew up as many Durban youngsters do. Mornings were spent at school, afternoons at the beach and holidays with friends at Jeffreys Bay. His father Graham was a board shaper, so there was a natural inclination to seek out the best waves. He may have all the trappings of a wealthy youngster now, but it wasn't always so. His precociousness on the board earned him clothing sponsorships, but many times he had to sell the clothes to pay to travel to surf contests. He worked in surf shops and general stores to scrape together what he could to pursue his dream. 'I just wanted to surf.'

It was an experience that taught him to never take anything for granted.

Smith's relentless spirit set him apart and he fast earned a reputation for being unafraid to do what it took to win: high risk, high reward became his mantra.

Defeat is something he has seldom encountered, but Smith has rationalised (and internalised) its meaning. 'A lot of people are scared to do their best, they're scared of defeat,' he says. 'Many don't go into things trying 100%, they don't put their neck out there, they're afraid. I'm not scared to lose. You can't win everything; there will be some serious losses.

'I realised that at the beginning of last year, when I learnt to lose, because that's where the good stuff happens inside and you learn about yourself. It's a learning curve. Growing up, I had never lost in my whole career, until last year. And when that happens, it's a bitter pill. You must accept losing before you can win.'

And winning is what he's done a lot of, with the Jeffreys Bay triumph representing the high-water mark of an already extraordinary career.

'I'm there for a reason and that's to do my job, which is to try and beat everyone. I don't really care who they are.'

Smith has a burning confidence, but he's never fallen for the hype, thanks primarily to his father who constantly emphasises the need to have fun and never take yourself too seriously. As manager, coach and mentor to Jordy, he is never far away.

'It was cool to be called a future great, but that puts a target on you,' says Smith. 'I just block it all out and people around me remind me who I am. They keep me humble.'

Inevitably, there have been comparisons with Kelly Slater, commonly regarded as the best surfer of all time. 'King Kelly' is a nine-time world champion and, significantly, an ally with whom Smith shares a birthday, albeit 16 years apart.

'I've known him practically my whole life, since I was seven or eight years old. He has nothing to hide from me and I have nothing to hide from him. I've been fortunate; with a lot of guys he either hates on them or they hate on him [sic]. I'm kind of neutral; I believe it's important to keep friends close and enemies even closer.'

Smith has carved out a very agreeable existence. The world tour takes him to exotic locations – Brazil, Tahiti and Puerto Rico among them – and of course he's a superstar among the Generation X-ers.

Three years ago, when the sports manufacturers were chasing his signature, Tiger Woods called him up on behalf of Nike. He gave a bewildered Smith the spiel about coping with pressure and hooking up with the right people.

'I wasn't sure what to say, but he was cool. I just cruised with it.'

Days later, he signed with O'Neill for a reputed seven-figure sum.

Prior to competing in Jeffreys Bay, Smith was in Malibu where he stayed with actor Owen Wilson for a fortnight and hung out with Ben Stiller. When he's in Hawaii, he shacks up with Jack Johnson, the soft rock musician.

To him, they aren't Hollywood A-listers, they're simply friends he seems to have known his whole life. Such is the life of a world surfing superstar.

No one pretends that surfing is overly hard work, so naturally Smith has begun to dabble in other areas. He has worked as a consultant and appeared in the *Blue Crush* movie franchise and he makes surfing films that can be purchased on iTunes or seen at smaller theatres. Most recently, he collaborated with Goldfish, the electro-jazz band who recognise Smith's pulling power in a market everyone is chasing down.

He picked up a tidy $15 000 for the win in Jeffreys Bay, but the real riches come from endorsements. The top echelon can expect to earn $500 000 to $1 million a year; enough to ensure a lifetime's supply of flip-flops and baggy shorts.

For all that, he's an uncomplicated youngster. Like many of his peers, he's a Harry Potter devotee. Less expectedly, he psyches himself up with Beatles music. But his other tastes and likes largely mirror those of contemporary South African 20-somethings. He's a regular guy who reaches out to his fans.

What he isn't is a regular surfer. Last year, off the coast of Indonesia, he blew the sport wide open when he performed the Rodeo Flip, the most high-performance manoeuvre ever executed on a wave.

'At the time no one had seen anything like it before,' he chuckles. 'They asked, "who's this kid?" I've perfected it and can now nail it seven or eight times out of 10 which is good consistency. It works like this: once you hit the top of a wave, you do a backflip and at the same time you spin the board fully, rotating 360°. You get it wrong and it's pretty tragic.'

It's these kinds of tricks that put him in elevated company, with any number of aficionados anointing him as the sport's likely flag-bearer for years to come.

Smith boasts a passport that would shame any high-flying corporate executive, but, even so, the best waves are found closest to home.

'I travel all over the world, but some of the best waves I've surfed have been in KZN. The most consistent waves anywhere are in South Africa,' he says. 'I can catch a four or five foot wave every day. But if it's the most perfect wave, I'd have to say Indonesia.'

A number of elements constitute a good wave: swell direction, banks and the reef. 'No wave is ever the same, so every time you stand on a board it's a whole new experience. You never get bored.'

The remarkable aspect of Smith's surge to stardom is that although he's already made it at 22, he could conceivably be there or thereabouts for another 20 years. Having reached the summit, he yearns to occupy it for a while longer. 'For the next 20 years that's what I'm gonna do,' he says with calm assurance.

Unlike so many other sports, where real life constantly intrudes, surfing's rate of attrition is low. It's not a bad life.

'I get to hang out at the beach,' says the world No 1. 'Sun. Waves. The girls on the beach do my back. Never a shortage of girls to sunscreen my back. I can't complain.'

He wouldn't dare.

Tiger Woods once phoned the surfer Jordy Smith and asked him to pledge his allegiance to sportswear manufacturers Nike. In Hawaii, Smith shacks up with a rock star and A-list actors are among his closest friends. At the age of just 22, he has Hollywood appeal and is widely regarded as the future of surfing. The other good news is that he is South African.

CASE FOR THE OUTCASTS
By Peter Roebuck

ZIMBABWE HAD FOR YEARS BEEN A SIMPLE TOPIC. RUTHLESS LIBERATOR turns into tyrant, becomes paranoid, slaughters rivals, suppresses people, crushes democracy, gets greedy, builds marble home, stashes plunder overseas, surrounds himself with toe lickers, marries femme fatale, bribes backers, militarises youth, tortures and rapes, rigs elections, controls media, talks about endless revolution, becomes deluded, blames enemies for starvation and bankruptcy and avoids crimes tribunal. It was as straightforward as a cowboy film with the hero in a white hat and the villain sporting darker attire.

It was the same in cricket. Inevitably significant institutions are driven by the same forces, and often the same people, as the corrupt state. Pakistan cricket reflects the nation at large. Each man for himself, and most of the money reserved for the army. Zimbabwe Cricket (ZC) was in cahoots with Zanu PF, and prospered from the liaison. Even now, in these more confusing times, ZC leaders flaunt their wealth. Clearly they are convinced that it was acceptable to make a fortune in a time of tyranny, to collect booty as a people starve and a game suffers. Better than anything else, their wealth confirms their connections.

Until a year ago it was easy, indeed compulsory, to condemn those ruling the roost at Government House and the offices of ZC. Only craven apologists and shallow Africanists defended either party. Of course the occupants talked cleverly, spoke with forked tongues. Sweet words left their mouths even as the schools and hospitals collapsed and the youth militia did its devilish work. Evil does not wear horns.

From the president downwards the presentation was plausible. Throughout it was designed to appeal to other parties nursing grievances. Always the attack was sustained. After all, it is not possible to defend the indefensible. Colonialism and colour, not corruption, lay behind the collapse of the country, and the weakness of its cricketing arm.

Now the position is more complicated. Knee-jerk reactions and round condemnations no longer suffice. The tyranny has given ground. Doubtless it was a tactical withdrawal, and quite possibly it is temporary, but it's a fact and needs to be taken into account. The new liberator, the MDC, has formed an alliance of sorts with its tormentor, and a joint government has been formed.

Predictably, Zanu PF retained control of the strategic and financial institutions and allowed their opponents to accept responsibility for health and education. In that regard both partners demonstrated their concerns; Zanu PF concentrated on money and power, the MDC on people. Despite gloomy forecasts, too, the alliance remains intact. Of course the tension has been palpable. Both sides anticipate betrayal. But the position has not deteriorated. There were no illusions to be shattered.

It has been three steps forward and two back. The abolition of the Zim dollar helped to reduce the level of wheeling and dealing. Insiders had been able to trade Forex between the official and the black market and could end up buying a Mercedes for US$100. When that path was finally blocked, the thieves turned their attention to diamonds, adding sparkling gems to their farms and plush houses on various continents. Next, the plan to nationalise anything left that makes money: mines, companies, whatever. There is no end to their greed. As the president of Liberia told an August audience of African leaders in 2008: 'Africa is not poor, just poorly managed.'

But the fact remains that things have changed. Democracy has put a foot in the door. ZC has changed too. Previously secretive, reviled and much investigated, it has suddenly thrown its doors open. Foreign coaches have been appointed, previously disgruntled past players have been invited back and put in positions of responsibility, a franchise system has been introduced, overseas players have signed on the dotted line and even hostile journalists have been chivvied along.

Famous players and coaches have been added to the roll. Allan Donald has taken charge of one of the franchises (not the one run by the fellow sacked not so long ago over a scam involving new cricket balls). Jason Gillespie has been chosen to coach a rival outfit. Alan Butcher, a well-rounded Englishman with a patchy coaching record, is guiding the national team. Heath Streak, Alistair Campbell, Grant Flower and Dave Houghton, all retired Zimbabwean players, are serving in various capacities. Brian Lara spoke at the annual awards ceremony held on 3 September. Neil Manthorp, a South African cricket writer of renown, is also working as ZC's media liaison officer, a conflict of interest but hardly an isolated case in the cricket community. It is an impressive line-up. If anything, the list is disconcertingly strong. Arguably ZC is trying too hard to impress. None of these fellows work for peanuts. And that begs the question. Where has all the money come from? Why is it suddenly available? Where was it last year when the players were poorly paid and fields went uncut for want of a mower?

Nothing has changed in the corridors of power at ZC. Peter Chingoka, the long-standing chairman, has proved as durable as his president, a friend of his father. Paul, his twin brother, was sacked from the Olympic Commission for corruption and was given a farm for his pains. Peter carries on, working the rooms, planning his moves, a survivor in some eyes, and a manipulator in others. Over the years he has been convicted on Forex charges, and swiftly released, has housed his family in London and has been banned from visiting various countries because he is regarded as a leading beneficiary of the tyranny. He remains an obstacle to ZC's full rehabilitation. As CP Snow put it, 'the past is not history; it's not even past.'

Chingoka stays behind the scenes. Ozias Bvute is the activist, a gregarious, forceful operator and, as managing director, the face of ZC. He denies putting fingers in the pie and points out that his wealth comes from his other job as a banker – his uncle is involved in Wachovia bank. The relationship is rewarding enough to permit the ownership of a property in New York and a luxury house in the plushest part of Harare. He also denies that he is hand in pocket with Zanu PF and objects to being called a thug, though he is widely regarded as the man responsible for causing Tatenda Taibu, Zimbabwe's best black player, to flee the country.

Bvute and Chingoka believe they have been much maligned. They point towards the KPMG report into ZC commissioned by the ICC, claiming that it gives them a clean bill of health, which is not quite the case. In fact the report is inconclusive, and on several occasions the auditors were obliged to rely on information provided by the ZC officials. At best the books were not well kept. But then the country itself had become a money trail. Moreover, the maligned are wearing rags, not Rolexes.

In any case it is perfectly possible to waste money legitimately. Mugabe himself regularly takes a large entourage on overseas jaunts, gives them US$5 000 a day from state coffers and stops in Cairo and elsewhere for a few days of shopping. Nice work if you can get it. ZC once sent 14 officials to accompany the 15 players involved in an U19 tour. Nepotism has been rife.

Chingoka and Bvute might indeed not be members of Zanu PF but they have benefited vastly from its patronage. A financier could not otherwise make his fortune in a time of decay. Nor can a cricket official without obvious sources of income invest a million dollars in a mining company.

But that is the past. It is possible that most of the allegations made against ZC officials were well founded and that such activities have ceased. What then? Certainly ZC has opened itself up to scrutiny. Cynics say they have fleeced the sheep and now are happy to let it frolic in the pasture. Sceptics suggest that the arrival of a unity government and the nomination of David Coltart as minister of sport concentrated minds. Coltart is respected across the spectrum as a man of intelligence and integrity. He is also a devotee of the game. Critics regard his appointment as a significant breakthrough. Perhaps, too, the incumbents are mindful of Mugabe's deteriorating health. Survivors know when to hold 'em and fold 'em.

Now comes the uncomfortable question. Are these reforms serious or merely a façade intended to liberate overseas accounts and retain power? Can the Zimbabwe government and ZC be taken at face value? Or is it merely a Prague summer?

At such times it is surely best to be guided by those on the ground. Years ago I asked Steve Tshwete whether protesters were right to object to South Africa's participation in the 1992 Cricket World Cup. He said 'Well, I am here.' Since he had spent 15 years behind bars for the cause his point seemed conclusive. In Zimbabwe's case, Coltart, Biti, Chamisa, Tsvangarai and company decided that the time had come to make a deal. They could not sit by any longer as the powerful stole elections and destroyed the nation. They were not naive; merely patriots seeking to save their fellow countrymen from further suffering.

Accordingly Zimbabwe ought to be allowed back into the front rank of cricketing nations. It's fruitless wasting any more time trying to remove the entrenched. Like Mugabe and his backers, they are not going anywhere. Better to acknowledge the improvements and take it from there. Sometimes it's no use waiting for a better day to dawn. Mugabe's mother reached three figures. Sometimes you have to work with what's on the table.

That does not mean Test status ought to be restored straight away. It was not lost solely because Zimbabwe had become a pariah state. Standards had also declined as experienced players were chased away or departed in high dudgeon. Gifted young black players were thrown into the pot before they were ready. At least Zimbabwe had a steady supply of them, the product of a development structure South Africa ought to copy. ZC identified promising boys at an early age and sent them to carefully chosen schools capable of instilling discipline and direction.

CASE FOR THE OUTCASTS

Although Zimbabwe remained competitive in the one-day arena they are lightweights in the longer version of the game. That is not going to change overnight. Nor are democratic nations going to forgive and forget in five minutes. For now the best ZC can expect is a gradual renewal of relations, cricketing and otherwise, with U19 and A team tours arranged. Progress has been made but it's fragile and the world will remain wary. After all, the present does look uncannily like the past. The same applies to ZC. The risks are high, another fixed election whose crookedness even the ANC might recognise, military intervention, more rape and pillage, more repression. But it's a step worth taking. What is the alternative?

South Africa's betrayal of the Zimbabwean people has been shameful. It sided with a liberation party long after it became the oppressor. Zanu PF's genius has been in ensuring that the legitimate desire for black liberation be manipulated to sanction the party's every monstrous move. It's a trick whose devil lies in its allure. Hunger, bad health, declining education, weak cricket teams, it's all worthwhile provided the cause is advanced. And provided the leaders are not affected. But the cause is democracy, or ought to be. Mugabe liked it until he became unpopular.

Now, with more legitimacy, Cricket South Africa has invited Zimbabwe to play a few ODIs. It is appropriate. The time is ripe. But it's important to remember that the real battle is not between creeds or colours, but between the tyrant and the common man. Mugabe's rhetoric about colonialism and renewing the African soul is a ruse. Meanwhile he fills his coffers and his people fill their coffins. Zanu PF consists of smooth-talking gangsters hell-bent on protecting their patch. Africa deserves better. In recognition of recent developments, cricket can open its arms to Zimbabwe but ought not to drop its guard.

Zimbabwe had been in cricket's international wilderness since 2006. They were about to make a short tour of South Africa, and not everyone agreed they should be touring, given the old apartheid struggle slogan of 'no normal sport in an abnormal country'. This was a case in support of them. Given the plundering of riches by government and the manner in which Zimbabwe is run, it seemed pointless to penalise their cricketers for something beyond their control.